8/841

THE ANTHROP   ER
INCOME UF
THE CASE C

Freidonberg
Anthropol
(studio)

ANNALS OF THE NEW YORK ACADEMY OF SCIENCES

Volume 749

THE ANTHROPOLOGY OF LOWER INCOME URBAN ENCLAVES THE CASE OF EAST HARLEM

Edited by Judith Freidenberg

The New York Academy of Sciences
New York, New York
1995

COVER: The front cover shows East Harlem and surrounding areas in 1992 and the back cover shows approximately the same area in 1962. The aerial photographs were provided by Lockwood, Kessler & Bartlett, Inc.

Library of Congress Cataloging-in-Publication Data

The anthropology of lower income urban enclaves : the case of East
  Harlem / edited by Judith Freidenberg.
       p.   cm. -- (Annals of the New York Academy of Sciences ; v .
  749)
     Includes bibliographical references (p.   ) and index.
     ISBN 0-89766-891-X (cloth : alk. paper). -- ISBN 0-89766-892-8
  (paper : alk. paper)
     1. Puerto Ricans--New York (N.Y.)--Social conditions. 2. East
  Harlem (New York, N.Y.)--Social conditions. 3. New York (N.Y.)--
  Social conditions. I. Freidenberg, Judith. II Series.
  Q11.N5 no.749
  [F128.9.P85]
  500 s--dc20
  [974.7'1004687295]   95-5500
                                                         CIP

CDP/PCP
Printed in the United States of America
ISBN 0-89766-891-X (cloth)
ISBN 0-89766-892-8 (paper)

ANNALS OF THE NEW YORK ACADEMY OF SCIENCES

Volume 749
June 26, 1995

THE ANTHROPOLOGY OF LOWER INCOME URBAN ENCLAVES
THE CASE OF EAST HARLEM[a]

Editor
JUDITH FREIDENBERG

CONTENTS

Part I. Ethnographic History of East Harlem: 1950–1992

[a]This volume is the result of a workshop held at the Museum of The City of New York in November of 1992.

Part II. Ethnography and National Culture:
A Comparative Perspective

Preface

This book is based on a workshop that I organized on the urban ethnography of East Harlem (November 19 and 20, 1992). Although those of us conducting fieldwork in the area knew of each other's work, there had never been an opportunity to exchange information about our research and ideas in a small group. When the Museum of the City of New York invited me to curate an exhibit based on my own fieldwork in the area, I realized the time had come to sustain formal and informal discussions with other urban ethnographers who had worked in East Harlem for the last four decades.

In the 1950s a research group consisting of Elena Padilla, Joan Mencher and others, studied the area with such methodology. The study population was Puerto Rican—in fact, a book by Padilla was entitled *Up from Puerto Rico*. Although there was regional diversity in the origin of the newcomers, some came from enclaves which were structurally similar to El Barrio. One such was studied by Helen Safa in the 1960s.

Since then, urban ethnography of East Harlem has continued. In the 1970s, Dehavenon started longitudinal fieldwork on hunger and homelessness. Bourgois and Freidenberg followed in the 1980s, responding to the increase in the drug trade in the area, and other social issues that affected the life circumstances of the Latino elderly, respectively. Later on, other important dimensions of the human condition in East Harlem were addressed by two teams: while Kornblum and Williams focused on the constraints of growing up in public housing, Torruellas, Ayala, and Pedraza, of the Center for Puerto Rican Studies, centered on the potential of literacy programs for action (the papers of the last two were not submitted for publication).

In addition to paying attention to context, the papers in this volume contribute to the writing of a social history of East Harlem—for example, Mencher describes how the recruitment of people for the newly constructed projects disrupted existing family structures in the 1950s. The work of Williams and Kornblum, on the impact of urban housing on social relationships in the 1990s, help us to get a diachronic view of social policy in action.

Finally, the contributions of discussants (Jones and Nash) and commentators (Fernández-Kelly, Foner, Montbach, Sørensen, and Vélez-Ibañez) build on the presentations and discussions with other urban ethnographers to reflect on the anthropology of low-income urban enclaves. I hope our dialogues at the workshop and in this book, stimulates all of us to continue our work with renewed enthusiasm and fresh perspectives.

JUDITH FREIDENBERG

Acknowledgments

I express my gratitude to the following organizations and individuals: The Wenner Grenn Foundation for Anthropological Research, for awarding me a conference grant to aid in the organization of the workshop that resulted in this publication; The Department of Community Medicine and the Department of Geriatrics and Adult Development, Mount Sinai School of Medicine, City University of New York, for enabling my own research in East Harlem, and its dissemination in scholarly circles; The Department of Community Relations, Mt. Sinai Hospital, for supporting my work in curating an exhibit at the Museum of the City of New York; colleagues who reacted positively to my conceptualizing of the workshop, read papers, collaborated in taping sessions, and discussed turning the workshop into a book: Anna Lou Dehavenon, Linda Winston, Joan Montbach; and last, but not least, The Museum of the City of New York, particularly its Director, Robert McDonald, the then Associate Director for Programs, Andrew Svedlow, and the Associate Director of Education, Cathy Benson, for graciously lending us their Auditorium to hold our discussions, and for initiating me into the fascinating world of museums.

I also gratefully acknowledge Peter Harris, Director of Educational Resources, CUNY Graduate Center who provided extensive assistance in the selection and processing of photographs appearing in this volume.

Last but not least, the enthusiasm expressed by Kurt W. Deushle, M.D., Chairman of the Department of Community Medicine throughout most of the fieldwork reported here, in thinking and documenting population issues in East Harlem, was both enlightening and contagious.

I deeply regret the loss of a scholar and a friend, Rosa Torruellas, a presenter in the workshop who worked on her paper in bed and died without seeing the project in print. I asked Rina Benmayor, her friend and long-term collaborator at the Center for Puerto Rican Studies, to write the text of the dedication to Rosa.

JUDITH FREIDENBERG

Rosa M. Torruellas (above left and below center)

Photographs provided by Lucas Andino Torruellas

Rosa M. Torruellas

IN MEMORIAM

We dedicate this book to the memory of Rosa M. Torruellas, a young anthropologist and researcher at the Centro de Estudios Puertorriqueños at Hunter College, CUNY. Rosa built and directed the El Barrio Popular Education Program in East Harlem until 1991, and dedicated the last two years of her life to writing as much as she could about this unique intervention-research experience. Rosa was deeply committed to linking knowledge, theory, and practice to the concrete needs of people. Her vision was to provide, in a participatory, collective, and mutually enriching manner, an empowering educational opportunity for Puerto Rican women and men. At the same time, the program provided a rich context to advance, through research, understanding of cultural resources, community policy needs, and strategies for action. Her writings evidence a deep understanding of the cultural intersection of class, gender, and ethnicity in the empowerment process. Rosa Torruellas left a powerful intellectual, political, and human legacy to inspire future generations of socially committed researchers.

Rina Benmayor, *Director of Cultural Studies, Centro de Estudios Puertorriqueños, Hunter College, City University of New York, 695 Park Avenue, New York, New York 10021*

Lower Income Urban Enclaves
Introduction

JUDITH FREIDENBERG
Center for Urban Research
Graduate Center, City University of New York
New York, New York 10036
and
Mount Sinai School of Medicine
City University of New York
New York, New York 10029

THE ANTHROPOLOGY OF LOW-INCOME ENCLAVES IN NEW YORK CITY

Some of anthropology's most important contributions to social theory have emerged from the ethnographic case. The relatively new field of urban ethnography in the United States[1] continues in that tradition, particularly in New York City, recently the site of more published ethnographic work than any other city in the United States (Sanjek 1990). The units of analysis for most ethnographic studies have been the neighborhood (for example, LaRuffa 1988), the ethnic group (for example, Wong 1982), the immigrant cohort (for example, Foner 1987), or the behavior of an ethnic population (for example, Harwood 1977). Few urban ethnographies of New York City, however, have sought to understand the meaning of the phenomena studied within larger socio-economic contexts—thus as social issues (for some exceptions, see Susser 1982; Williams and Kornblum 1985; Jones, Turner and Montbach 1992; Scharff 1987; Hopper, Susser, and

---

[1]A review of urban ethnography outside of the United States falls outside the scope of this paper. As Sørensen and Fernández-Kelly (this volume) illustrate for Scandinavia and Latin America, there are similarities and differences. It needs to be noted that an important similarity is that the political climate of the times relates to research topics. For example, it was not until the rural-urban migration in Latin America acquired gigantic proportions that a plethora of studies on the urban poor appeared. Policy makers, politicians, the general population, and the military sectors of society became alarmed at the impact—actual or imagined—that these demographic changes could have on the fabric of society. The fact that social scientists produced information on the poor and that they focused on issues of marginality, political organization, family patterns, and the like, should be seen within the context of this political and policy context.

1

Conover 1985; Lopez 1987; Dunlap 1992). A historical and comparative[2] perspective on the impact of these issues on the daily lives of the residents of low-income enclaves has also been lacking.

Thus, the urban ethnography of social issues in low-income enclaves in New York City lacks: 1) A comparative framework: the research site is one urban place; 2) A historical background: the center of the study is on the ethnographic present; 3) A focus on social issues, and thus on viewing phenomena from a policy perspective; and 4) An assessment of conceptual paradigms used to describe and explain the political economy of social issues. Given these characteristics, it is difficult to generalize from a particular case to the analytical category and to propose paradigms useful for generating theory and policy on low-income urban enclaves.

The present volume is based on the urban ethnography of one such locale—East Harlem—since the 1950s. It explores the substantive, methodological and policy dimensions of social issues affecting this low-income space using a comparative and historical perspective. Exploring the case from the vantage point of several ethnographers working at different points in time may enhance our understanding of larger socio-economic systems, and thus our ability to offer a paradigm for the study of low-income urban enclaves.

THE RELEVANCE OF TIME AND CONTEXT IN URBAN SPACE: EAST HARLEM AS A CASE

The Making of a Neighborhood[3]

Before the European migration to the shores of America, the geographical area we now name East Harlem was, according to historical record, inhabited by the Weckquaesgeks, part of the Delaware nation, who were hunters, trappers, and fishermen.

From the start of the European colonization, the history of East Harlem has reflected, in microcosm, that of New York City, the nation, and other corners of the world. The area has been home to successive waves of immigrants determined to achieve *their* version of the American Dream. Since the turn of the century, East Harlem has provided shelter for successive massive migrations from Ireland, Germany, Eastern Europe, Italy, the south of the United States, and Puerto Rico (Stewart 1972).

---

[2] For an exception, see Sullivan (1989).

[3] A fully updated version of the history of East Harlem, particularly from a socio-economic perspective, has yet to be written.

At the beginning of the period covered by this volume—the 1950s—the most massive wave of migration was from Puerto Rico[4] (Centro 1979). In the 1990s, the countries of origin of people that have made East Harlem their home are in Asia, particularly Korea, and Latin America, particularly Mexico.

The people of East Harlem can be characterized in terms of race, ethnicity, social class and country of origin. Given the visible differences between East Harlem and other urban spaces in the city, this neighborhood is a metaphor for other markers of social stratification in the United States. Two that are central to the arguments made in this volume are residence in a low-income area and the transformation of New York into a global city.

Residence in a low income area augments the difficulties of daily living: not only are the residents' needs greater but access to services and entitlements (Sexton 1965; de Ortiz 1992) becomes more problematic. East Harlem becomes a metaphor for the transformation of New York into a global city: the living conditions in the geographical unit reflect the structural and historical changes of the city, and its place in regional, national and international systems.

Geographical Location

Boundaries of neighborhoods, like people who inhabit them, change throughout time. In the 1950s, East Harlem was an area bounded by 99th Street on the south, 105th Street on the north, the East River on the East and Second Avenue on the West (Mencher, this volume).

By the 1990s, the geographical boundaries of East Harlem had expanded to 96th Street to the South, Harlem River and Hell's Gate to the North, the East River to the East and Fifth Avenue to the West (See MAP 1).

The officially designated boundaries of government agencies are usually not congruent. Thus, this geographical area contains three census tracts (10029, 10035, and 10037); two health areas (15 and 16); and several school districts. The lack of coordination among agencies undoubtedly increase the maze that a person in need of services negotiates.

East Harlem is also Community District #11 in the borough of Manhattan (See MAP 2). The profiles that follow compare changes in life conditions during the last decade in East Harlem, Manhattan, and New York City.[5,6]

---

[4] While the massive migration of Puerto Ricans in the 1950s originated in Puerto Rico, there had also been a steady immigration of Cubans and Puerto Ricans since the 1930s motivated by political exile rather than economic necessity.

[5] These profiles were prepared on the basis of data collected by the 1980 and 1990 census questionnaires, as analyzed by the Department of City Planning of the City of New York (Department of City Planning, 1992, A and B).

[6] Although various life circumstances will be discussed separately, the interrelationships between the variables will be noted when appropriate.

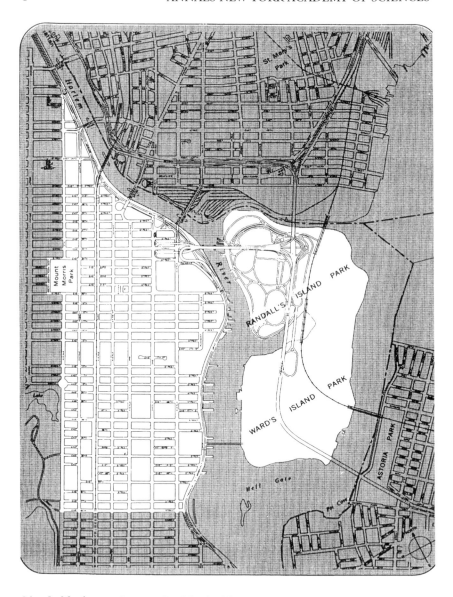

MAP 1. Manhattan Community District 11.

MAP 2. Community Districts in New York City.

Demographic Conditions[7]

The population of East Harlem totalled 130,770 persons in 1990, show-ing a decrease for the last decade in comparison to Manhattan and New York City. It has also changed in composition.

[7] The United States Bureau of the Census releases data on decennial Censuses of Population and Housing. There have been concerns about the adequacy of the data. According to the Department of City Planning in New York (City of New York, 1992,A:1): "The Bureau has acknowledged that these data reflect an undercount of the population . . . especially severe for Hispanics, Black Nonhispanics, Asians and Pacific Islanders, and Native Americans. The City of New York is pursuing litigation to compel the reporting of statistically corrected census data that would eliminate or substantially reduce that undercount."

In 1990, the population was distributed among the following Census-defined ethnic categories: 12.1% were White, 32.6% were Black, 53.0% were Hispanic and 2.3% were Asian/Other. The ethnic population categories that experienced the largest increases during the last decade were Asian (particularly Philippino) and Hispanic (other, than Puerto Rican, and particularly Mexican) (See TABLE 1, APPENDIX I) The high residential mobility and the doubling of the proportion of non-citizens reflect these demographic shifts (see TABLE 2)

The age pyramid has inversed: although the East Harlem population remains young (31% were 19 years old and younger in 1990), during the last decade the most rapidly growing age group was 85 years and over.

Living arrangements reflect population growth, availability of housing, and patterns of social organization. Thus, the increase of nonrelatives sharing quarters in 1990—which East Harlem shares with Manhattan and the city—is probably related to the decrease in the proportion of married families living with related children in East Harlem (TABLE 3).

SocioEconomic Conditions

East Harlem is one of the least affluent enclaves in Manhattan, as suggested by indicators such as gross income, educational attainment, labor force composition, occupational structure, and location of industries.[8]

The gross income of the people of East Harlem experienced little change during the last decade. By 1990, 40% of the total population was below the poverty level and, of those, 62% were below 200% of the poverty level. In actual currency, 40% had income levels of less than $10,000, and another 20% were under $20,000 per annum. These absolute indicators of poverty reflect characteristics of the larger society when examined from a relative perspective: thus, while median household income for East Harlem was $14,882 in 1992, it was $32, 262 for Manhattan, and $29, 832 for the city (City of New York, 1992:B).

The rates of school dropouts are high: in 1990, 51% of the population had not attained a high school degree. Finishing school and encountering structural constraints in entering the labor market are also influenced by the high rate of teen age pregnancies and single parent households.

---

[8] These indicators usually indicate social status and predict mobility in capitalist societies. However, allowances should be made for the discrepancies between ideology and opportunity structure. Thus, the rate of college-educated persons in the labor force has increased to unprecedented proportions in the United States. Yet employability correlates with both the educational attainment of the workforce and the political economy of the global city.

During the last decade, labor force participation by gender in East Harlem has remained constant for males, but has decreased for females, possibly a reflection of the increase of female-headed households with young children below the poverty level. For both males and females, unemployment rates have increased by 52% during the last decade, as compared to 20% for Manhattan and 31% for New York City (see TABLE 4).

Industries employing the civilian labor force reflect fluctuations in the City economy—for example, the flight of manufacturing industries and the increase in service industries. In East Harlem, there has been a marked increase in the percentage of persons employed in unskilled or semi-skilled occupations.[9] For both males and females, the armed forces have become a major source of employment (see TABLE 4). Unpaid family members have increased 600% during the last decade, as compared to 8% for Manhattan and 57% for the city (see TABLE 5).

The geographical location of the work site can often provide some indication of the relationships between a particular location and the employability of its residents. Among the workers of East Harlem, there was a 123% increase during the last decade among those that worked at home, as compared to 44% for Manhattan and 58% for the city (see TABLE 5).

Health Conditions

Community District 11 has one of the highest rates of live births to teenagers: 60% in 1988. In 1988, infant mortality rates were 21.7 per 1,000 live births, an increase from 17 over a two-year period. Although East Harlem constitutes 1.4% of the city's population, recent data indicate that the district will reflect the highest incidence of child abuse and neglect in the borough.

The death rate per 1000 was 12.5. While death rates for most causes have been going down, trends in the late 1980s show an increase of deaths due to AIDS, drug dependence, accidents and unidentified injuries. There was an 88.3 percent increase in AIDS between 1988 and 1990. In 1990, 13.4% of the adult population was HIV infected, and it was estimated that 18.8% of the adult population were intravenous drug users. Given the prevalence of intravenous drug use, the Health Systems Agency of New York City estimates that 60% of the adult population is at risk of contracting AIDS.

---

[9] It could not be stressed enough that the figures reported here reflect the populations reached by the Census. Thus, the informal economy, affecting individuals and particular industries, such as manufacturing sweatshops, are not reflected in these analyses.

Housing Conditions

An important correlate of housing is that it affects the quality of life of people, and the way people use both private as well as public space.[10]

In the 1960s and 1970s, large-scale projects were built in East Harlem, almost doubling the structures built in Manhattan and the rest of the city. In the 1990s, housing shortages are higher in East Harlem than in the rest of the city. Housing units in East Harlem have actually decreased by 16% in the last decade: units are lost to fire or abandonment, the city has virtually stopped the construction of public housing, tenements are left in various states of disrepair, and gentrification has opened some pockets that are not affordable to the local residents.

Scarcity of housing relates to the availability of residential space: in comparison to Manhattan and the rest of the city, East Harlem has less available units. The number of persons per room in occupied housing units, however, has increased at a faster pace outside of the district (see TABLE 6).

Despite higher rates of poverty, the median gross rent has increased at the same rate in East Harlem as in the borough and the city (see TABLE 7). Not only is absolute income lower but there are also fewer housing alternatives available to the large influx of new immigrants. Moreover, the gross rent as percent of household income has increased in East Harlem during the last decade, in contrast to both Manhattan and the rest of the city (see TABLE 8).

In East Harlem, very few individuals are homeowners. Sixty percent of the housing units are owned by the government.

THE ETHNOGRAPHY OF EAST HARLEM: 1950–1990

The rationale for the working conference that resulted in this book was threefold: First, to provide an opportunity for urban ethnographers who had worked on social issues in East Harlem to present their work. Second, to enhance the understanding of their work by sustained discussions with other urban ethnographers who had worked on structurally similar low-income urban enclaves elsewhere. Third, to explore the broader implications of their combined work for the urban ethnography of low-income urban enclaves.

---

[10] Bourgois (this volume) makes reference, for example, to two social categories of people: those who do and those who do not negotiate the streets at night. My own observations indicate that the elderly live in constant fear of the growing and unpredictable violence in the area, and that they feel particularly vulnerable to victimization by the younger generation.

By offering a forum for the exchange of ideas among urban ethnographers[11] who are or have worked[12] in a wide variety of research sites and within various theoretical paradigms, the conference was informed by the comparative perspective that has always been a distinctive feature of anthropology. The working group of urban ethnographers addressed a variety of social issues, such as the increase in urban poverty, changing demographic patterns, the living conditions of vulnerable populations—such as the elderly, children, the hungry, the homeless, substance abusers. They attempted to understand these social issues within a range of theoretical frameworks, such as theories of acculturation, culture of poverty, urban underclass, political economy, cultural materialism. They chose individuals, households, social networks, neighborhoods, localities, as units of analysis. The research topics they pursued included ethnicity and social class, local versus supralocal phenomena, marginality, national development, and processes of social articulation. By reviewing the conceptual frameworks employed in their work, the members of this working group were able to reflect on how best to understand and explain social issues in these kinds of locales.

CONCEPTUAL ELEMENTS OF A POSSIBLE PARADIGM TO STUDY LOW-INCOME URBAN ENCLAVES

Although I had initially presented the parameters for organizing our work, it was only after comparing and contrasting the written and oral contributions of the participants that I was able to reflect upon what seemed to emerge from our joint work: the conceptual elements of a possible paradigm for the urban ethnography of low-income enclaves.[13]

Place
The physical appearance of the neighborhood, the human behavior in the streets, the level of noise, the languages featured in signs over stores (See photographs in APPENDIX II)—all of these aspects of the environment translate into how people experience life circumstances, and how they artic-

---

[11] The urban ethnographers were trained in different disciplines: anthropology, sociology, history, psychology. Regardless of their training, they prioritized a specific dimension in their work, such as culture, economy, politics, policy, among others. The cross-fertilization of approaches allowed members of the working group to test the validity of insights they had developed in the field and to learn from each other.

[12] Although studying the same or similar enclaves, these ethnographers differed in terms of the theoretical and methodological frameworks influencing their thinking and practice at the historical period in which they conducted their studies.

[13] These elements are discussed separately but their interrelationships need to be explored more fully in each specific case.

ulate individual identity. Place is thus intimately related to the social construction of daily life.

A place is also a social field where power relationships are visually displayed. In understanding a place as an enclave, moreover, the structural
characteristics that create localities—for example, the labor market—are
given priority over a notion of "community," based on real or putative ties
among its members.

Context

Urban research problems become social issues when what is observed at
the local level is manifested in larger systems as well. Conceptualizing the
local level ecologically clarifies the interrelationships between "the local"
and "the supralocal" in terms of power (Leeds, 1973).

Patterns of social stratification are visible in New York City because social
strata reside in close geographical proximity—a few blocks mark the difference between poverty and affluence, even within the same neighborhood.[14]

New York is not only a large metropolitan center that epitomizes issues
that define current preoccupations of the nation. It is also a global city
(Sassen 1992), and thus a metaphor for larger systems.

By referring to the enclaves as "low-income," thus, reference is not solely made to poverty as income but as a social issue. As Castells (1983:124)
put it: "Poverty is the consequence, at the distribution level, of a basic pattern of relationships of production organized by class." These relationships
can be better understood in their historicity.

Time

The notion of enclave brings forth changing conditions at many levels.
A historiography that examines critically the political economy of phenomena, as different from chronological accounts, is what is needed to understand complex systems (Wolf 1982; Centro 1979).

Heterogeneity

As the profiles presented above clearly show, the people of East Harlem
are diverse. Thus, for example, if 60% of teenagers become parents, 40% do
not. Public imagination, feeding on journalistic accounts of social life and,
often, on easy generalizations by social scientists and policymakers, homog-
enizes the heterogeneous. How to deal with homogeneity and heterogeneity at the same time will become an important issue for urban
ethnographers.

---

[14] There is a marked difference, for example, between Lexington Avenue and
104th and Fifth Avenue and 104th, only three blocks from one another, and yet
they are both in East Harlem.

Policy

In low-income enclaves, where needs are greater, services provided by government agencies are less comprehensive or non-existent, and access is problematic, the interplay of supply and demand need closer examination than in other localities when making policy recommendations. And, as Montbach (this volume) points out, policies are historically and politically determined.

THE BOOK: OPENING DIALOGUES, ENGAGING DEBATES

The book replicates the historical and comparative framework used for cross-fertilizing ideas among the working group of urban ethnographers of low-income urban enclaves.

The contributions of the East Harlem ethnographers share the following characteristics:

A. Their study populations are geographically concentrated East Harlem.
B. Most have adopted a longitudinal perspective so that the focus is on process rather than solely on synchronic phenomena.
C. Ethnographic methods of inquiry, by themselves or in combination with others, are used.
D. Their research questions are formulated as social issues, in terms of relationships to the larger socio-economic context.
E. Their research seeks to shape social policy.
F. The researchers consider the links between the individual and the collective, the personal and the political, the researcher role vis-a-vis the research population.
G. The researchers also consider a range of theories advanced to explain the relative lack of socio-economic mobility in East Harlem (such as cultural and structural assimilation, cultural pluralism, internal colonialism, culture of poverty, underclass)

This book is divided into two parts: Part I deals with the ethnographic history of East Harlem in the period 1950–1992. Presenters Padilla, Mencher and Safa share their work during the 1950s and 1960s—at both ends of the massive migratory stream coming into East Harlem at the time from Puerto Rico. They describe their ethnographic work and its implications for issues central to both the study populations and their disciplines at the time. Presenters Bourgois, Freidenberg, DeHavennon, Torruellas, and Kornblum and Williams, who have worked in East Harlem more recently, share their work on the political economy of substance abuse, homelessness, the experience of living in, growing up and growing old in East Harlem. Part II deals with Ethnography and National Culture from a Comparative

Perspective. First, the views "from El Barrio," to borrow Lisa Peattie's (1968) phrase, are assessed by discussants Nash and Jones in reaction to the presentations and resulting discussions of the working group. The methodological and theoretical dimensions of the urban anthropology of low-income urban enclaves, based on the dialogues of the working group,[15] are the subject of the reflections of two urban ethnographers who have worked in New York City, Fernández Kelly and Sørensen, from a comparative perspective. Finally, the implications of policy and population issues for national contexts are examined by Montbach, Foner and Vélez-Ibañez.

This book is offered as a contribution to the continuing dialogue and debate on the anthropology of low-income urban enclaves, in light of the urgent and pressing problems that continue to affect the life circumstances of the people of East Harlem.

REFERENCES

CASTELLS, MANUEL
    1983   The City and the Grass Roots: A Cross-Cultural Theory of Urban Social Movements. Berkeley: University of California Press.
CENTRO DE ESTUDIOS PUERTORRIQUEÑOS
    1979   Labor Migration under Capitalism: The Puerto Rican Experience. New York: Monthly Review Press.
DEPARTMENT OF CITY PLANNING, CITY OF NEW YORK
    1992   A Portrait of New York City's Community Districts from the 1980 & 1990 Censuses of Population and Housing. A: Demographic Profiles. B: Socioeconomic Profiles
DE ORTIZ, CAROL
    1992   The politics of home care for the elderly poor: New York City's medic-aid-funded home attendant program. Medical Anthropological Quarterly 7 (1):4–29
DUNLAP, ELOISE
    1992   The setting for the crack era: Macro forces, micro consequences (1990–1992). The Journal of Psychoactive Drugs, May.
FONER, NANCY, ED.
    1987   New Immigrants in New York. New York: Columbia University Press.
HARWOOD, ALLAN
    1977   Rx: Spiritist as Needed: A Study of a Puerto Rican Community Mental Health Resource. Ithaca: Cornell University Press.
HOPPER, KIM, E. SUSSER, AND S. CONOVER
    1985   Economies of makeshift: Deindustrialization and homelessness in New York City. Urban Anthropology 14:183–236
JONES, DELMOS, JOAN TURNER, AND JOAN MONTBACH
    1992   Declining social services and the threat to social reproduction: An Urban Dilemma. City and Society 6:99–113

---

[15] APPENDIX III provides a list of participants of the working group.

LaRuffa, Anthony
1988 *Monte Carmelo: An Italian-American Community in the Bronx*. New York: Gordon & Breach.

Leeds, Anthony
1973 Locality power in relation to supralocal power institutions. In *Urban Anthropology*, A. Southhall, Ed., pp. 15–41. New York: Oxford University Press.

Lomnitz, Larissa
1977 *Networks and Marginality: Life in a Mexican Shantytown*. New York: Academic Press.

Lopez, Iris
1987 Sterilization among Puerto Rican Women in New York City: Public Policy and Social Constraints. In *Cities of the United States: Studies in Urban Anthropology*, Leith Mullings, Ed., P. 269–291. New York: Columbia University Press.

Peattie, Lisa
1968 *The View from the Barrio*. Ann Arbor: University of Michigan Press.

Sanjek, Roger
1990 Urban anthropology in the 1980's: A world view. *Annual Reviews of Anthropology* 19:151–186

Sassen, Saskia
1992 *The Global City: New York, London, Tokyo*. Princeton: Princeton University Press.

Scharff, Jagna
1987 The underground economy of a poor neighborhood. In *Cities of the United States: Studies in Urban Anthropology*, Leith Mullings, Ed. New York: Columbia University Press.

Sexton, Patricia
1965 *Spanish Harlem. Anatomy of Poverty*. New York: Harper.

Stewart, Donald
1972 *A Short History of East Harlem*. New York: Museum of the City of New York.

Susser, Ida
1982 *Norman Street: Poverty and Politics in an Urban Neighborhood*. New York: Oxford University Press.

Sullivan, Mercer
1989 *"Getting Paid": Youth Crime and Work in the Inner City*. Ithaca, NY: Cornell University Press.

Williams, Terry and William Kornblum
1985 *Growing Up Poor*. Lexington, KY: Lexington Books.

Wilson, William Julius
Studying inner city social dislocations: The challenge of public agenda research. 1990 Presidential Address. American Sociological Review, 1991, 56,1 (Feb. 1–14).

Wolf, Eric
1982 *Europe and the People without History*. Berkeley: University of California Press.

Wong, B.
1982 *Chinatown: Economic Adaptation and Ethnic Identity of the Chinese*. New York: Holt, Rinehart, Winston.

APPENDIX I

Table 1. A Comparison of Changes in the Population Characteristics of New York City, Manhattan, and East Harlem: 1980–1990

Characteristics	Changes 1980–1990 (in percentages)		
	New York	Manhattan	East Harlem
Total population	3.5	4.1	−3.5
White nonhispanic	−14.6	0.7	−19.3
Black nonhispanic	9.0	−10.1	−12.7
Hispanic origin or descent	26.8	15.3	6.4
Puerto Rican	5.2	−6.8	−4.0
Other	60.2	37.1	78.2
Asian & Pacific Islander—			
non-Hispanic	104.7	43.5	47.3
Chinese	92.1	37.5	5.3
Asian Indian	102.5	9.7	0.4
Korean	215.9	113.6	68.0
Philippino	70.3	44.9	158.1
American Indian non-Hispanic	80.4	17.2	3.5
Other non-Hispanic	15.6	−10.8	28.3
Aged under 5 years	9.5	14.8	10.6
5 to 9 years	2.7	6.2	3.3
10 to 14 years	−11.5	−11.5	−23.3
15 to 19 years	−16.5	−15.5	−33.5
20 to 24 years	−4.3	−7.6	−5.0
25 to 29 years	10.8	0.1	29.1
30 to 34 years	16.2	7.5	8.0
35 to 39 years	31.5	27.0	7.9
40 to 44 years	35.9	39.8	−0.4
45 to 49 years	17.1	24.4	−0.2
50 to 54 years	−8.8	−3.0	−8.0
55 to 59 years	−19.4	−12.3	−22.0
60 to 64 years	−7.1	0.1	−3.0
65 to 69 years	−5.6	−5.7	4.4
70 to 74 years	−8.1	−14.9	−8.2
75 to 79 years	1.0	−7.8	11.3
80 to 84 years	13.3	11.5	20.9
85 years and over	36.0	37.4	40.4
Female	2.3	3.7	−4.0
Male	5.0	4.7	−2.9
Persons 15 years and over	4.6	4.5	−2.7
Now married, except separated	−2.6	3.6	−17.7
Never married	15.3	11.3	9.4

Separated, widowed, divorced	2.8	-6.4	-3.7
Persons in households	3.0	3.3	-4.7
In family households	1.6	3.5	-6.4
in a family	-0.1	2.2	-8.6
householder	-1.3	2.0	-6.4
spouse	-8.7	-1.4	-26.3
own child	-37.6	-36.4	-25.8
other relative	228.0	176.5	21.2
nonrelatives	113.9	54.7	130.7
in nonfamily households	9.6	3.1	5.2
householder	5.2	1.5	0.0
nonrelatives	40.8	12.6	56.5

SOURCE: Adapted from: *Demographic Profiles. A Portrait of New York City's Community Districts From the 1980 & 1990 Censuses of Population and Housing.* City of New York. Department of City Planning, 1992.

Table 2. A Comparison of Changes in Selected Social Characteristics of New York City, Manhattan, and East Harlem: 1980–1990

Characteristics	Changes 1980–1990 (in percentages)		
	New York City	Manhattan	East Harlem
Nativity			
Foreign born	24.7	10.1	23.7
Citizenship			
Naturalized Citizen	-0.5	-6.3	-23.7
Not a citizen	52.1	24.6	98.0
Speaks a language other than English at home	19.3	10.7	-0.5
Residential mobility[1]			
Lived in same house	8.7	11.6	-5.2
Lived in different house in United States	-10.7	-8.8	-7.3
Lived abroad	33.5	6.2	18.0

[1] Residence five years prior to the census for people five years and older.
SOURCE: Adapted from: *Socioeconomic Profiles. A Portrait of New York City's Community Districts from the 1980 & 1990 Censuses of Population and Housing.* City of New York. Department of City Planning.

Table 3. A Comparison of Change in the Household Characteristics of New York City, Manhattan, and East Harlem: 1980–1990

Characteristics	Changes 1980–1990 (in percentages)		
	New York City	Manhattan	East Harlem
Total Households[1]	1.1	1.7	–4.1
With persons under 18	–1.4	–0.7	–9.4
With persons 65 and over	0.9	–1.8	7.3
Family Households	–1.3	2.0	–6.4
Married-couple family	–8.7	–1.4	–28.3
With related children	–8.5	–5.2	–34.2
No related children	–8.9	0.9	–16.4
Other Family	14.8	8.2	10.1
Male householder	41.0	18.1	20.6
With related children	58.4	29.2	35.6
No related children	31.4	12.4	10.2
Female Householder	9.6	6.1	8.7
With related children	4.1	2.1	3.7
No related children	20.7	13.1	22.8
Nonfamily Households	5.2	1.5	0.0
One person	1.7	–0.5	–3.4
Male householder	2.3	–2.9	–10.9
Female householder	1.2	1.4	1.9
Two or more persons	32.2	12.9	37.5
Male householder	31.5	9.8	34.0
Female householder	33.2	17.0	41.7

[1] "A household includes all the persons who occupy a housing unit. The occupants may be a single family, one person living alone, two or more families living together, or any other group of related or unrelated persons, who share living arrangements" (*ibid*:B-8).

SOURCE: Adapted from: *Demographic Profiles. A Portrait of New York City's Community Districts from the 1980 & 1990 Censuses of Population and Housing*. City of New York. Department of City Planning (see TABLE 1):B-8.

Table 4. A Comparison of Changes in Selected Education and Labor Force Characteristics of New York City, Manhattan, and East Harlem: 1980–1990

Characteristics	Changes 1980–1990 (in percentages)		
	New York	Manhattan	East Harlem
Education			
School Enrollment			
Elementary or			
High School	−4.1	−3.3	−13.7
College	41.3	29.3	33.2
School Attainment			
Less than 9 years	−34.4	−33.2	−35.9
Some high school	16.5	11.9	22.0
High school graduate	23.6	19.6	28.7
Some college	64.6	32.3	74.0
College graduate	44.5	37.4	60.1
Labor force			
Males 16 years and over	6.8	4.9	0.4
In the Labor force	9.2	7.7	9.8
In the civilian labor force	9.2	8.0	9.4
Employed	7.4	7.0	3.2
Unemployed	31.3	20.3	52.3
In the armed forces	−6.5	−36.8	178.6
Not in the labor force	1.2	−2.5	−10.6
Females 16 years and over	3.6	4.6	−3.9
In the labor force	18.1	14.4	10.5
In the civilian labor force	18.0	14.4	10.5
Employed	16.7	13.8	7.5
Unemployed	33.9	22.4	33.3
In the armed forces	126.2	126.5	118.2
Not in the labor force	−9.3	−7.3	−11.8
Labor force composition	13.2	10.9	10.1
Males	9.2	7.7	9.8
Females	18.1	14.4	10.5
Females 16+ with own children			
In the labor force			
Children under 6 years	45.2	43.8	27.3
Children 6–17 years	7.3	−1.6	−1.9

SOURCE: Adapted from: *Socioeconomic Profiles. A Portrait of New York City's Community Districts from the 1980 & 1990 Censuses of Population and Housing.* City of New York. Department of City Planning (see TABLE 2).

Table 5. A Comparison of Changes in Selected Employment and Commutation Characteristics[1] of New York City, Manhattan and East Harlem: 1980–1990

Characteristics	Changes 1980–1990 (in percentages)		
	New York	Manhattan	East Harlem
Industry			
Agriculture, forestry, fisheries & mining	36.7	26.2	54.3
Construction	69.8	62.5	104.6
Manufacturing	−26.7	−22.4	−33.1
Durable	−21.4	−14.9	−19.5
Nondurable	−29.5	−24.8	−40.7
Transportation	7.9	−9.3	−1.3
Communication & public utilities	−3.6	1.8	−29.0
Wholesale trade	−5.8	−4.8	4.1
Retail trade	10.7	3.9	−2.1
Finance, insurance & real estate	15.1	40.6	−3.2
Business and repair services	10.1	−2.6	25.0
Personal, entertainment & recreation services	20.4	4.2	−3.0
Professional and related services	37.4	33.2	27.9
Health services	30.7	18.0	18.3
Educational services	31.0	18.5	47.5
Other	52.0	56.4	28.6
Public administration	11.8	−4.3	17.5
Occupation			
Executive, administrative & managerial,	32.1	31.2	42.7
Professional specialty	31.9	22.6	40.2
Technicians & related support	41.4	26.2	81.7
Sales	28.1	37.4	25.7
Administrative support, including clerical	−7.6	−12.8	−2.1
Service	22.2	0.2	6.6
Private household	−5.1	−29.1	−28.3
Protective service	36.5	24.0	28.8
Other	21.5	0.7	6.9
Farming, forestry & fishing	4.0	−5.3	−11.8
Precision production, craft & repair	−0.6	−12.8	−21.7

Machine operators, assemblers & inspectors	−29.1	−31.8	−40.2
Transportation & material moving	19.9	6.6	8.7
Handlers, equipment cleaners, helpers & laborers	2.0	0.1	−1.3
Class of Worker			
Private wage & salary	9.8	9.8	2.8
Private not-for-profit wage & salary	—	—	—
Federal government	−16.9	−27.5	−20.6
State government	15.8	18.6	6.5
Local government	24.4	5.3	16.0
Self-employed	29.0	30.7	35.8
Unpaid family member	57.1	7.5	600.0
Place of Work			
Within New York City	—	—	—
within county of residence	—	—	—
Outside New York City	—	—	—
Mean travel time to work (minutes)	—	—	—
Means of Commutation			
Car, truck or van	22.5	19.0	17.2
Drove alone	34.8	41.6	17.5
Carpooled	−2.4	−10.6	16.7
Public Transportation	7.9	8.3	2.7
Bus, trolley, streetcar	7.0	−3.3	23.9
Subway	5.1	8.8	−7.9
Railroad	20.1	25.1	38.7
Taxicab	43.3	53.2	164.8
Ferryboat	—	—	—
Walked	6.2	10.7	9.7
Worked at Home	58.4	43.5	123.2
Other means	−14.5	1.0	40.5

[1] For employed persons 16 years of age and over
SOURCE: Adapted from: *Socioeconomic Profiles. A Portrait of New York City's Community Districts from the 1980 & 1990 Censuses of Population and Housing*. City of New York. Department of City Planning (see TABLE 2).

Table 6. A Comparison of Changes in the Housing Characteristics of New York City, Manhattan and East Harlem: 1980–1990

Characteristics	Changes 1980–1990		
	New York City	Manhattan	East Harlem
Total Housing Units	1.7	4.1	−10.2
Vacancy Status	12.7	37.6	−54.8
For rent only	20.5	86.1	−24.4
For sale only	157.7	228.8	−84.0
Not occupied[1]	2.1	13.6	−60.5
Occupied Housing Units	1.1	1.7	−4.6
Persons Per room			
One or less	−3.9	−1.6	−8.4
1.01	60.7	44.6	22.4
1.01–1.50	24.8	17.2	14.7
1.51–2	107.4	58.4	−4.9
2.01	283.7	161.2	83.2

[1] Rented or sold.

SOURCE: Adapted from: *Demographic Profiles. A Portrait of New York City's Community Districts from the 1980 & 1990 Censuses of Population and Housing.* City of New York. Department of City Planning (see TABLE 1).

Table 7. A Comparison of Changes in Selected Housing Characteristics of New York City, Manhattan and East Harlem: 1980–1990

Characteristics	Changes 1980–1990 (in percentages)		
	New York City	Manhattan	East Harlem
Year Structure Build			
1949, or earlier	-13.6	-11.5	-42.1
1950–1959	11.9	16.0	1.0
1960–1969	11.3	9.4	24.4
1970–1979	14.0	5.0	12.1
1980–1984	—[1]	—[2]	—[3]
1985–1990	—[1]	—[2]	—[3]
Year Householder Moved Into Unit			
1959, or earlier	-43.8	-46.0	-39.2
1960–1969	-39.8	-38.0	-41.0
1970–1979	-62.9	61.7	-58.0
1980–1984	—[4]	—[5]	—[6]
1985–1990	—[4]	—[5]	—[6]
Vehicles Available			
None	-3.8	-1.4	-5.6
1	-1.7	12.2	-0.4
2	33.6	40.1	62.5
3 or more	98.1	82.9	3.8
Gross Rent			
Median gross rent	25.9	22.4	24.8
Telephone Available			
Occupied housing units with a telephone	5.3	6.6	7.7
Mortgage Status			
Specified owner occupied units with a mortgage	17.1	146.1	109.1

[1] There are no data on 1980 on this characteristic so changes cannot be computed. However, from the 1990 census, we can see there was an increase of 2.9 in structures built 1980–1984 and of 3.3 for 1985 to 1990.
[2] *Idem.* An increase of 3.4 in structures built 1980–1984 and of 4.9 from 1985–1990.
[3] *Idem.* From 1980–1984, there was an increase of 5.0 in structures built, and from 1985–1990, there was an increase of 3.7 percent.
[4] *Idem.* From 1980–1984, there was an increase of 17.8 of householders moving into units. From 1985–1990, the increase was of 37.9 percent.
[5] *Idem.* From 1980–1984, there was an increase of 16.6 of householders moving into units. From 1985–1990, the increase was of 39.1 percent.
[6] *Idem.* From 1980–1984, there was an increase of 17.8 of householders moving into units. From 1985–1990, the increase was of 31.4 percent.
SOURCE: Adapted from: *Socioeconomic Profiles. A Portrait of New York City's Community Districts from the 1980 & 1990 Censuses of Population and Housing.* City of New York. Department of City Planning.

Table 8. A Comparison of Changes in Selected Income and Poverty Characteristics of New York City, Manhattan and East Harlem: 1980–1990

Characteristics	Changes 1980–1990 (in percentages)		
	New York City	Manhattan	East Harlem
Income and Housing			
Selected monthly owner costs as a percent of household income in 1989 Specified owner-occupied housing units	17.3	185.0	184.4
Less than 20 percent	15.2	219.1	152.4
20 to 24 percent	–3.3	68.9	40.0
25 to 34 percent	15.2	172.9	—
35 percent or more	40.5	172.2	316.7
Not computed	40.2	57.9	—
Gross Rent as a Percent of Household Income in 1989 Specified renter-occupied housing units	–5.9	–9.5	–4.2
Less than 20 percent	–11.9	–9.3	–20.9
20 to 24 percent	–10.0	–18.2	–15.8
25 to 34 percent	5.5	–3.2	48.9
35 percent or more	–4.6	–11.1	0.4
Not computed	8.1	5.2	–11.8
Poverty Status			
Below the poverty level	–0.5	–2.6	–3.2
Below 125% of poverty level	–5.4	–7.5	–8.0
Below 150% of poverty level	–8.6	–11.4	–11.4
Below 175% of poverty level	–9.7	–12.1	–13.2
Below 185% of poverty level	—	—	—
Below 200% of poverty level	–10.3	–13.0	–12.3
Families below the poverty level	–6.1	–4.8	–6.6
With related children under 18 years	–8.8	–5.8	–5.4
With related children under 5 years	–6.7	–1.7	1.2
With female householder, no spouse	–4–3	0.1	3.5
With related children under 18 years	–8.0	–2.2	1.6
Unrelated individuals 15 years and over below the poverty level	16.1	–2.3	15.9

SOURCE: Adapted from: *Socioeconomic Profiles. A Portrait of New York City's Community Districts from the 1980 & 1990 Censuses of Population and Housing.* City of New York. Department of City Planning (see TABLE 2).

APPENDIX II
PART I—EARLIER VIEWS OF EAST HARLEM

Playing dominos, "undated."(Kurt W. Deuschle Collection)

A panoramic view of *El Barrio*, undated. (Kurt W. Deuschle Collection)

Street scene, August 1971 (Kurt W. Deuschle Collection)

Market scene—probably *La Marqueta,* undated. (Kurt W. Deuschle Collection)

Market scene, August 1971. (Kurt W. Deuschle Collection)

One hundred and eleventh street, Betterment Block Association and Borinquen
Democratic Club—November 1965. (Kurt W. Deuschle Collection)

Street scene showing tenements, September 1977. (Kurt W. Deuschle Collection)

Tenement with clothes drying outside windows, November 1966. (Kurt W. Deuschle Collection)

Fixing "piraguas" in the street, August 1971. (Kurt W. Deuschle Collection)

Street intersection, November 1968. (Kurt W. Deuschle Collection)

Borinquen Towers, September 1977. (Kurt W. Deuschle Collection)

APPENDIX II
PART II—CONTEMPORARY VIEWS OF EAST HARLEM

Vacant lot with improvised shacks. (Photo credit: Edmundo Morales)

Street scene, 116th Street, undated. Unknown photographer.

Borinquén Neighborhood Center taken from 121st Street and Lexington. (Photo Credit: Judith Freidenberg)

View of *El Barrio* taken from 102nd Street and Fifth Avenue. (Photo Credit: Judith Freidenberg)

Buildings, highrises in background. (Photo credit: Edmundo Morales)

Vacant yard with abandoned cars. (Photo credit: Edmundo Morales)

A view from El Barrio: from 104th Street between Park and Lexington Avenues towards Fifth Avenue. (Photo Credit: Judith Freidenberg)

Botanica (Hispanic Herbal Store)—104th Street, 1991. (Photo Credit: Judith Freidenberg)

Entrance to dilapidated tenement: Park Ave at 117th Street. (Photo credit: Edmundo Morales)

Park Ave at 117th Street: An example of folk health care system. (Photo credit: Edmundo Morales)

Lexington Avenue at 104th Street: Playing dominos on the sidewalk and vacant yard with *casita*. (Photo Credit: Judith Freidenberg)

APPENDIX III
LIST OF CONFERENCE PARTICIPANTS[1]

Jorge Ayala
Centro de Estudios Puertorriqueños
Hunter College, CUNY
New York, NY 10021

Margaret Boone
4501 Arlington Blvd. Apt. No. 727
Arlington, VA 22203

Eloise Dunlap
Narcotic and Drug Research, Inc.
11 Beech Street
New York, NY 10013

Vivian Garrison
16 Ridge Road
Rumson, NJ 07760

Muriel Hammer
N.Y.S. Psychiatric Institute
722 West 168th St.
New York, NY 10032

Phillip Kasinitz
Sociology Department
Hunter College, CUNY
New York, NY 10021

Antonio Lauría-Perricelli
Centro de Estudios Puertorriqueños
Hunter College, CUNY
New York, NY 10021

Pedro Pedraza
Centro de Estudios Puertorriqueños
Hunter College, CUNY
New York, NY 10021

Jagna Wojcicka Sharff
327 West 101st Street
New York, NY 10025

Gisela Welz
Ludwig-Uhland-Institut für Empirische Kulturwissenschaft
Universitat Tubingen
Tubingen, Germany

Linda Winston
401 East 86th Street
New York, NY 10028

---

[1] These individuals participated in the workshop discussions with the presenters and contributors to this volume.

Retrospect of Ethnomedical Research among Puerto Ricans
Living at the Margin of East Harlem

ELENA PADILLA[1]

Saint Barnabas Hospital
183rd & Third Avenue
New York, New York 10453

The manifest purpose of the field research on which my book *Up from Puerto Rico* was based, was to provide sociocultural background information for a medical study of life stress, and for the operation of a family practice clinic model at a small first floor apartment in an old tenement building in a distressingly poor area of New York City. This was a multiracial/multicultural area where many Puerto Ricans who had recently arrived in the City lived.

CLARIFYING DOMAINS

Both for pragmatic and conceptual perspectives, upfront, all cross-disciplinary research requires a clarification of domains and interphases. Defining research problems relative to health in a sociocultural framework was a perplexing issue for the anthropologists. As challenging was to delineate effective roles for the anthropologists and for the physicians in the project. Since by funding source, the project was under medical auspices, in this sense, the anthropologists were clients of the physicians. At first, their expectation was for the anthropologists to function as support staff or consultants who could help them answer questions about their individual patients, their specific illnesses, and response to medical care. Puerto Rican patients seemed to have posed vexing medical problems for the physicians both by the manner in which they presented symptoms and by how they dealt with their health complaints and illnesses. The physicians were also

[1]Scholar in Residence, Saint Barnabas Hospital in the South Bronx and Professor Emerita, Health Policy and Management, Robert F. Wagner Graduate School of Public Service, New York University.

interested in doing research on how the health of families was affected by stresses produced by migration to New York City.

For the anthropologists, trying to meet or approximate physicians' expectations was not possible without field research. It was crucial to provide the physicians with a culture-bound, contextual framework and data base as dimension for their own clinical research. Physicians could then identify conditions and individual responses to life stress situations to help in managing the health care problems of their patients in their family practice setting. The physicians also appeared to need cultural translations of patients' presenting symptoms, diseases, and distress. While it was relatively easy to discuss these equivalencies, it was not easy to agree on how they were to be incorporated within an organized study. For the anthropologists, deciding how to do such research required a leap into unknown territory: we lacked any basic organized information about the people or how they lived, and the skills of team members in urban research and in ethnomedicine varied substantially. A balance had to be found between the kind of social research that the anthropologists could do and be trained to do and the physicians' expectations about the nature of the data and the work roles of anthropologists. This balancing act called for generating documented field data in accordance with research standards. The other side of this requirement was for the anthropologists to provide physicians with the kind of empirical information that they needed for their own work in consonance with their professional standards. A process had to be developed for disentangling the domains of work of anthropologists from that of physicians, since unless the expectations of physicians could be moderated and the anthropologists could manage the constraints posed by the culture of medicine and physician mystique, the possibility of protecting the integrity of the research was minimal.

At issue for both physicians and anthropologists was learning to discharge complementary role sets. In simple terms, the conceptual and empirical work processes of the physicians and those of anthropologists could not be commingled; physicians were professionally and technically oriented to patient care and the anthropologists to informants/respondents in sociocultural contexts. Operationally, anthropologists could only do competent field research if they defined freely the kinds of relationships that would allow them to gain rapport and trust from the area residents. Here also, confidentiality was a concern. Certain types of information collected by the anthropologists was at stake in the same way that personal medical information was privileged to physicians and other clinicians. In disentangling professional domains, both physicians and anthropologists had the fortuitous intervention of Professor Charles Wagley who was then chairman of the Columbia University Anthropology Department and a diplomat par excellence. Professor Wagley introduced and conducted regular interdisciplinary seminars and mediated in setting parameters and in resolving moot issues and misunderstandings. These seminars became a source of joint learning and stimulated tolerance in negotiating and resolving mutual concerns, helping all of us to shed our professional tribalism. This expedited the process of cross-disciplinary work as ideas and interests became specified and assessed, that is communicated.

PLANNING THE RESEARCH[2]

In many ways, this study was both an invention and an exploration in applying anthropology both to an urban area and to medicine, in learning to manage the tensions involved in the nature of interdisciplinary collaboration, and in assuring the intellectual integrity and quality control of research work.

The anthropological team included 5 to 7 graduate students who came and went throughout the period of field work. These students were not only dabbling in their first field experience but also intended to make their own individual contribution for their own doctoral dissertations. As project director, I was then a Ph.D. rookie in Anthropology. The study covered four main questions, and although these were not formulated explicitly at the outset, they evolved gradually into the parameters of the inquiry. The questions were:

1. How can ethnological methods be applied to learn about a population that lives in a given urban area but whose lives are linked both to city institutions and also to Puerto Rico?

2. Can social adaptations and cultural norms be studied stemming from positions in the family, and by extension, to other positions and roles outside the family identified in primary, interactive social contexts?

3. How do city institutional settings manage the latter relationships? and

4. How are these dimensions of social behavior related to definitions and actions involving health and disease?

From the above questions, many more emerged and were incorporated into the study, as would be expected from research in which the multiple variables involved cannot be identified beforehand by a principal investigator.

NATURE OF THE RESEARCH

This was not a typical anthropological study. For purposes of the study, it was necessary to invent a neighborhood—a social construct—defined by a system of recurrent social activities and of flows of relationships that influ-

---

[2]This article is only concerned with the anthropological segment of the study which I directed. Beatrice B. Berle, M.D. directed the medical segment and the family clinic.

enced the lives of residents in fateful ways. Technically, this neighborhood was defined by its mesh of social interactions, *i.e.* families, friends, gatherings in grocery stores, churches, building stoops, alleys and in street corners. Socially, this neighborhood was not like the section of East Harlem, (known as "El Barrio"), a few blocks northwards, where the dominant population was and still is Puerto Rican. The area studied was inhabited by members of different ethnic/racial groups with interactive social relations among them, with their conflicts tending to be interpersonal rather than racially or ethnically based. Puerto Ricans had become a major presence here and were the most visible and readily identifiable players. The neighborhood comprised some ten by five city blocks; north was an Italian neighborhood; to the west, public housing projects had been built where people from different racial/cultural backgrounds and different parts of the City lived. Southward, demolition of old buildings and new construction had proceeded for highly priced condominiums and cooperatives and east, was the East-River.

Although Puerto Ricans were our main interest, to describe the study as "of Puerto Ricans" or of the "Puerto Rican community" is misleading. It was a study of a slum urban area, where home was in rundown buildings in the midst of blight. This piece of East Harlem was like a beachhead or forefront for Puerto Ricans and others moving into the city, mostly from the southern states.

The study dealt not only with families and their functions, but also with their relationships to welfare and social services, work, the police and the courts, schools, churches, and medical care in the context of cultural norms, preferences, expectations and values of the population. Slices of specific social processes were also tapped: child rearing practices and socialization of children, cliques and drug addiction, *machismo* and relations between men and women; race relations, and the "we" or insider group identity solidarity and cultural definitions of health and disease. Political participation and expectations (for example conflict solution, constituency behaviors, voter registration, campaigning, elections, running for office, voting and demanding resources) were not a part of the social processes of the area. Ironically, even when a Puerto Rican councilman lived in the area and the Puerto Rican community in New York had a long history of community organization and active political participation, in this neighborhood, politics was not yet a vehicle for public problem solving. Except for a handful of white, Protestant American ministers who lived in the area and operated their own storefront churches there, neither politicians, or government or voluntary agencies reached out to the neighbors. The ministers had been instrumental in establishing the medical clinic, and acted as "brokers" with agencies for individual residents. The arms of government and of social and health agencies that touched them were guided by long standing Elizabethan principles regarding help for the "deserving poor." Residents of the area were considered "people in trouble," needing their help and control, with little if any room for kindling their empowerment. Their cultural differences were manifested in social inequality, discrimination and rejection of the residents. In a political sense, they were tools of a mobilization of bias that reinforced their status as clients rather than as citizens[3] in the sense used several years later by Osborne and Gaebler (1992):

> clients are people who are dependent upon and controlled by their helpers and leaders . . . Citizens . . . understand their own problems in their own terms (and) perceive their relationship to one another and . . . believe in their capacity to act.

In trying to cope with their life circumstances, residents formulated rationalities or explanations consistent with their own cultural orientations. These ranged from humor to bitter criticism of those that treated them as if they were their superiors. In their daily routines, they were likely to face barriers that interrupted their efforts to complete their daily tasks as when they were visited by a welfare worker, insurance bill collector, or school attendance officer. Their time frames were usually fragile. How to go around barriers had become a part of their corpus of social adaptations for solving problems in situations that posed threats or broke down their routines. For both adult men and women, the toll for these unexpected events and struggles with work or family was frequent illness, and confusion. The men mostly lost face and authority in the family as the women were gaining ascendancy and responsibility in keeping the family together.

The residents were in effect disenfranchised and recurrent struggles, which to outsiders would seem trivial, dominated their daily lives. Education for the children and work were of the highest value. The young went to school, at times without a coat in winter days. A high school diploma was the dream. As for work, most adults were "non participants in the labor force"; few had regular full time jobs and some worked full time for part time wages. Negotiating the institutional systems of the City was an integral part of their lives. There was no "feminization of poverty"; poverty was both male and female. Politically, and economically they were marginalized and powerless; the source of strength was in family, friends and common social understandings.

---

[3]See Lindbloom, 1982, for an analysis of the influence of social class and traditional biases in the American political culture. For Dye (1987), mobilization of bias within the political system curtails benefits for small and unorganized constituencies.

PUTTERING WITH METHODS

Given the range and focus of the study and considering the diverse interests of the researchers, modifications had to be made in applying ethnological methods. How does one study "an urban neighborhood," albeit one, invented for research purposes that is neither an organized sociopolitical unit nor a historically self-defined community but one which consists of segments of social structures and processes? How can one bring a culture of health dimension (*i.e.*, theories of health and disease, and social norms that lead to behaviors related to maintaining and restoring health and managing disease[4]) into this context?

The study required using a variety of data collection techniques. It became necessary to develop guides for interviews covering the scope of the study and to write questionnaires which although not consistently administered to respondents, were used to steer in-depth interviews, mass observation (events of a day in different street blocks) and participant observation. There was no way the anthropologists could select respondents randomly or control the selection of participants—those who participated did so freely, with the consequence of limiting the generalizability of findings. In today's language, we worked with multiple respondents on quota samples supplemented by hundreds of hours of observation by each field worker. Most field research was done during daytime, although it was also necessary for some of the researchers to be there late at night, since by midnight, the apartments, streets and stores lighted up—with people shopping, going to church services, chatting and, on warm nights,—strolling by the streets. This renewal of activity coincided with the return to the neighborhood of those who worked in 4 P.M.–11 P.M. shifts in hospitals and factories. There was also an underground business economy mostly operated by the few drug addicts who then lived in the area. In addition to being organized for stealing, selling, buying, processing, and getting high on drugs, addicts held street corner markets at dawn where, bargains from bananas to men's and women's suits could be bought cheaply.

Assembling and analyzing the data collected in the field, posed other unexpected challenges. New searches in the literature were necessary and further checking of the field data was required because of problems with incomplete information, inadequate documentation, internal consistency, and reliability. All poorly documented and conflictive pieces of information that could not be verified were discarded. The study was descriptive and

---

[4]See Weidman, 1976. Weidman used the concept "health culture" to encompass the phenomena associated with well being and sickness entailing values, beliefs, and blueprints for health action as well as the health care delivery system. In the study of East Harlem the culture of health was conceptualized operationally as including health/illness beliefs, and decisions and behaviors for restoring health.

applied. It did not derive from any explicit body of theory. Nonetheless, it was possible to identify theoretical issues that influenced the field research: among these were included using culture as a psychobehavioral analytical concept that "explained" the conduct of individuals; or culture, as a vector for attitudinal and psychosocial processes, and as a construct dealing with normative aspects of behaviors rooted in social learning. These divergent theoretical views also influenced the selection and analysis of data. The findings were shared with the physicians to use in their clinical analyses of families and stressors. One of the first products generated by the anthropologists was a vocabulary on health, symptoms and disease which covered over 100 items and which became a tool for the family practice clinic.

REFLECTING ON THEN AND NOW

This research activity provided an irradicable learning experience; yet, one can only draw vignettes of some of the many loose ends that still remain extant. As the Puerto Rican saying goes "a lot has rained," from the time the study was completed and published. Research theory and methods have advanced in ways that we could not have fathomed at the time of the study. Since that time, research has acquired new foci, new rules, technology and values in a climate dominated by ready made computerized data bases and multiple regression analyses which yield masses of interrelated findings in short time. In this equation, ethnological research has been at a disadvantage vis-à-vis those who finance the research enterprise and the kinds of macrolevel societal problems that have captured the contemporary *Zeitgeist*. Still, given the complexity of sociopolitical and economic systems, many questions regarding the importance of studying small sociocultural units of the macro society—ranging from how different types of family systems adapt to the functions of organizational culture of corporate businesses or social and health systems under conditions of rapid change—are unanswered.

The barrage of categories for characterizing minority groups and/or poor peoples calls into question both investigators' values and biases and point to the need for further social research. Is such a label as "culture of poverty" applicable to the section of East Harlem that we studied? Were they living in a "melting pot" of people trying to lose their identities "to become American"? Were they members of an "underclass" or a case study in "social disorganization"? The section of East Harlem that we studied, was an organized society in which living conditions were deplorable; it would be hardly appropriate to characterize its residents by labels based on their problems without considering their own solutions to their living circumstances. Although they were critical of those who treated them as socially inferior because of their values and language,—racial, linguistic or cultural differences were not a source of conflict among their social equals. In a social level, those differences were overridden by common understandings derived from their position in the society and common ways life. Still, this country has to catch up with the rapid pace and consequences of unplanned social change and large immigrations and is not in tune with energizing low income, minority communities with the economic and political elements of empowerment for "affirmative communities" of citizens rather than client.

Meanwhile, new social structures, values and social meanings have recast the Puerto Rican experience both in New York and on the island. For urban Puerto Ricans, traditional family roles and religious beliefs are no longer the central fulcrum of social control, having been supplemented and in many cases replaced by other societal mechanisms and processes. Although this is reflected in the varied ways of life of Puerto Ricans in this City, the sense of being Puerto Rican has been strengthened in spite of the Puerto Rican diaspora, with different generations living throughout the United States and other countries. The in-and-out movement of Puerto Ricans led a Puerto Rican leader to say that "we are no longer migrants; we are travelers." Also growing, has been a reaffirmation of Puerto Rican social identity. At the time of the study, Puerto Ricans identified themselves as Hispanic not as a form of self-denial but as a term of reference that in effect meant Puerto Rican. More recently, the terms "Hispanic" and "Latino" have tended to dilute the sense of identity of the Puerto Rican community hiding politically the largest ethnic group in New York City. Today, the designation of Puerto Ricans as Hispanic and Latino is not altogether positive since in the ethnic/racial political basis of this City, blurring Puerto Ricans with other ethnic national groups, conceals the Puerto Rican community politically and thus renders it invisible in the allocation of social, economic and political resources. Masking Puerto Ricans contributes to effective discrimination to the point that, although Puerto Ricans are the largest ethnic group in the City, Puerto Ricans are notoriously underrepresented in government, corporate business, communications media, and the professions, and are conspicuously missing from boards of educational and charitable foundations and other organizations. The political recognition of the Puerto Rican community *qua* Puerto Rican has yet to be established in New York and in other American cities where large numbers of Puerto Ricans live. Recognition of the Puerto Rican identity by public agencies is essential for the Puerto Rican community so that its leaders increase their political capacity to empower this community to address its needs and aspirations and redress them as citizens (see above). In spite of the efforts and accomplishments of Puerto Rican leaders and community organizations, an affirmative Puerto Rican community is yet to be developed.

Meanwhile, medical anthropology and ethnomedicine have come of age in scholarship and many anthropologists have built careers in this arena at universities, medical schools, hospitals, government, and business, articulating anthropology within those contexts. Interdisciplinary cooperation in research between anthropology and medicine has yet to gain fuller realization. A cleavage persists between health/human service organizations and poor people of color of diverse cultural backgrounds[8]. The organization of the health industry, its hierarchical authority structure, and the concentration of economic and political power in its hands, block the development and operation of services that focus on the health of communities taking into consideration the cultural diversity of their people. Can this be accomplished while health services continue to be oriented inwards towards professional imperatives rather than focusing outwards on the health of communities and interact collaboratively with those communities in improving their health statuses? With few exceptions, health care services are still planned and operated as if they were universally effective for all people and encourage passive behaviors on those seeking services. The need for health and mental health services that consider the linguistic and cultural diversity of the populations they serve is ever growing in spite of the rhetoric of "cultural sensitivity." Can problems of costs, quality, appropriateness and timeliness of care be controlled if sociocultural variables that guide health behaviors are not explicitly included in health care transactions? Anthropology can play a major role in the development of health care delivery organizations that are transculturally viable and applicable to clinical work, in bridging gaps between public health and medical-care, in the development of preventive and health promotion approaches, in adding dimensions to the assessment of needs for health care by populations, and for appropriate use of medical services. The agenda is still unfinished.

[8]Weidman's question as to whether new radical strategies would be needed to bring human service professionals to adopt a transcultural reorientation is still fresh. (See Weidman 1976; Fabrega 1970; and Sherer 1993)

REFERENCES

DYE, T. R.
  1987   *Understanding Public Policy*, 6th edition. Englewood Cliffs, NJ: Prentice Hall.
FABREGA, HORACIO, JR.
  1970   The study of disease in relation to culture. *Behavioral Science* 17:183–200.
LINDBLOOM, C. E.
  1982   The market as prison. *Journal of Politics,* May.
OSBORNE, D. AND T. GAEBLER
  1992   *Reinventing Government: How the Entrepreneurial Spirit is Transforming the Public Sector.* Reading, PA: Addison Wesley.
PADILLA, ELENA
  1958   *Up from Puerto Rico.* New York: Columbia University Press.
SHERER, J. L.
  1993   Crossing cultures: Hospitals begin breaking down barriers to care. *Medical Staff Leader.* July: 3.
STAFFORD, W.
  1990   The decades of poverty: A perspective on community development. *Economic Development and Law Center Report.* Summer/Fall:3–8
WEIDMAN, H. H.
  1976a   The transcultural view: Prerequisite to interethnic (intercultural) communication in medicine. *Social Science and Medicine* 138:85–87.
  1976b   On getting from "Here" to "There". *Medical Anthropology Newsletter.* November: 2–7.

Growing Up in Eastville, a Barrio of New York

A Retrospective View

JOAN MENCHER

Department of Anthropology
Lehman College
City University of New York
Bedford Park Boulevard West
Bronx, New York 10468

INTRODUCTION

From the early to mid-1950s, a number of studies were carried out among the various ethnic populations in New York City. In 1954, Dr. Beatrice Berle (a medical doctor) and Professor Charles Wagley from Columbia University conceived of the idea of doing a medical-cum-ethnographic study of a slum area in New York's East Harlem, an area that was bounded by 99th Street on the south, 105th Street on the north, the East River on the east and Second Avenue (where there had been a large urban renewal project earlier) on the west. Dr. Elena Padilla, who had worked on Julian Steward's study in Puerto Rico, was selected to direct the anthropological study, and four graduate students were given fellowships to work on the project. My own research started there in 1953–55 and was supplemented by short visits during 1956–58.

Dr. Berle set up a free clinic in the area, because it was recognized that the public hospitals and clinics serving the area were often not meeting the needs of the people in the barrio. Each of the anthropologists collected basic data from a sample of 25 households. Apart from these 25 families (which were visited repeatedly over the course of a year) approximately 250 other families were visited for brief periods of time to collect basic demographic materials.

The work on the project was divided in the following manner: I was assigned the study of the socialization of children from birth until the age of six, or the start of the first grade; Joan Campbell studied the effects of the school on the child between the age of six and the start of adolescence; Vera Green worked with adolescent girls; Dr. Edwin Seda and Mr. Wee worked with adolescent boys and young men; and Muriel White studied the elderly (defined then as people over 50). In addition, Elena Padilla and the four women anthropology students also worked with young adults, and Padilla and White interviewed social workers, hospital personnel and people connected with social service organizations in the area. I also interviewed school personnel, and spent considerable time observing families in the school and in both formal and informal nurseries, as well as organizations and people connected with Puerto Rican migrants, including the office of Puerto Rican affairs. At the time this project was conducted (in the mid-1950s) the economic situation in the United States and in New York City was still influenced by the second World War. The boom of the 1960s had not yet occurred, and funds for research as well as jobs for urban poor were limited. The end of World War II had suddenly released large numbers of men back into the work force from both the armed forces and war-related industries. It was a period of economic conservatism, growing cold war tensions, and the growth of virulent antisocialist rhetoric, culminating in the McCarthy witch hunts.

From the beginning it was recognized that the Puerto Rican migration was different from the European migration, because it involved issues of race and racial prejudice as well as ethnicity. At the time of our study, the only Hispanic population in that area was Puerto Rican. There were no Mexicans or Cubans or other Hispanics in our particular area. There were, however, some older women from earlier European migrations—elderly Italians and Irish women scattered throughout the Puerto Rican enclave, often in the same buildings. And there were also Black migrants from the American South. At that time the main Black population lived further north in Harlem. For the purpose of our research however, while we interviewed many of those families as well, we concentrated primarily on the Puerto Ricans. The researchers all worked out of Dr. Berle's clinic on 100th Street.

THEORETICAL PERSPECTIVE

Though there were many critiques of the national character studies carried out in the 1940s and the entire culture and personality school, including Julian Steward's critique in his introduction to *Peoples of Puerto Rico* (1956), and though under his influence anthropologists had begun to pay attention to both ecological and historical differences between subregions and classes, the full effects of colonialism and neo-colonialism had not yet been explored in detail. Analysis of political economy was considered dangerous. It was a period when Marxist or even socialist anthropology in the United States was almost non-existent, and witch hunts were still going on in many arenas of American life, including academia. At the time there was an interest in applied anthropology, but it was of limited scope and did not include a world systems or dependency analysis, nor any understanding of the complex interaction between macro-level and micro-level dynamics. We were not unaware of the role of social policy (city policy, state policy and national policy) in shaping the living conditions and life expectancies and experiences of the Puerto Rican migrants and their families, but lacked a theoretical orientation to relate the data to. Therefore, what emerged were individual recommendations or observations relating to specific programs, such as housing (discussed below), but no holistic theoretical statement.

In the mid-1950s, there had been no studies conducted in urban areas in Puerto Rico. The only background information that we had was from the rural areas. Yet, most of the migrants, even those who had come originally from sugar plantation areas or other rural areas, had lived in urban areas such as San Juan or Mayaguez for fairly long periods of time. In other words, they had already made an adjustment to urban living. And yet, urban living in Puerto Rico was not studied until Helen Safa worked there in the 1960s (see Safa 1974). During the project period I visited the University of Puerto Rico and talked with anthropologists working there, but was only able to obtain bits and pieces of information from studies in progress, or from students who had done mini-papers. Elena Padilla had carried out her doctoral research in the sugar cane area in the northern part of the island, so she had considerable insight, which she brought to the project and graciously shared with the team.

SOME OF THE FINDINGS FROM THE 1950S

Housing

In the mid-1950s, even though most families were living in extremely sub-standard conditions (where as one mother put it "my children think of rats as pets"), and though their apartments were often not heated[1] and smelled from uncollected refuse, many were reluctant to leave the tenements to go into public housing. Their reason was very simple: at that time there were many extended households in the tenements. The extended kin might not all be living in the same apartment, but generally lived in the same building, or next door, or across the street. This provided the advantages of continual interaction, sharing dinners, sharing child care, sharing money, clothes, and other items. The minute that the City of New York allotted public housing to a "family" these social ties had to be severed. No allowance or understanding was given to traditional extended family ties or social networks. A mother could be sent to Staten Island, a sister and her children to Brooklyn, another "family" to downtown Manhattan, another to Washington Heights, and so forth. The fact that doing this broke up

[1] The lack of heat in these building is not a thing of the past. In 1989, the City of New York's Housing Authority took over and renovated six of the buildings on 100th Street. Yet, it was reported in the *New York Times* of February 11, 1994 (page B4) that the main source of heat for many of these tenants is still the gas oven. One woman was quoted as saying that the temperature in her family's apartment had dropped as low as the 20's, and that she has had to keep her children home from school because it was too cold for them to get out of bed.

family ties, led to greater anomie, took children away from alternative nurturing figures, isolated households, and deprived women with newborn children of family help with child care, was irrelevant to the bureaucracy. When it was pointed out, the bureaucracy simply replied that it would make for more paper work and was not fair because people had to be moved according to the order in which they had applied, as well as meeting a variety of other criteria; that it was impossible to take personal networks into account.

What we clearly saw, however, was that public housing was breaking up all of the traditional ties people had. My research data, which focused on families with children under the age of six, showed that where people maintained complex familial and other social networks, they were much more capable of coping with emergencies or even the stress of daily life, despite extreme poverty, unemployment, or other problems. In many ways, the extended families were the most flexible in adopting new styles of child rearing, adjusting to the new environment, as opposed to the isolated nuclear households. Our data showed how differently households functioned when there was one additional woman available, whether it was a grandmother, a cousin, or a more distant relative, and how much more secure life was for children in those cases.

Occupations

At that time the only employment available to the men coming from Puerto Rico was in the tertiary sector in service occupations. A very high proportion of employed men were dishwashers, floor cleaners, or the like. Lacking education, even in Spanish, these were the only options available, and they were very difficult to get since there seemed to be an endless stream of applicants ready to take a job when it became vacant.

For the women at that time, garment factory work was a major source of employment. Today this kind of work is only available in the greater New York area for illegal immigrants who are afraid of being caught and will work far below the minimum wage. The sweat shops of Brooklyn, lower Manhattan and Queens tend to use people who speak only Chinese, or illegal Hispanic immigrants who are not free to complain about wages through legal channels. But in the 1950s, many Puerto Rican women had factory employment. This employment of women was beginning to undermine some of the more traditional family structures, in the sense that women could more easily obtain work that was steady and paid more than the male service sector jobs. Thus, in at least some of the families, there were periods when women had work and men did not. Considering traditional male values, this was perceived as an insult to the men's sense of dignity.

The Role of Religion

Our data also showed a connection between religious affiliation and family stability. In part because of the greater strictness about sex and marriage, in part because of Evangelical missionizing, there was a sharp distinction between households which belonged to the East Harlem Protestant Parish of Dr. Norman Eddy, as well as other storefront evangelical groups, and those which belonged to the Catholic Church. Among those I interviewed who belonged to the Catholic Church, there was a larger proportion of families with fewer personal problems. (These were families that I met through knocking on every fourth door in each apartment structure, *i.e.*, through taking a semi-structured random sample.) They were the ones where there was a greater likelihood that a father or a stepfather would be in the home; they were the ones whose children were kept in the house whenever they were not in school, and were never allowed to play on the streets; they were the ones who were less likely to present serious problems among teenagers, since the teenagers were either kept at home or had jobs to help the family.

The Catholic families were helped considerably by the Church. The priests went out of their way to get clothes for the children and to get all kinds of other things to help families that came to church regularly. The only Church in the neighborhood was Italian, that is the main priest and many of the parishioners were Italian. At that time, the priest was losing his flock as Italians moved away, and was eager for more parishioners. Thus, even though there were tensions and hostility between the Italian population and the Puerto Ricans, there was also an attempt to get as many of the Puerto Ricans to join the Church. Furthermore, many of the Puerto Rican Catholic families also managed to get some or all of their children into the parochial school that then existed on 105th Street.

The East Harlem Protestant Parish and the various local evangelical storefront churches were providing for a growing proportion of the people in the area. They were the ones who sponsored the Saturday night dances, who tried to break up the gangs or at least tried to mediate between them. But their role in the neighborhood cannot be underestimated since a large proportion of their parishioners included people from broken homes, addicts, gang members, deserted women, girls pregnant at sixteen, and those with similar problems.

Education

Even among those families that were not Catholic, many families attempted to send their children to the parochial school because it was clearly seen as conferring an advantage that would be realized when the children entered the workplace. The children were perceived as getting a better education. There was no question that it was much better run, and had much more parental involvement in education than the public schools. The major barrier was financial, since only those families that could get scholarships were able to afford the Catholic schools, and naturally such scholarships were given to parishioners first. Their classes were large, but in spite of this the children in those schools were seen to be learning more. These schools made the assumption that all children were educable—that all they needed was to work hard and be disciplined, and they could learn. Thus they placed a great deal of stress on the value of learning, on the fear of what would happen if one did not work hard and learn, along with a strong emphasis on moral values. They started from a much more positive assumption. The public schools start from the belief that children's innate intelligence determines their ability to learn and that the school was only required to take care of the child's mind, rather than an entire value system. In the Catholic Schools, the assumption is made that if children do not perform adequately, then it is an act of will, rather that the result of deficiencies in their background. The Catholic schools were aware of the problems of migration and assimilation, which gave them a big advantage. It was striking that while some of the children in the Catholic schools complained about the harsh discipline and the racism expressed by some teachers, and even said that they disliked school, most of the parents were quite happy about the school. From their point of view, what mattered was that their children were learning.

I spent a lot of time in the public schools. and found the attitudes of many of the teachers toward the migrants rather counter-productive. They often started with the assumption that what mattered most was maintaining quiet and order in the classroom, and controlling the students' basic unruliness. They saw their students as being unruly, that they were misbehaving. This was even true in the kindergartens. This negative assumption often became a self-fulfilling prophesy, and those teachers who did not think that way to start with were quickly socialized by other teachers to adopt that viewpoint. If they did not, they did not stay in the schools very long. Estelle Fuchs' (1967) study of the effect of the school on teachers clearly demonstrated how that worked. On the other hand, teachers in the public schools had much more paperwork, which took them away from classroom teaching and took up so much more of their time.

Drugs and Drug Use

Though drugs were used in Eastville in the 1950s the pattern differed greatly from today. To begin with, heroin was the only drug used, and it was used primarily by males. I still remember that all the vacant lots had garbage in them, which was used to make fires to sterilize needles. At that time, sterilization of needles was done very carefully. It was crude, but it was very overt. The war on drugs has made it harder to sterilize needles, which has led to the greater spread of AIDS and other diseases. In the 1950s even the most confirmed drug addicts sterilized their needles.

Gangs

The other thing that characterized the Eastville area at that time was the prevalence of youth gangs. There were numerous gangs operating in this area and they were an important part of adolescent life in those families where the children were allowed out on the streets. The East Harlem Protestant Parish tried to organize "dance parties," and would try to get young people from the gangs to come to these parties. Every Monday when I came to work I would find out who got stabbed, and who got beaten up, because of gang fights at the dances at the Parish on the previous Saturday night.

RANGE OF DIFFERENCES

The data from the 1950s pointed to many differences within the Puerto Rican migrant community and made it abundantly clear that the generalizations that were being made about the community as a whole were misleading. There had been a very large wave of Puerto Rican migration after World War II, particularly after relatively inexpensive air travel became available. Up to World War II most of the migration had been by sea, and it was limited. We were dealing with a new migrant population that was able to travel cheaply back and forth. It was very simple to go for the summer, or to send a child back to one's family or have members of a household in both places. It was easier then than it is today, with air-fares up and wages going down.

Our data clearly showed the effect of race and racial differences on adaptation to the city. Fair or white Puerto Ricans at that time tended to call themselves Hispanics, and often managed to move much more easily into the wider society. This was especially true for the children of the migrants who managed to finish high school or secretarial school or some kind of trade school. For those who were very dark, there was no option except merging with American Black culture. Yet they were rejected by many American Blacks, and felt doubly isolated. Those who were intermediate in color often suffered the most by trying to or wanting to pass and being rejected by a racist white society. While this is still true today, it was much worse during the 1950s before any of the movements of the 1960s and 1970s (civil rights movement, Black power movement, feminist movement, etc.) had occurred. There was some correlation between race and class among the Puerto Rican migrants of the 1950s, but sometimes race was overlooked if a person had a middle-class education. In this connection it is important to be aware of the fact that in any household, you could find children of every shade. Thus within the household itself, there was potential for tension between the fair sister and the dark sister. While this is a phenomenon found elsewhere in the world (for example in India, where the dowry of the darker sister is usually larger than that of the fair sister), nonetheless in the racial climate in the United States in the 1950s (as well as today) the psychosocial effects of this kind of tension within the household can often be devastating. This was especially true where one child found it easy to get a good job and another encountered racial prejudice.

LATER OBSERVATIONS

After working in East Harlem, I went to live and work in rural India. Many people from the United States that I met in India as well as upon my return asked me if I experienced any shock in going to India because of the poverty I encountered. They asked if I was bothered by the number of poor people, beggars on the streets, pavement dwellers, horrendous slums, and incredible rural poverty. Having worked in East Harlem, there was nothing in India that I saw that I found that shocking. When I am asked by Americans about poverty in India, I often suggest that they visit East Harlem. The things that I saw, the smells, the filth, the dirt I experienced in East Harlem were vividly in my mind when I worked in India. The combination of the smell of cooking pork fat, and babies' urine in an apartment that had to be heated by the gas stove because there was no heat was one that left an indelible memory for me. The mother whose children had been bitten by the rats they considered to be pets had an overwhelming impact on me because after all, we were supposed to be the richest country in the world. Furthermore, the breakdown of community and family structure exacerbated by idiotic public policy made their lives in many ways worse than anything I ever saw among the poorest landless untouchable agricultural laborers in India. Clearly this is a very personal observation. But it is important to note and understand because I do not believe it to be unique.

ACKNOWLEDGMENTS

The author is extremely grateful to Dr. Franklin Southworth for editing the paper and to Mr. Michael Mueller for transcribing the tape of the original meeting.

REFERENCES

ALBIZU, CARLOS
1956   The Influence of Social Class Membership Upon the Selection of Certain Rorschach Factors, Unpublished paper, Social Science Research Center, University of Puerto Rico.

APPLE, DORRIAN
1956   The social structure of grandparenthood *American Anthropologist* **LVIII**:656–663.

BERLE, BEATRICE
1958   *80 Puerto Rican Families in New York City: Health and Disease Studied in Context.* New York: Columbia University Press.

DIAZ, MANNY, (EARL FINO, LARRY GANGAWARE, *ET AL.*)
1953   The Attitude of Puerto Ricans in New York City to Various Aspects of Their Environment. Project #4317. New York: New York school of Social Work. (Mimeographed.)

FUCHS, ESTELLE
1969   (c.1967) *Teachers Talk: Views From Inside City Schools.* Garden City, NY: Anchor Books.

JAFFE, A.J., ED.
1954   *Puerto Rican Population of New York City,* New York Bureau of Applied Social Research of Columbia University.

MILLER, PAUL
1947   *Historia de Puerto Rico.* New York: Rand McNally Co.

MILLS, C. WRIGHT, CLARENCE SENIOR, AND ROSE GOLDSEN
1950   *The Puerto Rican Journey.* New York: Harper & Row.

PADILLA, ELENA
1951   *Nocora: An Agarian Reform Sugar Community in Puerto Rico.* New York: Unpublished Ph. D. Dissertation, Columbia University.

1958   *Up From Puerto Rico.* New York: Columbia University Press.

PETRULLO, VINCENZO
1947   *Puerto Rican Paradox.* Philadelphia: University of Pennsylvania Press

SAFA, HELEN ICKEN
1974   *Urban Poor of Puerto Rico: A Study in Development and Inequality.* New York: Holt, Rinehart, and Winston.

STEWART, JULIAN, ED.
1956   *The People of Puerto Rico.* Urbana: The University of Illinois Press.

WHITING, JOHN AND IRWIN CHILD
1953   *Child Training and Personality.* New Haven: Yale University Press.

APPENDIX
EXCERPTS FROM FAMILY LIFE AND CHILD REARING
PATTERNS IN EASTVILLE: EL BARRIO DE NUEVA YORK[2]

CHAPTER I
INTRODUCTION

The Problem

Anthropologists have long been concerned with problems of culture change. In this study, I shall discuss the question of culture change as it pertains to child rearing among Puerto Rican migrants living in Eastville, New York City. I shall show that, contrary to most expectations, those first generation families that are best able to function in terms of the ideals of their own culture are also the most accepting of change in child rearing behavior and attitudes.

The traditional Puerto Rican family is of the extended type. The majority of Puerto Rican migrants in Eastville grew up in extended families. However, largely because of accidents of migration, many conjugal families are forced into a nuclear structure in Eastville because their relatives have not moved to New York. Extended and nuclear families are thus found in about equal proportion here. I shall show that the presence of even one additional woman in the household is a crucial factor in Eastville Puerto Rican family functioning, and that this is due to the way in which relationships between individuals are structured when the expected form of the family is of the extended type.

The extended family in Eastville is a more stable and better integrated unit than is the newly emerging nuclear family. Members of extended families are more accepting of changes in attitude and behavior as it relates to child rearing. It is suggested that this greater ease of extended families in accepting new values in child rearing is directly related to their better integration and greater stability.

The Eastville Puerto Rican nuclear family, despite a striking structural similarity to the "American" family, is far more resistant to change in ideals about child rearing. I shall show that this is due to the fact that nuclear family living *per se* represents a departure from the ideal situation, leaving the mother without the expected assistance of mother-surrogates, and that this results in an exaggeration of traditional ideals. Mothers of these nuclear families do not know how to function without the usual mother-surrogates. Thus, living in a nuclear family is considered a "hardship." According to the

---

[2] These excerpts have been taken verbatim from my doctoral thesis which was never published. They have not been edited in any way.

norms of the Puerto Rican subcultures from which the migrants to Eastville came, the independent nuclear family represents a form of social disorganization. Thomas and Znaniecki state in general that:

> When the disorganization of a social group becomes the object matter of reflective attention on the part of its members, the spontaneous tendency immediately arising is that of strengthening the existing social system against the process of decadence. (Thomas and Znaniecki, 1927: 1213).

Because living in a nuclear family is seen by the adults involved as the break-up of the *familia* its members accentuate the traditional child rearing practices in their attempt to preserve as much as possible of the existing social system against the process of disorganization. Since the extended family is not subject to the stress experienced by the nuclear family, it is not as necessary for members of the extended families to accentuate traditional child rearing practices. Indeed it will be shown that the lack of stress in the extended family may be a factor in the more ready acceptance of new attitudes and practices of child rearing by its members.[3]

The following hypothesis is suggested: The family with the least status within the Puerto Rican subculture of Eastville will be the family most resistant to change, and will accentuate the traditional child rearing practices.

* * * *

I shall show that changes in ideals about child rearing are related both to the structure of the family (extended or nuclear) and to the status of the family within the subcultural setting of the *Barrio* (the neighborhood).

Child rearing in both nuclear and extended families will be compared to the traditional ideals about "how children should be raised" reported for Puerto Rico. In the course of these comparisons, I shall specify the characteristics of Eastville Puerto Rican child rearing during the first six years of the child's life. I shall also show that the Puerto Rican child in Eastville experiences a sharp discontinuity in its life experiences somewhere between the age of one and two, and that this discontinuity is related to a dichoto-

---

[3] In this study a distinction is made between the traditional form of the family in a structural sense and the adherence to traditional attitudes, beliefs and practices of child rearing. The traditions of child rearing referred to here include the traditional Latin American definition of role behavior for children in general including sexual role differentiation, as well as a relationship between parents and children characterized by social distance, respect, and total obedience. It is considered to be improper to be too friendly or relaxed with a child because then the child will "lose *respeto* for you." This traditional role is contrasted with the type of parent-child relationship which is characterized by less social distance and greater permissiveness. For a description of the traditional Latin-American patterns of sexual role differentiation see Chapter II, Part I A.

my in the mother's attitudes towards, and expectations of the "baby" as opposed to the "small child."

Furthermore, there are two other dichotomies that affect the life of the Puerto Rican child in Eastville. First, there is a dichotomy based on the status of the mother; Eastville Puerto Rican culture makes a sharp division between what is considered a "good woman" and a "bad woman." (The "bad woman" is one whose children are the result of casual liaisons rather than a permanent or semi-permanent relationship with one man.) The children of such a "bad woman" are isolated from other children even when they go to kindergarten, because of the stigma attached to the mother's behavior.

Second, there is a sharp division between families that "allow their children to play on the streets," and families that "keep their children *en la casa*" (in the house). I intend to show that approximately eighty-five percent of the children in Eastville are brought up *en la casa,* and that the families that "allow their children to play on the streets" are, by and large, the most socially disorganized, as well as the most traditional in terms of normative values.

* * * *

CHAPTER II
INTRODUCTION TO THE EASTVILLE DATA

Introduction

In examining the relevance of the studies done on the Island of Puerto Rico to our present study of Puerto Ricans in New York, it is significant to note that Mills, in a study of Puerto Rican migrants to New York, which will be discussed in a later section of this chapter, states:

> In the main, they [the majority of Puerto Rican migrants as of 1948] always lived in cities; only about one out of five can be considered rural in origin. The rest have merely changed the size and complexity of the city in which they live.
>
> Ninety-one per cent of all persons in the sample had lived in the island's urban centers before coming to New York...The later migrants...tend to have been recruited more heavily from the island's rural areas...The island's two largest cities—San Juan and Ponce—supply the mainland with the majority of migrants. (G.W. Mills, C. Senior, and R. Goldsen. 1950: 33).

While the increase in rural migration to Eastville, noted by Mills in the passage above, continued until 1954 (the year of the present study), the substantial majority of migrants continued to come from urban slums. The recent rural migration to Eastville has not been from all rural areas. Rather it has come predominantly from the sugar-producing parts of the island.

Thus, the majority of Eastville residents have come either from the slums of the big cities or from the coastal sugar areas. Furthermore, many of the migrants who have come from city slums report that they themselves were born in sugar-producing areas, or that their parents were.

Unfortunately, no study has been made of families in the large urban slums of Puerto Rico, so we have no data from those areas to compare with the data from Eastville, New York City.[4] However, Dr. Carlos Albizu and Mr. Fernandez-Mendez, both of University of Puerto Rico, have stated that it is their impression, based on pilot interviews in a slum near the University, that the majority of people dwelling in the slums of San Juan "had come there in the last twenty or thirty years, and seemed to have come primarily from the sugar cane regions of the Island." (Interview with Dr. Carlos Albizu and Mr. Fernandez-Mendez at the University of Puerto Rico, August 1956.) Further, Señora Delia Ortega de Pabon, who is engaged in a study of family patterns in three generations of the same family in three parts of the island—a sugar plantation area near Vega Baja; a slum of San Juan; and a wealthy section of San Juan—stated that there appeared to be many similarities in family functioning and child rearing between families in the sugar area and families in the city slum. (Delia Ortega Pabon. 1956). Therefore, in this study, I shall discuss the studies done in the sugar areas in greater detail than studies conducted in other regions of the island. Data from the other areas will be compared to the Eastville data only when there is no comparable data from sugar areas, and it will be noted in the text when this is done.

* * * *

The Puerto Rican Migrant

Prior to World War II, there was comparatively little migration to or from Puerto Rico. (A.J. Jaffe. 1954:5-7) Between 1900 and 1940, net migration from the island averaged only two to three thousand persons per year. Suddenly, at the end of the war, there was an enormous increase. Planeload after planeload of Puerto Ricans poured into New York's airports. There was another in 1950. (*op. cit.*:7) Migration from the island is, to some extent, sensitive to the economic cycles of the mainland: 1946,1948, and 1949, when migration fell off slightly from surrounding peaks, were years in which there was a similar decline in the American economy. All families used in this study came to the United States after 1945.

In 1948–1949, Mills, Senior and Goldsen did the first well-documented study of the Puerto Rican migrant in New York. It was a large-scale project that did not concentrate on a particular neighborhood. Five thousand Puerto Ricans living in Harlem and the Morrisania section of the Bronx

---

[4] Note: at that time no urban studies had been published. Subsequent to this thesis, Helen Safa (and later numerous others) carried out studies in urban slums.

were interviewed by a large staff of research workers. (Mills, Senior, and Goldsen:IX). The authors point out the difference in the problems of adjustment for Puerto Rican men who come here with some technical knowledge and mechanical skill and the more usual migrant who is totally unskilled. They distinguish between Puerto Rican migrants in terms of their ability to acculturate to the larger society, and point out that it is often the Puerto Rican who is of "intermediate" skin color who has the greater problem. The lighter migrants are readily able to assimilate to American white society and the very dark are compelled to assimilate to American Negro society. (*op. cit.*:27, 139–155) However, those of "intermediate" color resist assimilation to Negro society but are not accepted by the white society. They also note:

> The New York migrant's household often contains extended families: relatives other than the conjugal unit...the other half of the households consist of husband, wife and their children...it also fits the extended family pattern of the island...Generally, members of the Puerto Rican household in New York pool earnings in common purse. (*op. cit.*: 94)

* * * *

There are three kinds of slum-neighborhoods into which Puerto Rican migrants have moved in New York City. First is the neighborhood made up of rooming houses and apartments which have been broken up into separate dwelling units for individuals or families. Unmarried migrants with no established kin in New York gravitate toward this kind of neighborhood. So do families who need temporary quarters while they look for a permanent apartment. Families rarely stay in such neighborhoods more than a month or two. Second, there are neighborhoods where slum dwellings and wealthy residences are mixed. There has been no study of Puerto Rican migrants in neighborhoods of either of these types.

Eastville represents the third kind of slum neighborhood into which Puerto Rican migrants move upon arrival in New York. This is a neighborhood that consists exclusively of slum dwellings. It may be characterized as a lower-lower class "family" neighborhood, as distinguished from the one where the rooming houses flourish.

* * * * *

The study of socialization

In my interviews with informants particular emphasis was placed on questions about how individuals were socializing their young children, on questions about how they had cared for their children who were born in Puerto Rico before they migrated, and how this compared with the care of children born here, and also questions about the informants's recollections of her own and her siblings' upbringing in Puerto Rico. Since I did not record observations in the presence of the informants until the last four months, the early data came primarily from informal interviews, recorded retrospectively. During the last four months, I also recorded observations of mothers and other adults with the children.

In addition to the home visits, I also spent several hours a week in the local kindergarten, day care and nursery school classes, interviewing the teachers and the children and observing the children in the classes. Towards the end of the study, a sociogram was administered in each of the eight kindergarten classes in the neighborhood.

Children in the kindergarten were interviewed in groups. They were encouraged to talk about their family and about themselves. They also made up stories and told them to me. Many of these children were also seen outside the classroom, either in their homes or on the streets.

One of the purposes of the street observations was the verification of a hypothesis which I had formulated towards the beginning of the study, namely, that only a small number of disorganized families, who are also extremely assertive of traditional ideals, allow their children on the streets to play, and that better organized families in Eastville do not permit their children on the streets. One of the way in which I attempted to verify this hypothesis was to make a check of the children who were found playing on the street on given days. I questioned these children *about* their families and also about what they were punished for. In order to check further, as many of the families of these children were contacted as possible. On the basis of such checking on the streets, and in relation to all the rest of the data, I came to the conclusion that only about fifteen per cent of the children played on the streets all of the time and that the remaining group of children were primarily being brought up *en la casa*.[5]

Interviews with teachers and social workers in the area seemed to confirm this. One teacher in a kindergarten class said:

> Most of my children stay at home from the time they get home from school. They have so little opportunity to play. I guess that is the only thing mothers can do in a neighborhood like this. There are a few children who are on the streets all of the time. In this class it's David and his stooge Juan. But they are the only ones. The others stay home. But it's funny how a few can color the impression of people so, that they think it's true for the majority.

* * * * *

---

[5] For further discussion of methods used to check this hypothesis, see Chapter VII, section on "The Streets."

CHAPTER III
THE SETTING: A DESCRIPTION OF THE *BARRIO*

Eight o'clock on a summer morning. The sun, already hot, slants harshly down on the stark brick walls of the tenement buildings that line the narrow streets of Eastville, *El Barrio de Nueva York*. As the sun climbs, the bricks heat through, the dusty air steams, the tar oozes up between the paving stones on the streets and sticks to the shoes of passersby. Derelicts tumble blinking and scratching from dark areaways and the fringes of garbage-littered lots, where they had collapsed the night before. The people with jobs pour from houses and hurry down the hot street toward the jammed subway that will carry them to work. There is a lull. The day gets hotter. Slowly, the *Barrio* awakens. Angry voices from the hot, sticky, overcrowded rooms carry to the streets. Some dirty children assemble to play with bits of dirty paper in the gutter. Radios blare. Women collect on the stoops of the buildings. The streets fill up. Bums loiter by the lampposts. Women come out to make their small purchases of rice and beans and green bananas in the neighborhood *bodegas*. The hot, still air is full of sounds and smells.

Or the same block on a winter evening. All the windows drawn tight against the bitter wind that whips along the narrow street, the sidewalks almost deserted. A few short grim figures stride rapidly toward the subway. They are shivering. Inside the buildings, the cramped apartment is not quite heated by a kerosene burner. Seven children in a three-room apartment, sit shivering. No air, except the drafts that whistle through the warped window frames and under the narrow doors, bringing the cold. Unaired for weeks, the rooms reek of kerosene, of babies, of old garbage and stale fat. This, too, is the *Barrio*.

The world of Eastville[6] is bounded on the south side by a hospital still under construction. On the west, there is a housing project, also under construction: to the north is a neighborhood of somewhat wealthier Italian families, and to the east stretch blocks of lofts and warehouses used largely for commercial enterprises such as packing companies or fruiterers.

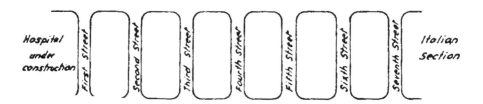

[6] Eastville, New York City is a neighborhood defined by the City both as a health area and a census tract. (See Appendix C for census and health area data.) Half of the tract was torn down at the time of the study to build a housing project.

However, none of the Eastville residents work in these companies. A few women work in garment factories just north of the *Barrio* in the Italian district, and a few others work in the "fish factory" in the Barrio itself.

On both avenues there are large stores, two supermarkets, liquor stores, and other retail establishments. These however, are of an impersonal "City" type, whereas the stores on the side streets are run more on the basis of personal relations. The stores on the side streets are owned and run by people of either Puerto Rican or American Negro origin. People gather and talk in these local side street stores, but they shop quickly in the big stores on the avenues, and quickly depart. Apple Avenue is usually deserted except during business hours. Broad Avenue is always very busy and active. People hurry back and forth along Broad Avenue at all hours of the day and evening, to the shops, to the schools, to places of work, to churches, and toward other contacts with the greater "City."

The side streets serve as gathering places for some of Eastville's inhabitants. The adults gather on the stoops of the tenement buildings while a few small children and adolescents play in the gutters and the garbage-filled lots. (We shall show in Chapter VII which children play on the streets.) There is a great deal of variation from street to street within Eastville with regard to which groups play on the street or lounge around talking.

Eastville consists primarily of two ethnic groups: the Puerto Ricans and the American Negroes. On First Street, one finds mostly Negro children playing. While many American Negro families live on Second Street, the dominant group of children and adults that "hang around" that street is Puerto Rican. Some Puerto Ricans from other streets come to Second Street to loaf or play. On Third Street, both American Negro and Puerto Rican children come to play on the south side, and the American Negro children on the north. American Negro children play on Fourth Street, and American Negro adults stand around talking. There is a group of American Negro mothers who gather on the north side of Fourth Street every afternoon, week in and week out, all through the year. Some of them live on Second Street, but they come to Fourth Street where they "feel more comfortable." One little Negro girl, whose mother is a member of this group, once saw the anthropologist walking by with a Puerto Rican woman who lives on Fourth Street, and her two small daughters. She exclaimed in amazement: "Are they your friends?" At being told yes, and that they lived on her block, she seemed to be very startled, as if she had ignored their very existence before that time.

* * * *

North of here, on Fifth Street, one finds Puerto Ricans living on the south side and Italians on the north. The Italians go around the corner to Sixth Street to relax, or else stay very carefully on their side of the street. There is a strong economic rivalry between the entrenched Italians and the invading Puerto Ricans which creates a far greater social distance between the two groups than mere ethnic difference could. Furthermore, there is a great deal of separation between the children of the two groups, since very few of the Italian children go to the public school, so the children of the two groups do not have the day-to-day school contact that would make for ease in social relations. Most Italian children go to the parochial school on Sixth Street.

Another feature of the side streets is a proliferation of store-front churches. While these are primarily American Negro institutions, rarely shared by the Puerto Ricans, they must be mentioned in any description of the neighborhood. Most of the Puerto Ricans are Catholic, and go to a Catholic church if they go to any church at all. A smaller number go to Protestant churches that have been set up by a group of ministers from Columbia University's Union Theological Seminary. This group runs store-front churches on Second, Fourth and Sixth Streets. However, they do not attract the majority of residents, who have remained nominal Catholics and who send their children for Catholic religious instruction.

Inside

The apartments in Eastville are very crowded. The largest apartments in the area have four rooms. This fact, added to that of large family size, produces a situation of extreme overcrowding. To illustrate this point I shall discuss the following: the largest apartment with the largest number of inhabitants; the largest apartment with the smallest number of inhabitants; and finally, the smallest apartment with the largest number of inhabitants.

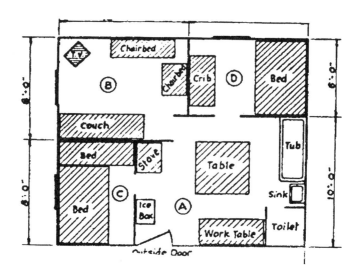

The Yaucos'[7] apartment represents the first example mentioned. The Yaucos have four rooms, and twelve people share them. Of the four rooms, only three are livable; the kitchen "A" (see figure) is too small for any sort of bed or couch when the appliances and kitchen table are installed. Mr. and Mrs. Yauco, their nine children, and Mrs. Yauco's mother sleep in the remaining three rooms. Five of the boys sleep in room "B"; the youngest boy (four and a half) sleeps in room "D" in a crib with Mr. and Mrs. Yauco. He does not sleep with the others boys because he still wets his bed. The two older girls, the baby girl, and Mrs. Yauco's mother sleep in room "C". There are no doors to any of these rooms, which are just large enough to get two small beds in. This means that nobody had a bed to himself except for the youngest boy.

In the largest apartment with fewest people, we find seven people living in an apartment like the Yaucos'. This is the home of the Nuñez family. Here Mr. and Mrs. Nuñez have a bedroom to themselves. Their two girls have one room and their two boys another, while Mrs. Nuñez's mother sleeps in the living room. However, it may be noted that this is a very rare occurrence in Eastville, the Yauco situation being far more common.

Finally, in the smallest apartment with the largest number of people, there are eight people living in an apartment with only two rooms. Here the mother's mother sleeps with the three older grandchildren on a small couch in the kitchen (the kitchen is about the same size as the one in the diagram, but the work table has been removed). The parents sleep in the "bedroom" with the three younger children and the baby. Since there is no room for a crib in the parents' room, the baby sleeps in the same bed as the parents.

Overcrowding, such as that found in the Yauco apartment, is not at all rare in Eastville. Indeed, even this last example while extreme, is typical. It is not uncommon to find a couple sharing an apartment with a sister of the wife and her children. This is particularly true if they have fewer than four children between them.

The buildings are all broken down six story walkups. The halls and stairs of the buildings are usually old, shaky and dirty. The walls are very thin between apartments, and any noise that a neighbor makes is clearly audible. Women complain bitterly about their endless, wearisome struggle against all sorts of bugs, mice and rats. One day at the Lorenzo home, while Mrs. Lorenzo was in the process of complaining about the mice, two ran out. Her little boy went over to them and started to play with them. With much embarrassment she said: "See what happens. What can I do? It is terrible to have mice and the worst is that he thinks they are pets."

---

[7] All names in this paper are fictitious. Spanish sounding ones have been chosen to give the flavor of the area.

In most apartments the bathtub is in the kitchen, as was shown for the Yauco apartment. It is only rarely that a family has a complete bathroom. On Second Street only one tenement building has apartments with separate bathrooms. There is also commonly only one sink in the kitchen in most homes. Few buildings have central heating. In the Northside Study (Diaz, Finch, Larry Gangaware 1953), eighty-five percent of those interviewed stated that they wished to move because of the overcrowding and poor facilities. Unfortunately, however, this is most difficult for Eastville residents since the majority of lowcost public housing that is presently going up does not provide apartments with a sufficient number of bedrooms for the average Puerto Rican family. (Jaffe 1954:50)

CHAPTER VIII
CONCLUSION

* * * *

Section 1. Analysis of Eastville Puerto Rican Child Life

During infancy, the Puerto Rican child in Eastville is indulged in all his needs. Babies are considered to be incapable of "doing wrong," and whatever a baby desires is given to him. Babies are picked up and fondled frequently by the adults and older siblings in the house. Bottle-feeding is the preferred form of feeding. The bottle is given freely whenever the baby wants it. All oral activity is encouraged. Bottle-weaning occurs late, usually at about the age of three. Women and older siblings are the main care-takers of the infant, though men may assist at times.

Infancy ends quite abruptly, either when a new sibling is born or, at the latest, when the baby is able to walk without assistance from others. With the end of infancy, a rigid regime of toilet training begins. Children are toilet trained harshly. Training in "being good," or ideal behavior, also commences at this time. The ideal small child is "good, quiet, respectful of adults, dependent on adults, never fights or takes the lead in anything." Children are considered to be *sin capacidad* [without capacity] and must be taught. This ideal has been shown to be changing at present. Sexual differentiation, though more emphasized than in the "American" family for this age group, is also declining among this group of Puerto Rican migrants.

Most children (about 85 per cent) are brought up *en la casa* until they start kindergarten. The remaining 15 per cent are allowed on the streets as soon as they can walk. We have shown that these children of the streets come from families that are most disorganized, and usually from homes without a father.

A small number of children go to the local day-care center. These children learn "American" ways at a much earlier age than the children who are brought up *en la casa*.

Eastville Puerto Rican families are rather isolated as far as friends are concerned. This may be in part correlated with the *anomie* described for slum areas in general, in part correlated with the typical Puerto Rican attitude toward friends reported in Chapter VII. Thus, in about 85 per cent of the families, where children are kept *en la casa,* the child's world is not enlarged beyond the family circle to any marked degree for the first five-and-a-half years.

The first large-scale contact such children have with non-familial children is in the kindergarten. There, for the first time, they are brought into contact with a large number of other children of both Puerto Rican and American Negro background. There is a greater tendency for the Puerto Rican boys to play with the American Negro boys than for the girls to mingle. This is primarily due to the fact that the American Negro boys, having grown up "in the streets", develop qualities of "toughness" and "aggressiveness" which the Puerto Rican boys, growing up *en la casa*, have been brought up to admire but forbidden to emulate in the household.

We also noted that most of these children experience a "spurt of independence" between the ages of five and seven. This is quickly stopped at home by punishment (both physical and mental). From seven until puberty, the child continues to be a "quiet and passive individual."

Section 2. Analysis of the Influence
of Family Organization on Child Life

Whiting and Child state in the conclusion to their cross-cultural study of child rearing that:

> A second aspect of social structure which appears to be related to child training practices is the structure of the family unit. Here the significant contrast is between extended families and nonextended families. . . . From the point of view of child training, what is likely to be significant about this contrast is the question of whether a young child's grandparents are or are not members of the immediate household. (Whiting and Child 1953:312)

We have shown that among Puerto Ricans in Eastville, families are about equally divided between these categories; there are extended and nuclear families in this population. The majority of the extended families have a grandmother in the household. Murdock and Whiting (Murdock and Whiting. 1951:13-34) showed in their study that the presence of grandparents tend to make for more stern imposition of rules. On the basis of our data, we must follow Apple (Apple. 1956:656-663) in suggesting that the question of sternness in the imposition of rules is related to the authority of the grandparents in the home. Since we have seen authority in the Puerto Rican family is related to the economic potential of the individual, the grandparent has little. Grandparents in Puerto Rican families in Eastville offer the young child a source of emotional refuge from the demands of the parents.[8] To a lesser extent, the mother's brother, mother's sister, and the mother's sister's husband also function in this capacity. In the nuclear family in Eastville, on the other hand, there is no adult with whom the child can interact in this manner.

In order to examine the functioning—in the area of child care—of the two forms of family organization within the same culture, it was necessary to choose a family system "in transition." However, because this family system is in transition, we must also deal with the variable of change from a rigid, traditional orientation in child rearing to a more flexible one. This variable affects the picture in the following manner: because the traditional Puerto Rican family pattern is of the extended type, we find that adults in the nuclear families in Eastville were themselves socialized, in the main, in extended families. Thus, the inability of the majority of nuclear families to find other means for dealing with changing aspects of child rearing may be related to their own experience. It might be suggested that, in a fully flowering nuclear family system (such as the "American" suburb), there are other institutions and persons who might take the roles that in the extended families are carried out by members other than the couple forming its core. However, in many Eastville cases, especially among the more traditional Puerto Rican families, there is no alternative to the extended family. The child in the nuclear family, therefore, experiences a much smaller field of interpersonal contacts.

* * * *

The most crucial ties for the Eastville Puerto Rican children are the following: child-mother, child-father, child-grandmother, child-older sibling, child-younger sibling, child-first cousins, and finally, child with members of the mother's generation in her family of orientation. In the few cases of patrilateral residence, we must also include the father's family members. However, in the great majority of extended families they are enlarged only through the mother's line. For the child in the nuclear family, the number and age of siblings is of much more crucial significance than in the extended family.

* * * *

The hypothesis may also be offered that children growing up *en la casa* in an extended family will learn how to get along better with non-sibling "other" children than those living in a nuclear family. This is related to the

---

[8] The one exception we have shown to this occurs when there is no man or father in the household.

fact that there are usually contemporaneous cousins in the extended family, and also to the fact that adults in extended families are more likely to have friends, also living in extended families, who have become "family friends." There is much visiting back and forth between these "family friends." The data from the kindergartens seem to support this hypothesis. The most popular of the children brought up *en la casa* were primarily from extended families.

One additional hypothesis may be suggested here. The child's emotional relationship to the parent is of greater intensity in the nuclear family, and there is less outlet for his negative feelings there than in the extended family as it functions among Puerto Ricans in Eastville. Two types of evidence support this hypothesis. One is the fact that grandparents show greater tolerance than parents for negative feelings on the part of the child, and that the grandparent-grandchild relationship is an easy one. The other evidence has to do with the child's attitude and adaptation in the kindergarten. Among children brought up *en la casa*, it is the child from the nuclear family who finds it hardest to overcome his initial fear of the teacher and who is most timid with the other children. On the whole, these are the least outgoing of all of the children in the kindergartens.

The Social Cost of Dependency
The Transformation of the Puerto Rican Working Class from 1960 to 1990

HELEN I. SAFA

Center for Latin American Studies
319 Grinter Hall
University of Florida
P.O. Box 115530
Gainesville, Florida 32611-5530

My interest in Puerto Rico started nearly 40 years ago, when I first went to the island in the summer of 1954 with a five week scholarship from New York University (NYU). Puerto Rican migration to New York City was starting in massive numbers at that time, and the NYU program was designed to acquaint teachers, social workers and other public employees working with Puerto Rican migrants with the island culture. I was a research assistant with the Puerto Rican Study, a massive program to test Puerto Rican children in the New York City schools in order to devise better educational methods and systems of bilingual instruction. So one might say that migration became the springboard for my initial introduction to Puerto Rico, although I have never conducted systematic research on Puerto Rican migrants on the mainland. I fell in love with the island during my visit, looked for a job, was hired by the Commonwealth government and stayed two years. I left to pursue graduate study in anthropology at Columbia University, with the help of a scholarship from the University of Puerto Rico, which then funded students for graduate work abroad in order to develop their own graduate programs in various fields.

The scholarship I received required me to return to Puerto Rico to work for the Commonwealth government for the same length of time I held the scholarship (two years). So when I finished my graduate course work at Columbia, I returned to Puerto Rico in 1959 to conduct my doctoral research, and was hired by the Puerto Rican Urban Renewal and Housing Corporation (CRUV), which was concerned with the problems of resettlement of shantytown residents into public housing in the San Juan metropolitan area. So I became a true applied anthropologist, responsible not only for scientific analysis but for policy recommendations that would be helpful to the government in public housing relocation. The data gathered through this research became the basis of my doctoral dissertation at Columbia, and after a follow up study 10 years later, in 1969, were published by Holt, Rinehart and Winston as *The Urban Poor of Puerto Rico: A Study in Development and Inequality.*

This rather lengthy introduction may help readers to understand why my analysis of the transformations Puerto Rico has undergone since 1960 is not purely academic. It is informed by nearly 40 years of intense involvement with the island, on both a personal and professional level. Although I have not lived in Puerto Rico since completing my doctoral research in 1960, I have returned frequently, and have witnessed firsthand the transformations wrought by rapid urbanization, industrialization, and migration. In 1980 I started research on Puerto Rican women garment workers, this time around Mayaguez, in the western end of the island.[1] This study was conducted with the assistance of a Puerto Rican anthropologist, Carmen Angélica Perez H., then a graduate student at Rutgers University, where I taught till 1980. Together we carried out a survey of 157 women workers in three different branch plants of the same garment firm in the Mayaguez region, while I returned in 1986 to conduct in-depth interviews with a subsample of 15 respondents. I have now completed a book comparing the results of this research with similar studies conducted on women industrial workers in the Dominican Republic and Cuba, which will be published in 1995 by Westview Press as *The Myth of the Male Breadwinner: Women and Industrialization in the Caribbean.* Several articles have already appeared on this Puerto Rican research (Safa 1981,1985,1990).

My aim in this article is to analyze the rapid transformation Puerto Rico has undergone from an agrarian to an urban, even post-industrial society in the 30+ years since the original research for *The Urban Poor of Puerto Rico* was conducted as a result of Operation Bootstrap, as the export-led industrialization process in Puerto Rico was called. The comparison is based on my own recent research in the 1980s on women garment workers as well as on secondary sources and the transformations I have personally witnessed during these years at both the macro and micro level. There are distinct regional differences between Mayaguez and the San Juan Metropolitan Area, where the previous shantytown study was conducted, and these should be kept in mind in making this comparison. Though Mayaguez is Puerto Rico's fourth largest city, it is more traditional and less proletarianized than the San Juan Metropolitan area, which shows much greater signs of social disintegration in terms of crime, violence, drug addiction, alcoholism, and divorce. Garment workers also represent an element of the Puerto Rican working class different from the more heterogeneous shantytown residents studied earlier, in part because the relatively permanent employment of women has enabled the family to enjoy greater economic stability and a higher standard of living than most of the poor. Despite these

---

[1] This research was funded by a small grant from the National Institute of Mental Health. The in-depth interviews conducted in 1986 were supported by a grant from the Wenner-Gren Foundation for Anthropological Research.

limitations, I think the comparison between my previous study of a shanty-town and the current study of women garment workers offers valuable insights into the transformations occurring in the Puerto Rican working class during this 30 year period.

I shall focus on three major changes during the past 30 years, all of which impact on Puerto Rico's migration process: 1) the overall economic changes wrought by Operation Bootstrap, including industrialization, migration and growing unemployment and dependency; 2) the increased importance of women in the labor force and as contributors to the household econo-my, which has weakened the man's traditional role as the principal bread-winner; and 3) the impact these changes had on political and social attitudes among the Puerto Rican working class, including their aspirations for them-selves and their children. I shall argue that the development strategies which Puerto Rico has pursued focusing on export-led industrialization have now totally integrated the island into the U.S. economy, and made the economy more dependent than ever on U.S. trade, investment, and assistance. This dependency is reflected in the continuing migration of Puerto Ricans to the U.S. mainland, which further integrates the two economies.

OPERATION BOOTSTRAP AND PUERTO RICO'S INDUSTRIAL TRANSFORMATION

When I started my research in 1959, Puerto Rico was in a period of rapid economic growth generated by Operation Bootstrap, as the industrializa-tion program was called. Operation Bootstrap was part of an ambitious government program to diversify the economy away from monocrop agri-culture (basically sugar) and to improve the level of living through increased employment and heavy investment in housing, health care, and education, in short an equity-with-growth development model. Puerto Rico went from being the "poorhouse of the Caribbean" to the "showcase of democracy," as GNP increased tenfold between 1950 and 1980 (Dietz 1988: 244). U.S. investment poured in, growing 219 percent from 1950 to 1960 and another 295 percent in the following decade, lured by low wages and tax incentives, later to be emulated by many other Caribbean and Latin American countries. Life expectancy increased from 46 years in 1940 to 73 in 1980, while the literacy rate rose from 68.5 percent in 1940 to 91.3 percent in 1976 (Dietz 1988: 30–308). In 1990, the median educa-tional level was 12.2 years, with about half the population completing high school (Depto. del Trabajo y Recursos Humanos 1991: 65).

The rapid economic growth in the 1950s and 1960s and improvements in the standard of living generated considerable optimism among the Puerto Rican urban poor. They professed a strong belief in the possibility of upward mobility based on individual initiative, thrift and education, and felt that the future held hope for themselves and their children. Though economic growth had not substantially altered their subordinate position in society, there was little sign of class consciousness or collective action among the Puerto Rican urban poor, who strongly identified with the progress achieved on the island. In the last chapter of my book, *The Urban Poor of Puerto Rico,* I analyze the reasons for the lack of class consciousness among the Puerto Rican urban poor in terms of several key factors, including their personalistic view of mobility, or tendency to view progress in terms of improvements in their own standard of living; the economic structure of Puerto Rican society, which was then open enough to absorb those who worked hard to get ahead; their personalistic view of poverty, which leads them to blame poverty on personal inadequacy such as laziness, ignorance, or vices like drinking and gambling rather than on class or other structural barriers; migration, which provides an outlet for those who do not succeed and siphons off the discontented; the tradition of dependency and docility created by 300 years of Spanish rule succeeded by American domination, which was actually reinforced by Operation Bootstrap and its reliance on external financing, markets, technology and raw materials; and the weakness of vehicles for creating class consciousness, such as unions or political parties, which have been used as mechanisms of co-optation rather than class solidarity. I concluded at that time that "Puerto Rico shows the limits of reform within a capitalist framework" (Safa 1974:109) and that the Puerto Rican case demonstrates that economic development alone will not eradicate poverty and social inequality.

In a subsequent article (Safa 1980) I analyzed class consciousness among the Puerto Rican urban poor from a feminist perspective, that is, I examined the same set of data on the shantytown from the point of view of women, who had been among my primary informants. I argued that for women, gender and class subordination intersect, and that the "primary obstacles to the development of class consciousness among working-class women in Latin America lie in the strict sexual division of labor, at home and on the job, their subordination within a patriarchal family structure, and in their restriction to the private sphere of domestic labor." I maintained that any attempt to develop class consciousness among working dass women must attack all three areas where women are subordinated: work, the family, and the community (Safa 1980: 82), an issue which is reinforced by my current research on Puerto Rican women garment workers. However, while Puerto Rican women in the shantytown clearly felt abused by men who failed to support them and confined them to the home and domestic responsibilities, the study suggested that the family should be considered not only as a source of subordination, but as a source of strength. Women in the shantytown maintained considerable authority and legitimacy in the family through their strong bond with their children and with extended kin and neighbors, which contributed substantially to shantytown cohesion and women's sense of self-esteem. In fact, I argued that the community or shantytown might serve as a more appropriate vehicle than the workplace for the development of class consciousness among the Latin American working class, as subsequent studies have reaffirmed (*e.g.,* Portes 1985).

By the early 1980s, there were clear signs of greater social disintegration, among the urban poor and other groups in Puerto Rican society. Drug use, crime and violence have increased rapidly, especially in the public housing projects or *caseríos* (as they were known then). My earlier book detected the loss of social control and cohesion in public housing as compared to the shantytown. As I then pointed out, in part the loss was due to the selection process for public housing, which favored the poorer families from the shantytown, including a high percentage of female-headed households. But public housing management reinforced dependency by taking control out of the hands of residents, who felt no identification with their community as in the shantytown. The high degree of violence today would probably make it impossible for a gringa to carry out fieldwork in a shantytown or public housing project as I did 30 years earlier. The family also shows signs of weakening, with an increase in divorce and female-headed households and the growing marginalization of men as economic providers. What happened in the intervening period to bring about these changes? How has the economic situation changed since the early 1960s, when the data for *The Urban Poor of Puerto Rico* was collected, and the early 1980s, when my new research on women garment workers was undertaken? What changes have occurred in family patterns and particularly in the role of women? Are the Puerto Rican poor still as optimistic or has class consciousness grown in the interval? In order to answer these questions, we need first to examine briefly the stages of Operation Bootstrap and its effects on the household and the national economy.

THE STAGES OF OPERATION BOOTSTRAP

Operation Bootstrap actually went through three stages, changing in focus from labor-intensive to capital-intensive in the mid 1960s, and initiating a third stage of high-tech industrialization in the mid 1970s. While different in emphasis, no one stage eclipsed the other, so that labor-intensive industries such as apparel continued to provide the major source of female employment in manufacturing in the 1980s. Although the industrialization program was initially designed to provide employment to men displaced from agricultural employment, women became the primary labor force in the labor-intensive factories attracted in the first stage such as apparel and food processing.

While growth in manufacturing output more than tripled from 1950 to 1980, it still could not offset the enormous declines in agriculture over this period. In 1940, agriculture employed 44.7 percent of the labor force and manufacturing 10.9 percent; in 1980, agriculture had declined to 5.2 percent, while manufacturing nearly doubled to 19 percent (Dietz 1986: 258). Some of this surplus labor was absorbed in services and particularly in public administration, but many workers migrated to the United States. Migration peaked in the 1950s, precisely when Operation Bootstrap was taking off, and continued at high levels until 1970, totaling in this twenty year period about 605,550 persons, a figure equivalent to 27.4 percent of the 1950 population (Dietz 1986: 286). Men slightly outnumbered women, and most were in the most productive age groups between 15 and 39. Despite this "safety valve," unemployment rates continued to hover around 12 to 15 percent from 1950 to 1970. But the decreasing and in some years reverse flow of migration in the 1970s increased unemployment rates considerably in 1980, especially for men (TABLE 1). Unemployment rates continue to be higher for men than for women, and in our sample survey of garment workers, 90 percent say it is easier for a woman than for a man to find a job. In addition, male labor force participation rates declined about 20 percent between 1950 and 1980, reflecting both the precipitous decline in agricultural employment, declining out-migration after 1970, and increasing levels of higher education, which kept young men (and women) out of the labor market. However, women were affected less negatively than men, and after an initial decline from 1950 to 1960, their participation rates increased again to 31.4 percent in 1990. Women were absorbed into export manufacturing, the public sector and the growing ser-

TABLE 1. Rates of Labor Force Participation and Unemployment for Females and Males in Puerto Rico, 1950–90

	Females		Males		Both
	Ages 14+	Ages 16+	Ages 14+	Ages 16+	
Labor force participation rates:					
1950	30.0		79.8		54.6
1960	20.1		71.5		45.5
1970		28.0		70.8	48.0
1980		27.8		60.7	43.3
1990		31.4		61.6	45.4
Percent of the civilian labor force unemployed:					
1950	13.1		15.3		14.7
1960	10.4		12.7		12.1
1970		10.2		11.0	10.7
1980		12.3		19.5	17.1
1990		10.7		16.2	14.2

Source: Estado Libre Asociado de Puerto Rico, Departamento del Trabajo y Recursos Humanos, 1991 Serie Histórica del Empleo, Desempleo, Grupo Trabajador en Puerto Rico 1947–1990. (These figures rely on sample population surveys conducted by the P.R. Department of Labor, but are generally deemed more reliable than the census.)

vice industry (Acevedo 1990). With growing rates of unemployment, men (and later women) migrated or some withdrew entirely from the labor force.

Growing male unemployment, higher wages, and the increasing cost of transportation was one of the factors which prompted the inauguration in the mid-1960s of the second stage of industrialization, focusing on capital-intensive industries such as petrochemicals and pharmaceuticals, which employed more men (Ríos 1990). Higher wages reflected the rising cost of living as well as efforts on the part of U.S. unions to close the wage gap between the mainland and the island. In 1950, the average hourly wage in manufacturing was only 28 percent of the U.S. wage, but the full extension of U.S. minimum wage laws to Puerto Rico in 1981 considerably reduced wage differences.

Capital-intensive industries were adversely affected by the oil crisis of the 1970s, which virtually eliminated the petrochemical industry, and the economic crisis which hit Puerto Rico and the United States in 1974. Capital intensive industries also did little to alleviate unemployment, even for men, and remained heavily dependent on U.S. investment. Investors, primarily external, absorbed an average of 75 percent of the net income from these capital intensive industries, and failed to develop backward or forward linkages to the Puerto Rican economy, so that these industries constituted an export enclave similar to the garment or sugar industries which preceded them (Dietz 1986: 254).

In an attempt to attract more stable industries catering to a highly skilled and better paid labor force, Puerto Rico in the mid-seventies initiated the third stage of industrialization, focusing primarily on high-tech industries such as electronics and scientific instruments. However, at this stage, manufacturing played a secondary role to the growth of the service sector, and industrial incentives were extended to include export-service industries such as investment banking, public relations, insurance, and computer services. Puerto Rico's role as the leading financial, administrative and trade center for the Caribbean was reinforced in 1976 by Section 936 of the U.S. Internal Revenue Code, which allowed U.S. subsidiaries in Puerto Rico to repatriate their profits free of federal taxes and made Puerto Rico into a major tax haven for U.S. manufacturing multinationals, including profits derived from production elsewhere (Pantojas-García 1990). However, this continued dependence of Puerto Rican export manufacturing on U.S. investment failed to generate self-sustained growth, despite the move into capital-intensive and high-tech industries.

Each of these stages in the industrialization process affected female employment. Women constituted the primary labor force in the early stages of labor-intensive industrialization, which required large supplies of cheap labor. More than half of all new jobs created between 1960 and 1980 went to women, and in 1988 they still constituted 47 percent of all workers in the manufacturing sector (Santiago-Rivera 1993: 147). Though capital-intensive industries favored male workers, women were also attracted to better paying white-collar jobs, particularly in the government, which became the principal source of employment in Puerto Rico by 1980.

The relatively high educational levels and low fertility levels among the Puerto Rican women in our 1980 sample results in part from conscious state policies to upgrade the labor force and reduce population growth. In 1980, 39 percent of all Puerto Rican women were high school graduates, which corresponds to the percentage in our sample, while fertility rates had declined to 2.8 births per woman, again approximately the same as the rates among our sample (Presser and Kishor 1991: 60–61).

Both higher educational levels and lower fertility levels contributed to an improvement in women's occupational profile and to their higher labor force participation rates. In addition, women are working more because of the rising cost of living, and the increasing unemployment and declining real wages among men, making it necessary for both husband and wife to contribute to the household economy. In our sample of Puerto Rican garment workers, nearly three-fourths claim their families could not survive without their working and the woman's salary never represents less than 40 percent of the total annual income, even among single women, and is usually higher among married women and especially female heads of household. Thus, Puerto Rico's form of export-led industrialization, by providing more jobs for women than for men, has contributed to the weakening of the man's role as primary breadwinner in many Puerto Rican households, leading to new patterns of authority and gender roles.

However, the increasing incorporation of women into the labor force could not meet the economic needs of many of the Puerto Rican poor, particularly given high unemployment and a rising cost of living. The percentage of households headed by women also increased from 16 to 19 percent from 1970 to 1980, due in part to a high divorce rate, to which the marginalization of men may have contributed. As a result, many poor families, including the working poor employed in low-wage industries such as apparel, became increasingly dependent on transfer payments to support themselves. These transfer payments are primarily federal funds in the form of social security and food assistance, which grew from 12 percent of personal income in 1950 to 30 percent by 1980. Food stamps, or "cupones" as they are known in Puerto Rico, began in the mid-1970s, and grew to reach 58.4 percent of the population in 1980 (Dietz 1986: 299). In our 1980 sample, only 19 percent of the households received food stamps, chiefly large families with many young children or female heads of household. While seen as subsidies to workers, these transfer payments are also aids to low wage industries like apparel that do not pay an adequate wage and might otherwise leave the island because of wage increases or a shortage of cheap labor. By providing alternative or supplementary sources of income, transfer payments further reduce a woman's dependence on a male wage, but increase her dependence on the state. Transfer payments combined with slow job growth also contributed to declining male labor force participation rates, resulting in a fall in the total population employed from 43 percent in 1970–71 to 33 percent in 1984–85. By 1983, over one-half of all families were without wage-earners (Amott and Matthaei 1991: 278).

These social support measures, in addition to ambitious government programs in housing, education, and health, helped to underwrite the costs of social reproduction for the working class, as well as to contain class conflict. State policy was directed at containing and co-opting the labor movement rather than repressing it as in other Latin American countries. Industrialization also led to a profound recomposition of the working class and paradoxically, to a weakening of the labor movement, as the strength of the militant labor union among sugar cane workers was sapped by the decline of the sugar industry and the increasing fragmentation and diversification of the industrial labor force. Fragmentation and competition between labor unions was accentuated by the rapid growth of AFL-CIO affiliates, in which the International Ladies Garment Workers Union (ILGWU) played a leading role. Though unionized, most women workers in our sample regard the ILGWU as a company union which does little to defend their interests or invite rank and file participation. The union's primary interest is in containing worker demands to retard the flight of garment plants to cheaper wage areas elsewhere, but as we shall see, they have not been very successful. In addition, the proportion of unionized workers in Puerto Rico as a whole dropped from 20 percent in 1970 to 6 percent in 1988, which can be partially blamed on unions' neglect of women workers (Santiago-Rivera 1989: 93)

The final blow to the labor movement and to the industrialization program came with Puerto Rico's loss of its comparative advantage as a source of cheap labor to Mexico and other Caribbean countries, who also offered tax incentives and even lower wages. In the 1960s, many countries such as Mexico, Jamaica, the Dominican Republic, and the newly industrializing Asian countries began to copy Puerto Rico's export-led industrialization strategy. High wages plus duty-free access to the United States, which most Caribbean countries acquired in 1983 through the Caribbean Basin Initiative, or CBI, eliminated Puerto Rico's one remaining competitive advantage, particularly in labor-intensive industries in which labor costs are a prime consideration. Puerto Rico has tried to counter this competition in manufacturing with the establishment of twin plants, utilizing funds accumulated under Section 936; these plants are similar to those along the U.S.-Mexican border, where the final and more skilled stages of the manufacturing operations are carried out on the island, with the initial labor-intensive stages in the Dominican Republic, Haiti, and other Caribbean islands.

But even with massive migration and transfer payments, Operation Bootstrap failed to provide sufficient income or jobs to sustain the population. Gross inequalities in income remain, with 55 percent of working families in 1980 and 1990 falling below the poverty level (Colón 1988: Table 4, p. 26). Families can no longer survive on a single wage, so that even when men are employed, their wives are generally also working. Women must often assume full economic responsibility if they are female heads of household or when their husbands are unemployed. Thus, not only has the industrialization program created a demand for female labor, but the continuing poverty of much of the population makes it necessary for women to work. Both demand and supply factors have weakened the man's role as breadwinner and have resulted in women becoming major contributors to the household economy. Compared to thirty years ago, Puerto Rican working women are more assertive and less subservient to male authority, but all carry greater economic responsibility in the household, as we shall see in the next section.

CHANGES IN GENDER ROLES

Permanent paid employment has given women garment workers a sense of independence which the shantytown housewives studied earlier did not enjoy, and has probably led them to expect more from men as well. At the time of our shantytown study in 1959, only one-fourth of the women in our sample had regular employment, but many worked sporadically when their husbands were unemployed, or a child was ill, or the family was faced with other financial emergencies. They considered themselves to be supplementary wage earners (Safa 1974: 28).

In contrast, most women in our 1980 sample of employed women consider themselves to be full economic providers on a par with men. The majority of married women in our sample maintain that they share household decisions with their husband and that they are now both heads of the household. This is a significant change from the patriarchal patterns prevalent earlier in the shantytown. In my 1959 study, husbands often refused to let their wives work, or even leave the house alone to visit relatives, and made the major decisions regarding household purchases or the children's education (Safa 1974: 44). Men also represented the family to the outside world, whereas most women today act as their own spokespersons. Since both are working, earnings today are usually pooled for household expenses and husbands no longer have exclusive budgetary control, as was common when the man was the sole breadwinner.

Most of the husbands of women garment workers now accept their wives working and no longer consider it a threat to their authority, because they realize it is impossible to live on a single wage. However, while authority patterns are changing, the sexual division of labor has remained relatively intact, with women doing most of the household chores. Teresa remarks: "En los quehaceres de la casa, usted sabe que los hombres son vagos para los oficios, los oficios de la casa. . . . Me hace falta, pero pa' tener que pelear con él, pues mejor yo me quedo callada y nos llevamos así, bien, así. El dice que los oficios de la casa es de la mujer." (In terms of household tasks, you know that men are lazy for those jobs, home jobs . . . I need help, but to have to fight with him, well it's better to keep quiet and we get along alright that way. He says that household tasks are for women). Few of the married women in our sample pressured husbands to do more than the shopping and pay the bills, even when the men were no longer working. This is changing somewhat among younger married women, where a greater percentage of husbands help out, reflecting generational changes in gender roles. However, even among the children of our respondents, it is the daughters who most frequently help their mother with household chores.

Male unemployment and outmigration, combined with the rising cost of living, has added to the importance of the woman's contribution to the household economy. Since the 1950s, high unemployment led to heavy outmigration from the western region of Puerto Rico, where this study was conducted, particularly among men because of the decline in male agricultural employment (Monk 1981: 41). In our entire sample, 62 percent of the women have husbands who have lived in the United States, and 46 percent have brothers who are currently living there, but the percentage of sisters and women themselves who have migrated is considerably less. Some of our respondents are return migrants who have lived in the United States for periods of several years, and returned because of difficulties in finding employment there or for family reasons. For example, the Flores family returned in 1974 after living in New York for 25 years because they feared the effect of crime and drugs on their teenage children. All four of their children live at home and the three oldest have gone to the University. They built a beautifully furnished three bedroom house on a *parcela* which they bought for $12,000, with savings they brought from New York. As a unionized blue-collar worker, Mr. Flores earned $600 a week in New York, and his wife did not work after they were married. However, since his weekly salary is now only $250, and with their children still in school and the high cost of living, Mrs. Flores is also working.

The contribution women make varies considerably by marital status and household composition, which affects the number of wage earners in the household and total household income. The highest household incomes are found among single women, where over 40 percent of the households have annual incomes over $14,000.[2] These young single women workers are generally members of large rural households, where there are usually two and often three to five persons working. These large rural Puerto Rican households tend to maintain strong patriarchal traditions and to follow a strict sexual division of labor, which is supported by the extended family setting. Men are not expected to participate in housework or childcare as long as there are other women around to carry out these chores. In Irma's

---

[2] In 1980, when this survey was conducted, the average family income in Puerto Rico was $14,762 (Puerto Rico Planning Board: 1987, p. 2).

household, for example, the father only does the shopping and pays the bills, while she, her mother, and sisters share the rest of the household chores. Her father is retired and receives social security, while both she and her sister (as well as several cousins) work in the same factory.

Like Irma's family, these rural Puerto Rican households are part of a tightly knit network of kin and neighbors, who help each other out in child care, house building, shopping, *etc.* Over 80 percent of the entire sample and 95 percent of the younger women in our sample have relatives living nearby, most of whom they see daily. Over 55 percent of the women have relatives working in the same factory, and they often travel to work together. The strong kin and neighborhood ties found among the garment workers, especially those living in the rural area, resemble the cohesive patterns found earlier in the urban shantytown. In both cases, solidarity is not so much with fellow workers as with female kin and neighbors, who constitute for these women their most important reference group.

There is little evidence of class or gender consciousness among these young, single Puerto Rican women. They have not been working very long, and are generally satisfied with their jobs. Though they are aware of problems on the job and in the larger society, such as inflation and the movement of industry to other areas, young women do not identify with these issues. Like the shantytown youth studied earlier, these young women are concerned with getting ahead, finding a husband and having a family, all matters which do not challenge the existing gender ideology or system of class inequality. However, most young women like Irma plan to continue working after marriage, which differs from earlier norms in which married women (especially with children) engaged only sporadically in paid employment, depending largely on their husbands as the main breadwinner (Safa 1974: 27–28).

Older Puerto Rican women workers are less optimistic about the future and tend to be more isolated and alienated. They are more worried about losing their jobs than younger women, who are better educated and have more alternatives. Older women are also more isolated from kin, particularly female heads of household, who are more likely to live in the city, and have fewer relatives living nearby. Over half of the female heads of households in our sample live in small households of one to three persons, which represents a distinct change from earlier patterns of household composition in the shantytown, where older women never lived alone, but were incorporated into an extended family (Safa 1974:38). It appears that paid employment, plus social security and pensions after retirement have enabled older women to become more independent, though they retain close family ties.

Evarista, for example, is an older female head of household who has worked for more than twenty years in the garment industry. She now lives alone in public housing, and brought up five children on her own, after she and her husband separated. Her mother lived with them and watched the children while she worked, but she died recently and Evarista has taken her grandson in to live with her, while his divorced mother lives nearby. Despite the struggle she had bringing up five children on her own, Evarista says it is better not to be dependent on a man. "Porque que yo coja un hombre y que yo tenga que, que mantener ese hombre, pasar malos ratos y maltrato, pues me quedo sola veinte mil veces. Me encuentro mejor sola porque así sola yo tiro pa' donde quiera y no tengo que estarle pidiendo." (Because if I take a man and have to maintain that man, suffer bad times and bad treatment, well then I stay alone twenty thousand times. I feel better alone because alone I go where I want and don't have to be asking him). Evarista expresses clearly the greater autonomy that older working women may achieve, and the resistance of female heads of households to re-marriage.

Like Evarista, two-thirds of the female heads of household in our sample would prefer not to remarry. They see men as restricting their freedom rather than as assisting them with the responsibility of raising a family. It is difficult to know whether men have become more irresponsible, as some women suggest, or whether women's expectations of men have increased and they are no longer willing to accept male abuse and domination, as some of the younger women interviewed in 1969 also suggested (cf. Safa 1974: 91–92). It is clear that paid employment, while not necessarily the cause of marital breakdown, may enable the woman to leave an unsatisfactory marriage by providing her with an alternative source of income.

Most of the female heads of household in our sample are divorced or separated from their former husbands (only four are widows), which again differs from the pattern 30 years ago, in which divorce was rare and even separated women represented less than ten percent of our shantytown sample (Safa 1974: 79). This reflects the rise in the Puerto Rican divorce rate, which increased from 23.8 per 100 marriages in 1950–59 (the time of the previous study) to 46.4 in 1982 (Muñoz Vasquez and Fernandez Bauzó 1988: 20). It also reflects a decrease in consensual unions, which in our original study represented over one-fourth of all shantytown women respondents, while in the study of garment workers, the figure is reduced to 4.5 percent. This lower percentage of consensual unions affects the divorce rate, since the dissolution of a legal union results in divorce, while consensually married couples merely separate. In the current sample, 70 percent have been married in a church or civil ceremony (especially the former) compared to 54.3 percent in the earlier study (Safa 1974: 39).

The reasons for the recent rise in legal marriage and divorce in Puerto Rico are not clear, and certainly bear more investigation. It may be related to public welfare and other legal regulations which give legally married women greater rights than those in consensual union to public financial aid and claims on the previous husband's pension and other benefits. The change may also reflect differences in the class composition of the sample studied, since legal marriages are associated with higher class status. Shantytown residents had a larger percentage of very poor households earning less than $500 a year compared to the largely working class garment workers in the current study, the poorest of whom had annual family incomes of $5000 or more. This also reflects the ten-fold increase in per capita income noted earlier between 1950 and 1980, but in terms of purchasing power, this increase is much smaller.

We cannot assume that paid employment is the only factor bringing about these changes in gender roles, especially since we do not have a control group of non-working women with whom to compare our sample. Undoubtedly, additional factors noted in this paper contributed to this shift, such as the large number of families who have lived in the United States, higher levels of education, higher divorce rates as well as the virtual total transformation of Puerto Rico from an agrarian to an urban, industrial society. These changes contributed to decreased fertility rates, which, as we noted earlier, fell drastically from 1950 to 1980 (Presser and Kishor 1990: 15). In our sample, nearly 65 percent of the women have three children or less, with a mean under two, while in the families where they grew up, 85 percent had more than three children, sometimes reaching to ten or more. It was common for earlier generations of Puerto Rican working class families to have a large number of children and send them to work at an early age. In the shantytown, although the average number of children was three, 39 percent of the families had four or more children (Safa 1974: 38). Almost 85 percent of the married women with children in the garment worker sample use some form of contraception, and about half of them have been sterilized, which was also the preferred form of birth control in the earlier shantytown study. Smaller family size is undoubtedly linked to improved employment opportunities for women (Presser and Kishor 1980), since most of the women in our sample could not assume the responsibility for a large family and continue working.

Improved educational levels, lower fertility levels, and the independence of earning their own income has also made women more conscious of their rights as workers and more disposed toward gender equality. It is possible that exposure to the women's movement in the United States and in Puerto Rico has also influenced their attitudes. Ninety percent of our sample think a woman should earn the same as a man, and eighty percent think education is equally important for both sexes. Nevertheless, 44 percent of our sample continue to feel that women with children should not work outside the home, though daughters are less negative than wives or female heads of household, again reflecting generational differences. Many of the women say a mother's employment should depend on the age and number of the children, on who is available to take care of them, and on how badly the family needs the added income. Clearly, in their own case, the economic need to work prevailed over their continuing strong sense of responsibility as mothers. The high level of unemployment and other changes in the occupational structure have for some time now weakened the economic role of the man, but strengthened the importance of women as key contributors to the household economy.

POLITICS, CLASS AND MOBILITY

While the working class women in our sample have begun to challenge male authority in the home, they have made much less progress at the level of the state or the political process. In part this stems from a general disillusionment with politics, as governments change, with little improvement in the overall situation of high unemployment and rising cost of living. As the middle-aged husband of Juanita, himself a government employee, noted: "To' el gobierno que viene y el que sale, lo que quieren es to' pa' ellos y el pobre que, que uno se muera . . . A nosotros nos aumentaron el trabajo, los chavos, no." (Every government that comes and goes, what they want is everything for themselves, and the poor, one could die . . . They increased our workload, but not our money.)

Eighty percent of the working women in our sample think that political parties in Puerto Rico have paid little attention to the needs of working women, and sixty percent think there is nothing they can do about it. Their vote in the 1976 election (the last before the 1980 survey was conducted) was almost equally tied between the two major political parties, the Popular Democratic Party (PPD), which favors a continuation of the Commonwealth status, and the New Progressive Party, PNP), which favors statehood. The PPD or Populares has apparently lost some of the strong support it enjoyed in the shantytown earlier, where residents relied on the PPD (then in power for nearly twenty years) for services ranging from water and electricity to jobs and bail in exchange for their political allegiance and support (Safa 1974: 73–4). The Puerto Rican working class is still heavily dependent on the government for a range of services and transfer payments, but the PNP has gained electoral support and adopted a more populist image. The Populares lost their unchallenged dominance in 1968, when the first PNP governor was elected, and Puerto Rico is now a truly two party system.

Both the PNP and the PPD have argued that Puerto Rico is too small and poor to survive on its own, while economic and political dependence on the United States has grown. This has weakened the working class's ability to challenge U.S. hegemony and reinforced their sense of dependency, which as in the earlier study, is manifest among both PNP and PPD supporters. Monserrate's husband, who has lived in the United States for 25 years, is an ardent supporter of statehood, noting: "Puerto Rico tiene que ser estado, no le dé más vuelta . . . Entonces de lo único, a los mas pobres lo único, la ventaja es la independencia, la estadidad. . . . Cuando uno es un niño y el papá es grandote y está defendiendo a uno. Puerto Rico es muy pequeño como le dije para poder ser independiente, ve? . . . Yo digo que si es independiente pues me voy para Miami." (Puerto Rico has to be a state, there is no alternative . . . Then the only thing, for the poor the only thing, the advantage is independence, is statehood. . . . When one is a child and the father is very big and is defending you. Puerto Rico is very small as I told you to be independent, see? . . . I say if it is independent I am going to Miami.) The way in which he equates the relationship between the United States and Puerto Rico with father and son reveals the omnipotence with which many Puerto Ricans regard the United States, which he continuously refers to as "la gran nación" (the great nation). He also appears to equate independence with statehood. Many statehood supporters reject commonwealth status as a continuation of colonialism and feel Puerto Rico would enjoy more rights and autonomy as a state. Monserrate's husband claims that in the United States people are more conscious of their rights and protest to their Congressmen, while Puerto Ricans are more apathetic. "Aquí nadie se ocupa de nada, y ese es el problema que tenemos." (Here no one bothers about anything, and that is the problem we have.) The women in our sample are seldom so vocal about their political opinions, perhaps because they still think of politics as a male domain.

Because of their concern with unemployment and inflation, more than half of the women in our sample say it is not easy to advance in Puerto Rico, and nearly half say it is more difficult now than it was five years ago. Still 78 percent of our respondents think it was even more difficult for their parents, most of whom had less than an eighth grade education. As in the shantytown, many of their fathers worked as agricultural laborers, sometimes cutting cane, or in other manual labor jobs. Three-fourths of their mothers were reported to be housewives, which corresponds to our earlier shantytown study, in which only one-fourth of the women were gainfully employed at the time of the study.

Several of the older garment workers interviewed had been part of the extensive home needlework industry prevalent in Puerto Rico in the 1920s and 1930s, which led to a rise in women's labor force participation of 26.1 percent, one of the highest during this century (Baerga 1992:127). Many of these home workers were married, and considered their wages as supplementary, although in one survey, they constituted the only wage in a majority of the households surveyed (Manning 1934). Generosa, who sewed at home with her mother and sisters, remembers the extensive poverty that existed in Puerto Rico when she was a child and left for the United States in 1951 at age 18: "En aquel tiempo en Puerto Rico se vivía una pobreza enorme. En aquel tiempo sí, de aquel tiempo a éste, ha habido . . . un cambio grande. Que en Puerto Rico antes las casas todas eran de madera. Y no había ni luz eléctrica más que en algunos sitios, no había agua." (At that time in Puerto Rico, there was enormous poverty. At that time yes, from that time to this, there has been . . . a great change. Before in Puerto Rico all the houses were of wood. And there was no electric light except in a few places, there was no water.) Now all of our respondents have running water and electricity, and sixty percent own their own home, which they have often built with their own labor, especially in the rural area. As in the shantytown earlier, investment in homes is one of the major forms of savings, particularly for rural households. Most of the homes are well equipped, and almost all have washing machines and television sets, and 69 percent have stereos. Only about a quarter of our sample have telephones, which are still not available in some rural areas, but 80 percent have cars, which they use daily to get to work. This compares favorably with the few amenities shantytown residents enjoyed thirty years ago. Although most had a radio and television and even refrigerators, few had flush toilets or washing machines, stereos, cars or telephones, and most of their income was spent on food (Safa 1974:16; 30). Among garment workers, many of these consumer items are bought on installment, which explains why 83 percent of our respondents have debts. Consumer debt in Puerto Rico as a whole rose from $237 million in 1963 to $3, 276.4 million in 1983 (Dietz 1986:261), showing that our sample is indicative of a more general trend.

The nicest homes are often found among return migrants, who saved while in the United States to build and furnish a house in Puerto Rico. Their higher standard of living and competition for jobs have caused some resentment among less privileged neighbors, although Monserrate's husband says it has diminished with time, as more migrants have returned. He remarked: "Había más antes cuando nosotros llegamos. Se nos tenía como una clase aparte, que éramos, tú sabes como algo aparte, pero lo cual es una gran mentira. . . . Yo para mí me siento tan americano como vamos a decir, como Eisenhower, como el apple pie y tan puertorriqueño como el coquí . . ." (There was more (discrimination) when we arrived. They had us like a class apart, like we were, you know like something apart, but this is a big lie . . . I personally feel as American as let's say, like Eisenhower, like apple pie, and as Puerto Rican as the *coquí*.[3]) Like many statehood supporters, he feels no contradiction between identifying as American and Puerto Rican at the same time.

Changes in class status are indicative of the progress most of our respondents feel they have made. While most shantytown residents saw themselves as poor, over half of our respondents identify as working class, while over half say their parents were poor. For our respondents, class status is based largely on annual family income and home ownership. About one-third of our sample identify as middle class, and three-fourths of them own their home and two-thirds have annual incomes over $12,000. Class status also varies by life cycle, with 71 percent of young women identifying as working class, while a greater percentage of women over 30 identify as middle class. These are generally married women whose husbands also earn a good salary (over $175 a week), so that they are likely to fall in the higher income brackets. Less than one-quarter of the female-headed households, who are generally poorer, identify as middle dass.

---

[3] A *coquí* is a small tree toad unique to Puerto Rico, which has come to symbolize much of national culture

Parents clearly have high aspirations for their children, and have struggled hard to give their children a good education. Of the small number of children of our respondents who have completed their schooling (36 boys and 38 girls), half of these have gone on to college, and almost all of these college-educated youth are identified by their parents as middle dass. A good number of these college-educated children are in white-collar professional or clerical jobs. In comparison, better educated youth in the shantytown in 1969 generally aspired to finish high school and to learn a trade like beautician, secretary or carpenter (Safa 1974: 95).

However, parents complain that even children with a college education cannot find a job. Monserrate's son and daughter both studied at the Colegio de Mayaguez, a branch of the University of Puerto Rico, but her daughter is planning to leave for the United States after graduation, because of the lack of employment. Monserrate complains: "Los jóvenes se van porque ahora mismo todos los que se gradúan tienen que irse a buscar para allá trabajo porque aquí no se consigue." (The young are going because right now all who graduate have to go to find work there, because here you can't find any.)

As Monserrate notes, unemployment is particularly acute among the young, even those with a college education, and has resulted in increased migration. Unemployment among youth aged 16–19 in 1990 was 36.4 percent, and from 1981 to 1985 reached over 50 percent (Depto. de Trabajo y Recursos Humanos 1991: 32). Nearly half the migrants between 1970 and 1980 were between the ages of 16 and 24, of whom about a third were students. Migration in 1986 reached 46,619 persons, its highest peak since 1957, and included a higher percentage of professionals and other white-collar workers (Puerto Rican Planning Board 1987: 35–42). The lack of employment possibilities and need for out-migration, even for college graduates, helps explain why over a third of the women in our sample say it is harder for their children to advance than it was for them, although sixty percent claim it is easier. At the time of our earlier study, migration to the mainland also represented an outlet for the young dissatisfied with life on the island, where the occupational system even then failed to keep up with educational expansion (Safa 1974: 76).

Women are conscious that their paid employment has contributed substantially to their own family's standard of living as well as the social mobility of their children. The progress they and their children have made in terms of education, occupation, income levels, home ownership and furnishings reflects in part the overall improvement in living standards in Puerto Rico since 1950, but the added income provided through female employment has also played a critical role. However, these women are beginning to express serious doubts regarding the possibility of sustaining this progress in the face of continuing high unemployment and the rising cost of living. But they have yet to translate these concerns into greater political activism.

CONCLUSIONS

Clearly paid employment has played an important role in increasing gender consciousness among Puerto Rican working class women. It has contributed to their family's improved living standards and to their (sometimes misplaced) faith in education as a vehicle for upward mobility. It has enhanced their sense of self-worth to the point that they no longer depend on men as the sole or even primary breadwinners and are proud and confident of their contribution to the household economy. And it has increased their awareness of issues such as unemployment, inflation and even gender discrimination, though they remain quite apathetic in their response to these problems.

While these women have seen real improvement in their own lives and in Puerto Rican society as a whole during the period of Operation Bootstrap, their optimism is giving way to pessimism as they see progress becoming more difficult and fear that the future may not hold the same promises for their children that they once envisaged. Yet they feel that political parties, like labor unions, pay little attention to the needs of working women, and that politics remains a male domain in which women have little voice. At the same time, as public expenditures mount, there has been an erosion of state support for the costs of social reproduction, which played such a crucial role in mitigating class conflict and underwriting low wages during the earlier stages of the industrialization process. Low-income Puerto Ricans are paying more for public housing, education and medical care, but are increasingly dependent on transfer payments such as social security and food stamps. While this has lessened dependence on male wages, poor women are now increasingly dependent upon the state, thus substituting public patriarchy for the private patriarchy which existed previously.

As in the shantytown studied earlier, the only arena where Puerto Rican women feel they have some legitimacy is in the family. Partially as a result of paid employment, working class women have gained a greater voice in household decisions and control over the budget, although they continue to do much of the housework. At the household level, women also have the support and assistance of the female kin group, while comparable working class women's solidarity groups are lacking in the workplace and in the political arena. The assistance of the female kin group and particularly the mother proves essential to the growing number of female-headed households who must struggle to support a family on their own. The marginal role of men in the family, even in their primary role as breadwinners, has tended to reinforce the traditional matrifocal nature of the Puerto Rican working class family (Safa 1974: 36), as well as to erode the last vestiges of deference to male authority in the household.

Thus, while male authority in the household has begun to weaken, it still remains largely unchallenged at the level of the workplace and in politics. Here I would argue that the fault lies more with the lack of support women workers receive from labor unions, the government, and political parties than with the women themselves. While the Puerto Rican working class women studied here appear quite resigned to the subordination they suffer from these public institutions, they are also hampered by a paternalistic company union which makes no attempt to build worker solidarity, and a government which fears the effect of labor unrest on foreign investment. Despite the long and extensive involvement of women workers in Puerto Rico's development process, they are not given the same legitimacy as workers as men, and continue to be regarded as subsidiary or supplementary breadwinners. Thus, the gender ideologies implanted in these institutions are as important as those generated in the home in maintaining women's subordination.

Political parties, the government, and labor unions have also retarded the growth of class consciousness among the Puerto Rican working class, as they did thirty years ago in the shantytown, but their message has changed. During the early period of Operation Bootstrap, when economic growth was strong, these institutions sold the Puerto Rican poor on the American dream, where upward mobility was possible for everyone as long as they worked hard enough, saved their money, and gave their children a good education. Now with the failure of Operation Bootstrap and economic stagnation, the dream has faded, yet this study suggests that the Puerto Rican working class appears more resigned than ever to their inability to challenge the status quo. Why? Because with the total integration of the Puerto Rican economy into the United States, Puerto Ricans feel more dependent than ever on maintaining these links. Dependency on the United States in terms of investment, trade, transfer payments and aid to the Commonwealth government has increased, while many Puerto Ricans now shuttle back and forth to the mainland in a pattern of circular migration. Migration has assumed alarming proportions among the young, among whom even the college educated cannot find a job on the island. Migration and transfer payments now coopt the working class into greater dependency on the United States and replace the buffer which expanding opportunities and economic growth once provided. Though pessimism among the Puerto Rican working class is growing with the failure of Operation Bootstrap to create self-sustained growth, it has not translated into a marked increase in class consciousness capable of challenging the United States and elite hegemony on the island.

REFERENCES

ACEVEDO, LUZ DE ALBA
  1990   Industrialization and employment: Changes in the patterns of women's work in Puerto Rico. *World Development* **18** (2):231–255.

AMOTT, TERESA AND JULIE MATTHAEI
    1991   *Race, Gender and Work: A Multicultural Economic History of Women in the United States.* Boston: South End Press.
BAERGA, MARÍA DEL CARMEN
    1992   Puerto Rico: From colony to colony. In *Creating and Transforming Households: The Constraints of the World Economy.* Paris: Cambridge University Press, Editions de las Maison des Sciences de L'Homme, pp. 121–144.
COLÓN, ALICE, MARYA MUÑOZ, NEFTALÍ GARCÍA, AND IDSA ALEGRIA
    1988   Trayectoria de la participación laboral de las mujeres en Puerto Rico de los años 1950 a 1985. In *Crisis, Sociedad y Mujer: Estudio Comparativo entre Países de América (1950–1985).* Habana, Cuba, Federación de Mujeres Cubanas.
DEPARTAMENTO. DE TRABAJO Y RECURSOS HUMANOS, ESTADO LIBRE ASOCIADO DE PUERTO RICO.
    1991   *Serie Historico del Empleo, Desempleo y Grupo Trabajador en Puerto Rico.* Informe Especial Número E-74. San Juan: Department of Labor and Human Resources.
DIETZ, JAMES
    1986   *Economic History of Puerto Rico: Institutional Change and Capitalist Development.* Princeton, NJ: Princeton University Press.
MANNING, CAROLINE
    1934   The Employment of Women in Puerto Rico. *U.S. Department of Labor, Bulletin of the Women's Bureau,* no. 18.
MONK, JANICE
    1981   Social change and sexual differences in Puerto Rican rural migration. *Papers in Latin American Geography in honor of Lucia G. Harrison.* Muncie, Indiana. Special publication of the conference of Latin Americanist Geographers, Vol. 1: 28–43.
MUÑOZ VASQUEZ AND FERNANDEZ BAUZÓ
    1988   *El Divorcio en la Sociedad Puertorriqueña.* Río Piedras, PR: Ediciones Huracán.
PANTOJAS-GARCÍA, EMILIO
    1990   *Development Strategies as Ideology: Puerto Rico's Export-Led Industrialization Experience.* Boulder, CO: Lynne Rienner Publishers.
PORTES, ALEJANDRO
    1985   Latin American class structures: Their composition and change during the last decades. *Latin American Research Review* **XX** (3):7–39.
PRESSER, HARRIET B. AND SUNITA KISHOR
    1991   Economic development and occupational sex segregation in Puerto Rico: 1950–1980. *Population and Development Review* **17** (1):53–85.
PUERTO RICO PLANNING BOARD
    1987   *Socioeconomic Statistics.* San Juan: Bureau of Statistics, Puerto Rico Planning Board.
RÍOS, PALMIRA N.
    1990   Export-oriented industrialization and the demand for female labor: Puerto Rican women in the manufacturing sector, 1952–1980. *Gender and Society* **4** (3).

SAFA, HELEN I.
  1980   *The Urban Poor of Puerto Rico: A Study in Development and Inequality.*
         New York: Holt, Rinehart and Winston, Inc. (now Harcourt, Brace,
         Jovanovich).
  1981   Runaway shops and female employment: The search for cheap labor.
         Signs 7, Winter.
  1985   Female employment and the social reproduction of the Puerto Rican
         working class. In *Women and Change in Latin America: New Directions
         for the Study of Sex and Class in Latin America.*, pp. 84–105. J.F.
         Bergin and Garvey Publishers.
  1990   Women and industrialization in the Caribbean. In *Women, Employment,
         and the Family in the International Division of Labor.* S. Stichter and J.
         Parpart, Eds. New York: Macmillan.
SANTIAGO-RIVERA, CARLOS
  1993   The Puerto Rican labor movement in the 1990s. In *Colonial Dilemma:
         Critical Perspectives on Contemporary Puerto Rico,* Edwin Meléndez
         and Edgardo Meléndez, Eds. Boston: South End Press, pp. 143–156.

The Political Economy of Resistance and Self-Destruction in the Crack Economy

An Ethnographic Perspective

PHILIPPE BOURGOIS

San Francisco Urban Institute
San Francisco State University
1600 Holloway Avenue
San Francisco, California 94133

The long-term transformation of the U.S,. economy from manufacturing to service has had profoundly dislocating effects on the lives of inner-city residents. Although researchers have argued extensively over the details of the statistics, they virtually all recognize that the disruptions caused by the loss of factory jobs in urban centers is a driving force behind inner city polarization (Sassen-Koob 1986; Waldinger 1991; Wilson 1987). In contrast, public "common sense" in the United States is not persuaded by this structural economic analysis. Neither upper-middle class white suburbanites, nor black and latino working-poor urbanites are convinced that the statistics on human suffering—from infant poverty to male adolescent murder rates to adult substance abuse—are fundamentally driven by the loss of stable factory jobs. The result has been a polarization around culture in public discourse and a lack of political will to address the apartheid-like concentration of poverty in major urban centers. Academics—and specifically anthropologists—have failed to engage these debates in a politically engaged manner, perhaps in part because the relationship between individual practice and structural exigency is poorly understood.

STRUCTURAL CONSTRAINTS OF THE NUYORICAN EXPERIENCE

The Puerto Rican experience of migration to New York City—specifically to *El Barrio*—during the post-World War II period provides an almost classically worst-case scenario for how processes of discrimination and economic exploitation confine vulnerable populations to geographically segregated communities that are then engulfed by violence, crime, and poverty. Second- and third-generation Puerto Rican immigrants in inner city New

97

York—Nuyoricans—are the descendants of an almost century-old colonial relationship between the island of Puerto Rico and the mainland United States. This historical process of marginalization is crucial for understanding daily life on the streets of *El Barrio*.

Almost immediately after invading Puerto Rico in 1898 the U.S. government sponsored a monumental transformation and dislocation of the Island's rural economy. Land and power was concentrated into the hands of large U.S.-owned agro-export companies. Hundreds of thousands of small farmers left their small plots in the hills to seek wage labor employment on the immense plantations that overtook much of Puerto Rico's coastal plains. Soon after World War II, many of these uprooted farmers—whose *jíbaro* or "hillbilly" identity has been reconstructed to symbolize "traditional" Puerto Rican culture—subsequently left the sugarcane fields in search of the new factory jobs that U.S. corporations were establishing in the Island's biggest towns. Less than a generation later, most of these newly urbanized immigrants and their children migrated to New York City in search of factory jobs.

In the fifteen years following World War II, an average of 40,000 people left Puerto Rico annually. Over 75,000 left in 1953 alone, and another 586,000 Puerto Ricans followed in the 1960s (Bonilla and Campos 1986:29; Maldonado-Denis 1980:145). Approximately a third of the population moved permanently to the United States. Significantly this already large figure camouflages the disruptions that occurred in the lives of the tens of thousands of emigrants who returned home after years of living abroad (Ortiz 1986:616). In any case, by the early 1990s, almost as many self-identified Puerto Ricans were living on the U.S. mainland as on the island of Puerto Rico itself (Institute for Puerto Rican Policy 1993). Few other countries in the world have exported such a large proportion of their population over such a short period of time to such a culturally hostile and economically alien host.

The Puerto Rican diaspora spurred by the destruction of Puerto Rico's small-farmer rural economy was a "voluntary" labor migration. The problem is that most of the immigrants went to New York to find jobs in precisely the economic sector that was, once again, about to disappear: light industry (Rodriguez 1989). Just as Puerto Ricans arrived looking for factory work, New York City was embarking on a structural transformation that rendered local manufacturing obsolete. In the decades since 1950 the City became a finance-driven logistical nodal point for the multinational corporations that have been closing their local production plants to relocate overseas where labor is cheaper.

To summarize, over the past three or four generations, the Puerto Rican people—especially those living in New York—have passed through almost a half dozen distinct modes of production: 1) from semi-subsistence peasants on private mountain plots or local haciendas; 2) to export agricultural laborers on foreign-owned, capital-intensive plantations; 3) to factory workers in urban shanty towns; 4) to sweatshop workers in ghetto tenements; 5) to service sector employees in high-rise inner-city housing projects; 6) to underground economy entrepreneurs on the street. This marathon sprint through economic history onto New York City's streets has been compounded ideologically by an overtly racist "cultural assault." Literally overnight the new immigrants—many of whom were enveloped in idealized *jíbaro* identities emphasizing interpersonal webs of patriarchal *respeto*—found themselves transformed into "racially" inferior cultural pariahs. Ever since their arrival they have been despised and humiliated with that virulence so characteristic of North America's history of polarized race relations.

The historic structural transformations imposed upon the Puerto Rican *jíbaro* translate statistically into a tragic profile of unemployment, substance abuse, broken families, and devastated health in America's inner cities. No other ethnic group except perhaps American Indians fares more poorly in the official statistics than do mainland U.S. Puerto Ricans. This is most pronounced for the majority cohort living in New York City where Puerto Ricans have the highest welfare dependency and poverty rates and the lowest labor force participation rates of any group (Rosenberg 1990; Center on Budget and Policy Priorities; Lehman 1991). More poignantly, the Puerto Rican statistics cover some of the most humanly painful experiences ranging from the fastest growing HIV infection rates, the highest rates of bedridden disability, the most deaths due to cirrhosis of the liver, the greatest per capita proportion of heroin and crack addicts, to the highest rates of suicide attempts (Giachello 1990; Lambert 1990; Rosenwaike 1983).

THE ETHNOGRAPHIC SETTING

These contemporary expressions of historical dislocation formed the backdrop for my five years of participant-observation fieldwork on street culture in the "crack economy" and early 1990s (Bourgois 1995). For a total of approximately three and a half years I lived with my wife and young son in an irregularly heated, rat-filled tenement in East Harlem, better known locally as *El Barrio* or Spanish Harlem. This 200 square block neighborhood is visibly impoverished located in the heart of the richest city in the Western Hemisphere—literally a stone's throw from multi-million dollar condominiums. Although one in three families survived on public assistance in 1990, the majority of *El Barrio*'s 110,600 Puerto Rican and African-American residents fell into the ranks of the working poor. They eke out an uneasy subsistence in entry-level service and manufacturing jobs in one of the most expensive cities in the world.

In my ethnographic research, I have not focused on the majority sector of the "working poor" population of East Harlem. Instead, I am exploring the ideologies (*i.e.*, the power-charged belief systems) that organize "common sense" on the street—what I call "street culture." Consequently, over the years, I developed my closest relationships with the addicts, thieves, dealers, and con artists who have carved out public hegemony on the stoops and housing project benches surrounding my tenement. Specifically, I have focused on a network of some 25 street-level crack dealers operating on and around my block.

Such an intensive examination of street participants risks exoticizing the neighborhood and may be interpreted as reinforcing violent stereotypes against Puerto Ricans. On the other hand, case studies of the "worthy poor" risk "normalizing" the experience of class and racial segregation and can mask the depths of human suffering which accompanies rapid economic restructuring. Furthermore, the legally employed majority of *El Barrio* residents has lost control of the streets and has retreated from daily life in the neighborhood. To understand the experience of living in the community the ideologies of violence, opposition, and material pursuit that dominate street life—much to the dismay of most residents—have to be addressed systematically. Furthermore, on a subtle theoretical level the almost caricatural responses to poverty and marginalization that the dealers and addicts represent, provide privileged insight into processes which may be experienced in one form or another by major sectors of any vulnerable working class population experiencing rapid structural change anywhere in the world and at any point in history.

My central concern is the relationship of the street dealers to the worlds of work—*i.e.*, the legal and illegal labor markets —that employ them and give meaning to their lives. I hope to show the local-level implications of this global-level restructuring of capital and, in the process, record the words and experiences of some unrepentant victims. In a nutshell, I am arguing that the transformation from manufacturing to service employment—especially in the professional office work setting—is much more culturally disruptive than the already revealing statistics on reductions in income, employment, unionization, and worker's benefits would indicate. Low-level service sector employment engenders a humiliating ideological—or cultural—confrontation between a powerful corps of white office executives and their assistants versus a mass of poorly educated, alienated, "colored" workers.

SHATTERED WORKING CLASS DREAMS

All the crack dealers and addicts in the network I frequented worked at one or more legal jobs in their early youths. In fact, most entered the labor market at a younger age than the typical American. Before they were 12 years old they were bagging groceries at the supermarket for tips, stocking beers off-the-books in local *bodegas*, or shining shoes. In fact, many dropped out of school in order to make money to obtain the childhood "necessities"—candy, sneakers, basketballs, baseball cards—that most pre-teenagers from more affluent communities are able to buy with their allowance money. For example, Chino, the night manager at a video games arcade that sells 5 dollar vials of crack on the block where I lived, pursued a traditional working class trajectory in his early adolescence. He dropped out of junior high school to work in a local garment factory:

> I was like 14 or 15, playing hooky and pressing dresses and whatever they were making on the steamer. They was cheap, cheap clothes.
>
> The boss was Spanish and shit, but I don't know if she was the main man. She just ran the whole factory and I just worked for whatever she gave me at the end of the week. Her husband was a dope fiend, but he was the one that picked the money up from the white owners downtown.
>
> My mother's sister was working there first and then her son, my cousin Hector—the one who's in jail now—was the one they hired first, because his mother agreed: "If you don't want to go school, you gotta work."
>
> So I started hanging out with him. I wasn't planning on working in the factory. I was supposed to be in school; but it just sort of happened.

This factory was so marginal that little Chino actually became the agent who physically moved it out of the inner city. In the process, he became merely one more of the 445,900 manufacturing workers in New York City to lose their job as factory employment dropped 50 percent from 1963 to 1983 (Romo and Schwartz 1993). Of course, instead of understanding himself as the victim of a structural transformation, Chino remembers with pleasure and even pride the extra income he earned for clearing the machines out of the factory space:

> Them people had money, man. Because we helped them move out of the neighborhood. It took us two days—only me and my cousin, Hector. Wow! It was work. They gave us 70 bucks each.

Not coincidentally, as I was taping these reminiscences, Caesar—who was Chino's lookout at the crack house door—interrupted with an almost identical story. Like Chino, Caesar obtained his first job through his family connections and their social network. Once again, however, his sweatshop job was among the most marginal and least desirable of New York's manufacturing sector:

> I worked in a factory before too. That was my first job. My uncle got me the job when I dropped out of school. My moms told me I either get a job or go back to school.
>
> I liked'ed it at that time, but I lost a lot of weight because it used to be stupid hot in there. They used to give us these salt pills and shit.
>
> They used to plate metal, like paint fake jewelry. But the company moved too.

In other words, despite being in the most marginal cohort of the traditional factory-based working class, the families of these crack dealers subscribed to mainstream working class ideologies about the dignity of engaging in "hard work" versus education. Caesar's repetition of the same type of youthful work experience as Chino is important, not merely because it provides a second example, but rather because it illustrates the type of working class memories still alive in what have become the hard-core lumpen of the inner-city. As unemployed mid-twenty year-olds they do not have a global structural perspective on the dearth of adequate entry-level jobs available to high school drop-outs in New York. At the same time they are frequently accused of slothfulness by their mothers and even by friends who are working legally. Eventually, therefore they begin to suspect that they might indeed be "stupid, lazy victims" who do not want to work hard and help themselves. Confused, they take refuge in an alternate search for career, meaning, and ecstasy in substance abuse.

Caesar's friends on the street—most of whom are also crack addicts and/or sellers—confirm the glory of Caesar's early factory employment days. While his former companions struggled in hostile schools, he assumed an enviable figure working "with his uncle chroming" in the adult male realm of the factory floor. Unlike the other 16-year-olds who remained in school, he had money, "fly clothes," and was able to "party hard." For poor adolescents, the decision to drop out of school and become a marginal factory worker, is attractive. More importantly, had Caesar and Chino not been confined to the weakest sector of manufacturing in a period of rapid job loss their teenage, working class dream might have stabilized.

Formerly, when most entry-level jobs were found in factories, the contradiction between an oppositional street culture and traditional working class shop-floor culture—especially when it was protected by a union—was less pronounced. Factory work is inevitably rife with confrontational hierarchies; nevertheless, on the shop-floor, surrounded by older union workers, high school dropouts who are well-versed in the latest and toughest street culture styles can function effectively. In the factory, being tough and violently macho has high cultural value; a certain degree of opposition to the foreman and the "bossman" is expected and is considered masculine.

In contrast, this same oppositional street identity is nonfunctional in the service sector that has burgeoned in New York's expanded finance-driven economy because it does not allow for the humble, obedient, social interaction that professional office workers demand from their subordinates. A qualitative change has occurred in the tenor of social interaction in service-sector employment. Workers in a mail room or behind a photocopy machine cannot publicly maintain their cultural autonomy. Most concretely, they have no union; more subtly, there are few fellow workers surrounding them to insulate them and to provide them with a culturally based sense of class solidarity. Instead they are besieged by supervisors and bosses from an alien, hostile, and obviously dominant culture. When these office managers are not intimidated by street culture, they ridicule it. Workers like Caesar and Chino appear inarticulate to their professional supervisors when they try to imitate the language of power in the workplace and instead stumble pathetically over the enunciation of unfamiliar words. They cannot decipher the hastily scribbled instructions—rife with mysterious abbreviations—that are left for them by harried office managers. The "common sense" of white collar work is foreign to them; they do not, for example, understand the logic for filing triplicate copies of memos or for post-dating invoices. When they attempt to improvise or show initiative they fail miserably and instead appear inefficient—or even hostile—for failing to follow "clearly specified" instructions.

Their "social skills" are even more inadequate than their limited professional capacities; They do not know how to look at their fellow co-service workers—let alone their supervisors—without intimidating them. They cannot walk down the hallway to the water fountain without unconsciously swaying their shoulders aggressively as if patrolling their home turf. Gender barriers are an even more culturally charged realm. They are repeatedly reprimanded for offending co-workers with sexually aggressive behavior.

The cultural clash between white "yuppie" power and inner-city "scrambling jive" in the service sector, is much more than style. Service workers who are incapable of obeying the rules of inter-personal interaction dictated by professional office culture will never be upwardly mobile. In the highrise office buildings of midtown Manhattan newly employed inner-city high school dropouts suddenly realize that they look like idiotic buffoons to the men and women they work for. A gender dynamic exacerbates the confusion and sense of insult experienced by young, male inner-city employees because most supervisors in the lowest reaches of the service sector are women. Street culture does not allow males to be subordinate across gender lines.

"GETTIN' DISSED"

On the street, the trauma of experiencing a threat to one's personal dignity has been frozen linguistically in the commonly used phrase "to diss" which is short for, "to disrespect." Significantly, one or two generations ago ethnographers working in rural Puerto Rico specifically noted the importance of the traditional Puerto Rican concept of "*respeto*" in mediating labor relations:

> The good owner 'respects' (*respeta*) the laborer . . . It is probably to the interest of the landowner to make concessions to his best workers, to deal with them on a respect basis, and to enmesh them in a network of mutual obligations (Wolf 1956:235; see also Lauria 1964 and Totti 1986).

Puerto Rican street-dealers do not find "respect" in the entry-level service sector jobs that have increased two-fold in New York's economy since the 1950s. On the contrary, they "get dissed" in their new jobs. Chino, for example, remembers the humiliation of his former, racially charged work experiences as an "office boy." Note also how he expresses his frustration in explicitly sexist language:

> I had a prejudiced boss. She was a fucking "ho'," Gloria. She was white. Her name was Christian. No, not Christian, Kirschman. I don't know if she was Jewish or not. [Note Chino's difficulty in reading the ethnic markers that differentiate white people.]
>
> When she was talking to people she would say, "He's illiterate," as if I was really that stupid that I couldn't understand what she was talking about.
>
> So what I did one day was, I just looked up the word, "illiterate," in the dictionary and I saw that this bitch is saying to her associates that I'm stupid or something, I'm stupid! You know like [pointing], "He doesn't know shit."
>
> Well, I am illiterate anyway.

Although Chino resented being called illiterate, the most profound dimension of his humiliation was being obliged to look up in the dictionary the word used to insult him. In contrast, in the underground economy, Chino does not risk this kind of threat to his self-worth:

> My boss, Big Pete [the crackhouse owner] he would never disrespect me that way. He wouldn't tell me that because he's illiterate too, plus I've got more education than him. I've got a GED. I got it in jail.

In order to succeed at Gloria Kirschman's magazine publishing company Chino would have had to submit wholeheartedly to her version of professional office culture, but he was unwilling to compromise his street identity. He refused to accept "Gloria's" insults and he was unable to imitate her culture; hence, he was doomed to a marginal position behind a photocopy machine or at the mail meter. The job requirements in the service sector are largely cultural—*i.e.*, having a "good attitude"—therefore they conjugate powerfully with racism:

> I wouldn't have mind that she said I was illiterate. What bothered me was that when she called on the telephone, she wouldn't want me to answer even if my supervisor who was the receptionist was not there. [Note how Chino is so low in the office hierarchy that his immediate supervisor is merely a receptionist.]
>
> When she hears my voice it sounds like she's going to get a heart attack. She'd go, "Where's Renée?"—Renée Silverman, that's the receptionist, my supervisor. "Why are you answering the phones?"
>
> That bitch just didn't like my Puerto Rican accent.
>
> OK, I don't have the education to type, so I will not type. But don't "diss" me for answering the phones.
>
> I used to answer it pretty well, man. I thought maybe it was important.

Chino took revenge by affirming the culture that so offended Gloria:

> And then, when I did pick up the phone, I used to just sound *Porta'rrrican* on purpose.

In contrast to the old factory sweatshop positions, these just-above-minimum-wage office jobs require intense proximal interpersonal contact with the middle and upper-middle class. Young men like Chino and Caesar simply do not have the "cultural skills" demanded by their white, college-graduate supervisors and bosses. Proximal contact across class lines, and the absence of an autonomous working class space for eight hours a day in the office can be a claustrophobic experience for the disoriented, young inner-city worker. Caesar specifically interpreted it as an affront to his dignity that challenged his definition of masculinity:

> I had a few jobs like that [referring to Chino's "telephone diss"] where you gotta take a lot of shit from bitches and be a wimp.
> I didn't like it but I kept on working, because "Fuck it!," you don't want to fuck up the relationship. So you just be a punk [shrugging his shoulders dejectedly].

One alternative way to survive at a work place that does not tolerate a street-based cultural identity is to become bicultural: to play politely by "the white woman's" rules downtown only to come home and revert to street culture within the safety of one's tenement or housing project at night. Tens of thousands of East Harlem residents manage this tightrope, but it often engenders accusations of betrayal and internalized racism on the part of neighbors and childhood friends who do not have—or do not want—these bi-cultural skills.

This is the case, for example, of Ray, a rival crack dealer whose black skin and tough street demeanor disqualify him from legal office work. He quit a "nickel-and-dime messenger job downtown" in order to sell crack full-time in his project stairway shortly after a white woman fled from him shrieking down the hallway of a high-rise office building. Ray and the terrified woman had ridden the elevator together and coincidentally Ray had stepped off on the same floor as her to make a delivery. Worse yet, Ray had been trying to act like a debonair male and suspected the contradiction between his inadequate appearance and his "chivalric" intentions was responsible for the woman's terror:

> You know how you let a woman go off the elevator first? Well that's what I did to her but I may have looked a little shabby on the ends. Sometime my hair not combed. You know. So I could look a little sloppy to her maybe when I let her off first.

What Ray did not quite admit until I probed further is that he too had been intimidated by the lone white woman. He had been so disoriented by her taboo, unsupervised proximity that he had forgotten to press the elevator button when he originally stepped on with her:

> She went in the elevator first but then she just waits there to see what floor I press. She's playing like she don't know what floor she wants to go

to because she wants to wait for me to press my floor. And I'm standing there and I forgot to press the button. I'm thinking about something else—I don't know what was the matter with me. And she's thinking like, "He's not pressing the button; I guess he's following me!"

As a crack dealer, Ray no longer has to confront this kind of confusing humiliation. Instead, he can righteously condemn his "successful" neighbors who work downtown for being ashamed of who they were born to be:

> When you see someone go downtown and get a good job, if they be Puerto Rican, you see them fix up their hair and put some contact lens in their eyes. They fit in. And they do it! I seen it.
>
> They turn-overs. They people who want to be white. Man, if you call them in Spanish, it wind up a problem. I mean like, take the name Pedro— I'm just telling you this as an example—Pedro be saying, [imitating a whitened accent] "My name is Peter." Where do you get Peter from Pedro?
>
> Just watch how Spanish people fix up their hair. When they get nice jobs like that, all of a sudden, you know, they start talking proper.

At the same time however, Ray feels defensive about his "failure" in the white world of work:

> I guess if I stay in the street too long after I'm off work that keeps me from talking proper. But it's not like I was ever an official hoodlum.
>
> I might have sold PCP and marijuana and crack and cocaine, but I have a home base.
>
> Even though I have been in the street, I went to Catholic schools. I was never stupid. I was just stereo typed [sic] because of my race.

RESISTING EXPLOITATION

Third-and-second generation Spanish Harlem residents born into working class families do not tolerate high levels of "exploitation." In the new jobs available to them, however, there are no class-based institutions to channel their resistance. They are caught in a technological time warp. They have developed contemporary mainstream American definitions of survival needs and emotional notions of job satisfaction. In short, they are "made in New York"; therefore, they are not "exploitable" or "degradable." Both their objective economic needs as well as their personal cultural dignities have to be satisfied by their jobs. They resist inadequate working conditions. Finally, they are acutely aware of their relative deprivation vis-à-vis the middle-level managers and wealthy executives whose intimate physical proximity they cannot escape at work.

At the same time that young men like Chino, Caesar, and Ray recognize how little power they have in the legal labor market, they do not accept their domination passively. They see themselves as resisting exploitation. In New York's finance-driven service economy, however, these involuted forms of resistances become especially self-destructive, given the all-importance of "attitude" in closed corporate quarters. Entry-level office workers have to be ready to perform diverse tasks with zest and initiative—whatever their supervisor might order—whether it be brewing coffee or picking up a silk blouse from the cleaners.

The traditional modes of powerless resistance—footdragging, disgruntlement, petty theft, *etc.*—which might be appropriate in traditional peasant or even proletarian settings contradict the fundamental "technological" requirement for enthusiastic "initiative" and "flexibility" that service sector jobs demand (*cf.* Scott 1985). In manufacturing, resistance can be channelled through recognized institutions—unions—that often reinforce class consciousness. In fact, oppositionally defined cultural identities are so legitimate on the shop floor that they even serve to ritualize management/worker confrontation.

In the service sector, on the other hand, there is no safe way to express cultural nonconformity. Stealing on the job, for example, is the avenue for "powerless revenge" most favored by Caesar and Chino. They both were skilled at manipulating the Pitney-Bowes postage meter machines and at falsifying stationary inventory to skim "chump change." Even though they were never caught, from the employer's perspective, this petty theft made Caesar and Chino even more inadequate workers. Not only did they scowl and argue with supervisors, but they were suspected of dishonesty.

Chino particularly enjoyed reminiscing about his successful pilfering in the mail room run by Gloria Kirschman—his literate nemesis. Ironically his "errand-boy" scam involved forging and exchanging receipts in order to double-invoice and cross-charge—skills that are not usually associated with illiteracy:

> You remember that lady that used to complain about me answering the phones and being illiterate? Well she had this petty cash money box but she didn't keep good inventory. And she was always bitching at me.
>
> When I first started working there, I used to bring all the receipts from everything. And, I used to borrow money sometimes from petty cash and I would have to pay it back when I get paid. She was so fucking cheap always bitching because the receipts' not in the right place.
>
> So one time, I just took eighty dollars from the petty cash box and that lady never figured it out because the lady was *stupid*.
>
> I didn't steal it, just like that. I knew the ropes to the place, so when she sent me out on a big xerox job. I called the place in advance to get the price . . . [continues with complicated story of double invoicing]. Nobody figured it out. [chuckle]
>
> That stupid bitch didn't keep an accurate record of anything, man. She was *stupid*, man. She bitches so much and she wasn't even doing anything correct.

Chino was apprehensive lest Gloria Kirschman, once again catch him off guard and "disrespect" him without his being immediately aware. Consequently, when he was ordered to perform mysteriously specific tasks such as direct mailings of promotional materials that required particular conjugations of folding, stuffing, or clipping, he activated his defense mechanisms. The urgency of the precision with which she oversaw the logistics of these mailings seemed overbearingly oppressive and insulting to him. Gloria appeared almost superstitious in the rigor and anxiety with which she supervised each detail, and Chino refused to accept the "flexibility" that these delicate mailings required—i.e., late night binges of collating and recollating to make bulk-rate postage deadlines coincide with the magazine's printing and sales deadlines. Furthermore, to Chino, it was offensive to have to bring over the assembled promotional packets to Gloria's home for a last minute late night inspection:

> It would be late and I would be at the office to do these rush jobs: collate them, staple them, fold them in the correct way . . . whatever way she said. It was always different. And it had to be just the way she wanted it. I'd stuff them just the right way [making frantic shuffling motions with his hands], and then seal the shit.
>
> I used to hate that. I would box it and take it to the 38th Street Post Office at 10:30 at night.
>
> But then sometimes she would call me from home and I would have to bring papers up to her house on 79th Street and 3rd Avenue [Manhattan's silk stocking district] to double check.
>
> And she would try to offer me something to eat and I would say, "No, thank you." Because she would try to pay me with that shit; 'Cause she's a cheap bitch.
>
> She'd say, "You want pizza, tea, or cookies." She had those Pepperidge Farm cookies.
>
> But I wouldn't accept anything from her. I wasn't going to donate my time man.
>
> She thought I was illiterate. She thought I was stupid. Not me boy, charge *every penny*. From the moment I leave the office that's overtime all the way to her house. That's time and a half.
>
> I used to exaggerate the hours. If I worked 16, I would put 18 or 20 to see if I could get away with it. And I would get away with it. I'm not going to do that kind of shit for free.
>
> And that bitch was crazy. She used to eat baby food. I know cause I saw her eating it with a spoon right out of the jar.

If Chino appeared to be a scowling, ungrateful, dishonest worker to Gloria, then Gloria herself looked almost perverted to Chino. What normal middle-aged woman would invite her 20-year-old employee into her kitchen late at night and eat baby food in front of him?

Chino's victories over his employer Gloria were pyrrhic. In the cross-cultural confrontation taking place in the corridors of high-rise office buildings there is no ambiguity over who wields power. This unequal hierarchy is constantly reasserted ideologically. For example, the routine criteria used to discipline office support staffs is often interpreted as a personal affront rather than as "helpful feedback" by the inner city employee receiving the performance evaluations—even if it is positive. When someone like Caesar, Chino, or Ray is "terminated" the personnel report generally contains an insulting notation: "lack of initiative," "inarticulate," or "no understanding of the purpose of the company." Even Chino realizes that in street-English such a phrase implies, ". . . she's saying to her associates that I'm stupid. . . ."

Caesar and Chino have no frame of reference to guide them through service employment because their social networks only have experience with factory work. In their first factory jobs, both Caesar and Chino were guided by older family members. Still today, for example, Chino's mother is a sweatshop/homework seamstress and Caesar's uncle is a factory foreman in the Midwestern town where his metal-chroming company relocated. In contrast, the only socialization available to Caesar and Chino in the service sector comes from equally isolated and alienated fellow workers. Caesar, for example, who has always been precocious in everything he has done in life—from dropping out of school, to engaging in street violence, to burglarizing, to selling drugs, to abusing women, to becoming a crack addict— immediately understood the impossibility of his supervisors maintaining an objective quality control in the mail room where he worked prior to being hired by Chino at the crack house:

> I used to get there late, but the other workers wasn't never doing shit. They was *lazy* mother fuckers—even the supervisor.
>
> They all be sitting, asking each other questions over the phone, and fooling with video games on the computer. And that's all you do at a place like that.
>
> My boss, Bill, be drinking on the sneak cue, and eating this bad-ass sausage.

Finally, the fragility of entry-level job tenure in the service sector is the immediate precipitating factor in Caesar and Chino's retreat from the legal labor market. When they were not fired for "bad attitude," they were laid off owing to economic retrenchment. The companies employing them fluctuated with the whims and fashions of rapidly changing "yuppie fashions." Chino, for example, lost two different positions in fragile companies that folded: 1) Gloria Kirschman's trendy magazine; and 2) a desk-top publishing house.

Surprisingly, in his accounts of being laid off Chino publicly admitted defeat and vulnerability. On repeated occasions I had seen Chino brave dangerous violence on the streets and in the crack house. I knew him capable of hard-hearted cruelty, such as refusing to pay for his pregnant fifteen-year-old girlfriend's abortion or of slowly breaking the wrist of an adolescent who had played a prank on him. Downtown, however, behind the computer terminal where he had held his last job "in printing," he had been crushed psychologically by the personal officers who fired him. Ironically, I registered on my tape recorder his tale of frustration, humiliation, and self-blame for losing his last legal job as a printer only a week after recording with him a bravado-laced account of how he mugged a drunk Mexican immigrant in a nearby housing project:

> I was more or less expecting it. But still, when I found out I wanted to cry, man. My throat got dry, I was like . . . [waves his hands and gasps like a man drowning] You see, I had went to pick up my check—I don't know if I had missed the night before, or something, I just knew I had got paid that day, and I went to pick up my check.
>
> So when I went in, before getting my check, there was a little hassle and they called me to the office, I was like, "Oh *shit!*"
>
> I couldn't get through to them. I even told them, "I'll let you put me back to messenger; I will take less pay; just keep me employed. I need the money; I need to work. I got a family.
>
> But they said, "Nope, nope, nope." I left.
>
> I just stood right outside the building; I was fucked, man. All choked up. *Me jodieron* [They jerked me].

As a knife wielding mugger on the street, Chino could not contrast more dramatically with the panic-stricken employee begging for a second chance that legal employment had reduced him to:

> I was with Rico and his girl, Daisy. We saw this Mexican sleeping on the floor in the lobby of my aunt's building. He was just probably drunk. He looked like he had a job, maybe, because a homeless would not have had a gold ring.
>
> As soon as I saw him, I just went, '*Tu tienes la hora* [You got the time]?' And as he got the time [Making the motion of looking at a wristwatch], I grabbed him by the back of the neck, and put my 007 [knife] in his back [making the motion of holding someone in a choke hold from behind], I put it in his back—right here [pointing to his own lower back]. And I was jigging him *HARD* [grinning for emphasis at me and his girlfriend, who was listening, rapt with attention]!
>
> I said: '*No te muevas cabrón o te voy a picar como un pernil* [Don't move mother-fucker or I'll stick you like a roast pork].' [More loud chuckles from Chino's girlfriend.].
>
> Yeah, yeah, like a piece of pernil—a pork shoulder . . . like how you stab a pork shoulder when you want to put all the flavoring in the holes.
>
> The Mexican panicked. He looked like he wanted to escape, but the more he tried to escape, the more I wouldn't let go and the more I was jigging him.
>
> And I had a big 007. I wasn't playing, either, I was serious. I would have jigged him. If he would have made an attempt, I would have went like 'Chkkk' [making a painful grimace as he twisted his wrist forward in an imaginary slow-motion stab].
>
> And I'd regret it later, but I was looking at that gold ring he had. [Chuckle].

> I put the Mexican to the floor, poking him hard, and Rico's girl start-
> ed searching him.
> I said, 'Take everything, man! Search for everything!'
> She found his chain. I said, 'Yo, take that asshole's fucking ring too.'
> He was going: [imitating a high pitched whine] *'Oh no, por favor, por
> favor!'*
> It must have been like a thing he treasured, maybe. He was saying 'take
> whatever else, but not the I ring.' I said, fuck that shit, you don't have
> enough money homeboy. Daisy take the fucking ring off his finger.

After she took the ring we broke out. We sold the ring and then we cut-out
on Daisy. We left her in the park; she didn't get even a cent. She helped for
nothing. [More chuckling.]

THE NEW IMMIGRANT ALTERNATIVE

The flooding of cocaine and then crack onto U.S. streets during the
1980s infused new energy into the underground economy making drug
dealing the most vibrant equal-opportunity employer for young males in *El
Barrio.* Normally, in order to fill jobs adequately in the expanding service
sector, New York's legal economy should have to compete for the hearts
and minds of the growing proportion of the inner city's "best and bright-
est" who are choosing to pursue more remunerative and culturally compat-
ible careers in the underground economy. A wave of cheaper, more docile,
and disciplined new immigrant workers, however, is altering this labor power balance. These immigrants—largely undocumented—are key agents in
New York's latest structural economic adjustment. Their presence allows
low-wage employment to expand while social services retrench. This helps
explain, for example, how the real value of the minimum wage could have
declined by one-third in the 1980s while the Federal Government was able
to decrease the proportion of its contribution to New York City's budget
by over 50 percent (Berlin 1991:10; Rosenbaum 1989:A1). The breakdown
of the inner city's public sector is no longer an economic threat to the
expansion of New York's economy because the labor force that these public subsidies maintain is increasingly irrelevant.

Like the parents and grandparents of Chino and Caesar, many of New
York's newest immigrants are from isolated rural communities or squalid
shanty towns where meat is eaten only once a week, and where there is no
running water or electricity. In downtown Manhattan many of these new
immigrants are Chinese, but in East Harlem the vast majority are Mexicans
from the rural states of Puebla and Guerrero. To them, New York's streets
are still paved in gold if one works hard enough.

Half a century ago Chino's mother fled precisely the same living conditions these new-immigrants are only just struggling to escape. Her idealized
childhood reminiscences of her natal village evoke the time warp of

improved material conditions, cultural dislocation, and crushed dreams that is propelling her second-generation son into a destructive street culture:

> I loved that life in Puerto Rico, because it was a healthy, healthy, healthy life.
>
> We always ate because my father always had work, and in those days the custom was to have a garden in your patio to grow food and everything that you ate.
>
> We only ate meat on Sunday's because everything was cultivated on the same little parcel of land. From there we got our eggplant, our beans, our cilantro, our . . . [lists several more traditional Puerto Rican subsistence vegetables and herbs]. That way we saved our money.
>
> We didn't have a refrigerator, so we ate *bacalao*, [salted codfish] which can stay outside and a meat that they call *carne de vieja* [shredded beef] and sardines from a can.
>
> But thanks to God, we never felt hunger. My mother made a lot of cornflour. And to save money, whenever there were beans left over, she would strain them; mash them; make a little soup; and add a little corn-flour. So we were never hungry.
>
> Some people have done better by coming here, but many people haven't. Even people from my barrio, who came trying to find a better life [*buen ambiente*] just found disaster. Married couples right from my neigh-borhood came only to have the husband run off with another woman.
>
> In those days in Puerto Rico, when we were in poverty, life was better. Everyone will tell you life was healthier and you could trust people. Now you can't trust anybody.
>
> And what I liked best about life in Puerto Rico was that we kept all our traditions, like our Christmas . . . our feasts.
>
> We didn't have Christmas decorations, because if you had two dollars to buy Christmas lights, then you brought food with the money. You couldn't waste money on Christmas lights when you needed it for milk, food, and other things.
>
> In my village, everyone was either an Uncle or an Aunt. Everybody had to be an Uncle or an Aunt. And when you walked by someone older, you had to ask for their blessing. It was respect. There was a lot of respect in those days.

Ironically, at sixty, Chino's monolingual Spanish-speaking mother is the only one of her family who can still compete effectively with the new immi-grants who are increasingly filling Manhattan's entry-level labor market. She ekes out a living on welfare in her high-rise housing-project apartment by taking in sewing from undocumented garment industry subcontractors.

Rather than bemoaning the structural adjustment which is destroying their capacity to survive on legal wages, street-bound Puerto Rican youths celebrate their "decision" to bank on the underground economy and to cultivate their street identities. Caesar and Chino repeatedly assert their pride in their street careers. For example, one Saturday night after they fin-ished their midnight shift at the crack house, I accompanied them on their way to purchase "*El Sapo Verde*" [The Green Toad], a twenty dollar bag of powder cocaine, sold by a reputable outfit three blocks away. While waiting for Chino and Caesar to be "served" by the coke seller I engaged three undocumented Mexican men drinking beer on a neighboring stoop in a conversation about finding work in New York. One of the new immigrants was already earning 500 dollars a week fixing deep-fat-fry machines. He had a straightforward racist explanation for why Caesar—who was standing next to me was "unemployed":

> OK, Ok I'll explain it to you in one word: Because the Puerto Ricans are stupid! Stupid! Do you understand? They're brutes because look at that guy [pointing at Caesar] he knows English. And look at his body. He's got a body that at least should get him a job as good as mine. And he doesn't have it because he's a brute. That's all.
>
> Puerto Ricans like to make easy money. They like to leech off of other people. But not us Mexicans! No way! We like to work for our money. We don't steal. We came here to work and that's all [original quote in Spanish].

Instead of physically assaulting the employed immigrant for insulting him, Caesar turned the racist tirade into the basis for a new, generationally based, "American-born," urban cultural pride. In fact, in his response, Caesar ridicules—what he interprets to be—the hillbilly naivete of the Mexicans who still believe in the "American Dream." He spoke slowly in street-English as if to mark sarcastically the contrast between his "savvy" Nuyorican identity versus the limited English proficiency of his detractor:

> That's right, m'a man! We is real vermin lunatics that sell drugs. We don't want no part of society. 'Fight the Power!'[1]
>
> What do we wanna be working for? We came here to this country and we abused the freedom because Puerto Ricans don't like to work. We rather live off the system. Gain weight, lay women.
>
> Okay, maybe not all of us, 'cause there's still a lot of strict folks from the old school that still be working. But the new generation, no way! We have no regard for nothing. The new generation has no regard for the public bullshit. We wanna make easy money and that's it.
>
> When we was younger, we used to break our asses too. [Gesturing towards the Mexican men who were straining to understand his English] I had all kinds of stupid jobs too . . . advertising agencies . . . computers.
>
> But not no more! Now we're in a rebellious stage. We rather evade taxes, make quick money and just survive. But we're not satisfied with that either. Ha!

At twenty-three years of age Caesar takes refuge in an abusive sense of superiority for no longer believing in the new-immigrant's American Dream.

---

[1]"Fight the Power" was a best-selling song in 1990 by the African-American rap group, "Public Enemy."

CONCLUSION: ETHNOGRAPHY AND OPPRESSION

America was built on racial hierarchy and on blame-the-victim justifications for the existence of poverty and class distinctions. This makes it difficult to present ethnographic data from inner-city streets without falling prey to a "pornography of violence" or a racist voyeurism. The public "common sense" is not persuaded by a structural economic understanding of Caesar and Chino's "self-destruction." Even the victims themselves psychologize their unsatisfactory lives (Sennett and Cobb 1972). Most concretely, political will and public policy ignore the fundamental structural economic facts of marginalization in America. Instead the first priority of Federal and local social "welfare" agencies is to change the psychological—or at best the "cultural"—orientations of misguided individuals (Katz 1989). Through the early 1990s the few policy efforts to address the need for reform in the delivery of public services have been fundamentally driven by the business world's definition of "cost effectiveness" and by a positivist science's naive, apolitical search for a "magic bullet" to cure a history of class inequality and cultural domination (Landau 1988).

Researchers in the United States have allowed the gap to grow between their hegemonically "liberal" intellectual community and a conservative popular political culture. From the late 1970s through most of the 1980s inner-city poverty was simply ignored by all but right-wing academics who filled a popular vacuum with empirically flawed "best sellers" on the psychological and cultural causes of poverty in order to argue against the "poisonous" effect of public sector intervention (cf. Murray 1984; Gilder 1982). Their analyses coincide with the deep-seated individualistic, blame-the-victim values so cherished in American thought.

There is a theoretical and methodological basis for anthropology's reticence to confront devastating urban poverty in its front yard. Qualitative researchers prefer to avoid tackling taboo subjects such as personal violence, sexual abuse, addiction, alienation, self-destruction, etc. for fear of contributing to popular racist stereotypes. The hegemonic explosion of postmodern theory in anthropology in the 1980s and 1990s has exacerbated this tendency despite the claims of many of its practitioners to being "subversive." Deconstructionist politics have tended ultimately to confine themselves to hermetically sealed elite academic discourses on the "poetics" of power and representation. The debates are most relevant to alienated, suburbanized intellectuals; they do not resonate with the urgent social crisis of the inner city unemployed. The "critical self-reflection" that postmodernism promised and that the social sciences desperately need to be effectively politically engaged has largely degenerated into the almost psychoanalytic narcissistic ruminations of the privileged upper crust of a hyper-literate post-industrial society. Most importantly, the useful deconstructionist insight that realities are subjectively constituted within fields of power is often interpreted dogmatically, thereby rendering it impossible to hierarchize, or even categorize, experiences of injustice. This subtly denies—or worse yet aestheticizes— the "very real" existence of pain, suffering, and exploitation across race, class, gender, age, sexuality, or any other socially vulnerable category that propels power relations. It also allows a paralyzing righteous self-critique to replace political engagement. An obsession with "subversion" through form—*i.e.*, evocative vocabularies, playful syntaxes, polyphonous voices, and heteroglossia—has replaced a concern for political relevance.

In contrast, the more atheoretical, policy-oriented fringe within urban anthropology, sometimes referred to as "the new ethnography" explicitly confronts inner-city social crises—homelessness, AIDS, teen pregnancy—in the hopes of concretely improving daily living conditions. This pragmatic, advocacy anthropology tends to be pater/maternalistic and sanitize its "subjects" with exclusively sympathetic portrayals that idealize victims. The commitment to contribute responsibly to "policy debate" stifles a more complexly critical perspective on marginalization and resistance. Indeed, defining policy as the political arena for engagement demobilizes both theory and practice.

Regardless of the political, scholarly, or personal motivations, anthropology's cautious and often self-censored approaches to social misery have obfuscated an ethnographic understanding of the multi-faceted dynamics of the experience of oppression and ironically sometimes even serve to minimize the depths of human suffering involved. Cultural production theory's focus on the way contradictory and complicated forms of resistance often lead to personal self-destruction and community trauma provides interesting insights (Foley 1990; Fordham 1988; MacLeod 1987; Willis 1977). One major problem with these ethnographically based, Gramscian-influenced attempts to grapple theoretically with ugly realities is that they glorify resistance in an almost self-conscious effort to escape a "blame the victim" interpretation of their ethnographic presentations (Bourgois 1989). Ironically, just as a postmodern obsession with literary criticism ultimately denies the reality of exploitation, the hallucination of everyday resistance or of counter-hegemonic popular currents glamorizes the dominated.

Much of the problem is rooted in the nature of the ethnographic endeavor itself. Engulfed in an overwhelming whirlpool of personal suffering it is often difficult for ethnographers to see the larger relationships structuring the jumble of human interaction all around them. Structures of power and history cannot be touched or talked to. Empirically this makes it difficult to identify the urgent political economy relationships shaping everyday survival. For my own part, in the heat of daily life on the street in *El Barrio*, I often experienced a confusing anger with the victims, the victimizers, and the wealthy industrialized society that generates such a record toll of unnecessary human suffering. For example, when confronted with a pregnant friend frantically smoking crack—and condemning her fetus to a post-partum life of shattered emotions and dulled brain cells—it was impossible for me to remember the history of her people's colonial terror and humiliation or to contextualize her position in New York's changing economy. Living the inferno of what America calls its "underclass," I—like my neighbors around me and like the pregnant crack addicts themselves—often blamed the victim.

Our challenge is to overcome these partial perspectives when researching painful human contexts rather than to follow the mainstream academic option of desisting from researching social misery. This obliges us to confront the contradictions of oppression. Perhaps if we could be engaged politically in what we study we might improve our theoretical/analytical capacity for relating individual actions to historical process. This might be particularly appropriate in the context of the U.S. inner city where many of the central contradictions of a post-industrial society around race, class, and gender reveal themselves by violently defying resolution and political vision despite superabundant wealth and technology.

ACKNOWLEDGMENTS

The author would like to thank the following institutions for their support: The Harry Frank Guggenheim Foundation, The Russell Sage Foundation, The Social Science Research Council, The National Institute on Drug Abuse, The Wenner-Gren Foundation for Anthropological Research, The United States Bureau of the Census, San Francisco State University, and the San Francisco Urban Institute. Finally, this could not have been written without the typing of Harold Otto, Henry Ostendorf, and most importantly, Charles Pearson.

REFERENCES

BERLIN, GORDON
    1991   The Poverty Among Families: A Service Decategorization Response. New York: Manpower Demonstration Research Corporation. Photocopied Report.
BONILLA, FRANK AND RICARDO CAMPOS
    1986   *Industry and Idleness.* New York: Centro de Estudios Puertorriqueños, Hunter College.
BOURGOIS, PHILIPPE
    1989   Crack in Spanish Harlem. *Anthropology Today* 5(4):6–11
    1995   *In Search of Respect: Selling Crack in* El Barrio. New York: Cambridge University Press.
FOLEY, DOUG
    1990   *Learning Capitalist Culture; Deep in the Heart of Tejas.* Philadelphia: University of Pennsylvania.
FORDHAM, SIGNITHIA
    1988   Racelessness as a factor in Black students' school success: Pragmatic strategy or pyrrhic victory? *Harvard Educational Review* 53:257–293.

GIACHELLO, AIDA L.
  1990   Selected Health Characteristics of Hispanic Children and Adults in the
          United States. Fact sheet presented to the Inter-University Program for
          Latino Research/Social Sciences Research Council Grantee meetings,
          Miami, March 1991.
GILDER, GEORGE
  1982   *Wealth and Poverty.* New York: Bantam.
INSTITUTE FOR PUERTO RICAN POLICY
  1993   The "Parallel Plebiscite" on Puerto Rico's Status: A Reassessment. New
          York: Institute for Puerto Rican Policy Brief, August. (Pamphlet, 6
          Columns).
KATZ, MICHAEL B.
  1989   *The Undeserving Poor: From the War on Poverty to the War on Welfare.*
          New York: Pantheon Books.
LAMBERT, BRUCE
  1990   AIDS Travels New York-Puerto Rico 'Air Bridge.' *The New York Times,*
          15 June, p. B1, col. 3–6.
LANDAU, MADELINE
  1988   *Race, Poverty, and the Cities: Hyperinnovation in Complex Policy
          Systems.* Berkeley: University of California Press, Institute of
          Governmental Studies.
LAURIA, ANTHONY JR.
  1964   '*Respeto,*' '*relajo,*' and inter-personal relations in Puerto Rico.
          Anthropological Quarterly 37(2):53–67.
MACLEOD, JAY
  1987   *Ain't No Makin' It: Leveled Aspirations in a Low-Income Neighborhood.*
          Boulder, CO: Westview Press.
MALDONADO-DENIS MANUEL
  1980   The ideology of colonialism: Emigration and neo-Malthusianism in
          contemporary Puerto Rican society. In *Sourcebook on the New
          Immigration: Implications for the United States and the International
          Community.* New Brunswick, NJ: Transaction Books.
MURRAY, CHARLES
  1984   *Losing Ground: American Social Policy 1950–1980.* New York: Basic
          Books.
ORTIZ, VILMA
  1986   Changes in the characteristics of Puerto Rican migrants from 1955 to
          1980. *International Migration Review* 20(3):612–628.
ROMO, FRANK AND MICHAEL SCHWARTZ
  1993   "Post-Industrial Society Revisited: Prospects for a service-based econo-
          my." In *Explorations in Economic Sociology.* Richard Swedburg, Ed.:
          335–373. New York: Russell Sage Foundation.
ROSENBAUM, DAVID E.
  1989   Bush and Congress Reach Accord Raising Minimum Wage to $4.25.
          New York Times, 1, November, pp. A1–2.
ROSENBERG, TERRY J.
  1990   Changes in household composition and income strategies of poor
          women in New York City. Madison WI: Institute for Research on
          Poverty, Discussion Paper No. 924–990.

ROSENWAIKE, IRA.
  1983   Mortality among the Puerto Rican born in New York City. *Social Science Quarterly,* March.
SASSEN-KOOB, SASKIA
  1986   New York City: Economic restructuring and immigration. *Development and Change* (London: SAGE) 17:85–119.
SENNETT, RICHARD AND JONATHAN COBB
  1972   *The Hidden Injuries of Class.* New York: Vintage Books
TOTTI, XAVIER F.
  1986   A face-threatening act: Ideology, language, and power in the Caribbean. Paper presented at the 85th Annual Meeting of the American Anthropological Association, December 3–7.
WALDINGER, ROGER
  1991   Beyond the Split Labor Market: Job Competition and the Persistence of Conflict. UCLA. Department of Sociology. Unpublished manuscript.
WILLIS, PAUL
  1977   *Learning to Labor: How Working Class Kids Get Working Class Jobs.* New York: Columbia University Press.
WILSON, WILLIAM JULIUS
  1987   *The Truly Disadvantaged: The Inner City, the Underclass, and Public Policy.* Chicago: University of Chicago Press.
WOLF, ERIC R.
  1956   San Jose: Subcultures of a 'traditional' coffee municipality. In *The People of Puerto Rico.* Julian H. Steward *et al.,* Eds.:171–264, Urbana: University of Illinois Press.

Policy Ethnography in East Harlem
Methodological Issues

JUDITH FREIDENBERG

Center for Urban Research
Graduate Center, City University of New York
New York, New York 10036
and
Mount Sinai School of Medicine
City University of New York
New York, New York 10029

PEOPLE AND POLICIES: A PARADIGM

Anthropology and public policy are intimately related: anthropology reflects a point of view on the articulation of human beings in the world that stems from a fascination with seeing ourselves in "the other" and "the other" in ourselves. Public policy, on the other hand, is predicated upon assuming what is normative in society and directing change to a better situation. Both anthropology and public policy are cultural constructions of what society is, might and should be, based on the social experience of practitioners who are, in most cases, members of intelligentsia, rather than of non-elites.

Yet the two disciplines fail to connect in ways that would result in changes in the life conditions of people. Anthropological research does not inform public policy. On the one hand, social issues of interest to policy-making are not described experientially. Anthropologists usually transform their informants' voices into "data" that freeze lived experience, yet the specific ways people make sense of their lives is relevant to the planning of service programs that policymakers intend to implement. For example, the meaning that women bestow on pre-natal care, as well as their actual experience with clinics, and their reasons for using them in a particular way could be predictive of utilization patterns of nonusers. Policies, however, are usually based on descriptive statistics on the characteristics of the user population. Both types of information are relevant to planning clinics that would attract the appropriate consumer population.

When anthropologists provide information to policy makers on social issues, it is awarded less importance and considered too "soft" to have an impact on policy outcomes. What is clearly needed in an integration of quantitative and qualitative data that addresses the needs of both the target population and the policymaker. Methodologically, there has been an over-emphasis on quantification of data, resulting in an unintended effect—that of silencing the voices of those from whom we gather information. Policy research could benefit from study designs that combine qualitative and quantitative methodologies. I am not advocating here use of quantitative or qualitative methodologies or their sequential use. Rather, I am suggesting exploration of the contributions that studies which incorporate a diversity of methodologies might make to enhancing an understanding of policy issues. For example, while collecting information on expenses, an ethnographic subject might report that her family helps "when there is a need," yet be unable to provide a monetary value to "need." Understanding of the informant's definition of need then becomes crucial if we are to pursue research on monetary exchanges within social units from a quantitative perspective.

Anthropologists primarily share their findings with other academicians, rather than with practitioners and policy makers. This leaves providers, program planners, and policymakers largely ignorant of informants' perspectives on social issues: Policymakers are either unaware of the cultural construction of social issues by low-income populations or examine them too early or too late in the policy process. Thus, the people that anthropologists study usually have little chance of having their voices make a difference in the formation of public policies that directly affect their daily lives. It is no wonder, therefore, that policies often do not fit the informants' needs. A further corollary of informants not being seen as they see themselves is that the general public is not dissuaded of its stereotypes.

Public policymakers, on the other hand, do not share the process of policy formation with anthropologists. Often anthropologists interested in policy analyze the implementation of macro-policies at the local level, while at the same time failing to see the forest for the trees by examining the *process* which results in policy-making. Yet policy is a process that is constructed from below, and debated by different sectors of national society on an everyday basis.

Recently, policymakers have expressed a need for an "insider's" perspective and have welcomed reports that include case studies. However, policymakers tend to listen to *individual* consumers, and thus construe the relationship between consumer and policy in linear terms. As social scientists, anthropologists focus on *populations*, generalizing from the case to the group, analyzing experiences lived in diverse contexts, and interpreting behavior as social issues. They approach population problems as a process, and thus in non-linear terms. It is in this role that anthropologists can fulfill an important role for policy-making.

Anthropologists can narrow the distance between informants and policy makers by focusing on the process of constructing informant-defined, policy-relevant anthropological knowledge on social issues. This paper provides a case study of this paradigm. First, I document my experience with methodologies designed to elicit social issues from informants. Second, I reflect on a museum exhibit as a means of disseminating social issues to diverse sectors of national society. Third, I consider possible contributions of anthropology to enable grassroots perspectives inform policy-makers. I illustrate with public programs in which the social issues were considered within and across ethnic and social class lines by individuals at various levels in the policy making process. Finally, I elaborate on the process of constructing policy-relevant anthropological knowledge for policy formulation and implementation.

PRODUCING ANTHROPOLOGICAL DATA ON SOCIAL ISSUES: THE FIELDWORK

Between 1988 and 1990, I conducted research to understand patterns of health seeking among a sample of 48 informants representative of the 1980 census population of Hispanic elderly who reside in East Harlem. The study sample had the following characteristics: 56% were 75 years of age and over while 44% were between 65 and 74; 60% lived alone, 40% lived with others; 65% were women, while 35% were men. Median income was about $500 a month. Almost all informants were Puerto Rican, and all were born either in Puerto Rico or in Cuba and had migrated to New York as young adults.

Throughout the process of collecting data, I tried to continue hearing the peoples' voices while thinking about policy issues. As different from other ways of categorizing reality, cultural voices can be better understood by a process of successive approximations, in which the researcher tests the validity of what "she believes she knows" with what "the population seems to know". Recently, some researchers have used the term "cultural sensitivity" to characterize strategies in research that attempt to capture an "inside perspective". Rogler (1989), for example suggests that, to enhance the cultural sensitivity of survey research, one should begin with, and use the insights derived from, ethnography—the face to face documentation of the culture of the population being studied—to develop culturally informed survey methodology.

Ethnography can be construed as a process of obtaining and validating culturally sensitive data and as a means of developing strategies of interviewing to further explore and probe deeper into findings. Two culturally sensitive research methodologies were used to collect the East Harlem data. One was the development of a three-stage strategy for assuring the cultural sensitivity of an ethnographically informed survey instrument. In the first stage, a survey instrument based on long-term ethnographic fieldwork was developed. In the second stage, the survey instrument was validated ethnographically, by means of pre-testing on the ethnographic sample using survey-like procedures. In the third stage, in collaboration with an epidemiologist, the cultural sensitivity of the survey instrument was tested by analyzing the congruence between the ethnographic and the survey data. In this experiment, the results were statistically significant (Freidenberg *et al.*, 1993).

The second culturally sensitive research methodology was the development of visual instruments as projective interviewing techniques (FIGS. 1-3). While I was collecting data through long-term and repeated interviewing to understand patterns of health seeking, I was struck with what the informants mostly talked about when I was not directly structuring our conversation through interviewing. They were talking about circumstances that they thought forcefully influenced their lives. I derived certain hypotheses about the meaning of what they were saying and then asked myself what procedure I could develop to confirm or disconfirm my hypotheses. I decided that presenting the informants with a visual representation of their social surrounding[1] as a projective instrument might diminish the intrusiveness of my presence as outsider and enable the informants in "looking at the photos" to "see the issues," and thus become analysts, interpreters, and social critics themselves.

What I called a "visual instrument"[2] finally consisted of a group of 20 photographs, 15 of my informants in their own social environments, two documenting a higher socioeconomic status than they enjoyed in New York, and three more depicting the conditions of elders in a Latin American country. I re-interviewed some of the informants, asking them to look at the photographs and tell me what was on their minds. Presented with photographs documenting the physical and social ecology of El Barrio, the informants identified several social issues related to growing old within that setting. Presented with photographs of middle class New York, and of a low-income neighborhood in Latin America, they reflected upon "self" by comparison to "other."

DISSEMINATING ANTHROPOLOGICAL DATA ON SOCIAL ISSUES: THE EXHIBIT AS CONVERSATIONS ON WALLS

The next step in this process was to identify a medium that would convey the messages communicated when "conversing with the photographs" while, at the same time, addressing the following questions: How can

---

[1] Photographs have long been used by anthropologists for what Collier (1986) has called "the rich recovery of data,"—the eliciting of serendipitous information that ethnographic observation and interviewing may fall short of drawing out.

[2] Credits for the photographs in the visual instrument go to sociologist Edmundo Morales and photo-journalist Federico Naiflesch. I added some of my photographs to the exhibit.

Figure 1. (Growing Old in *El Barrio* -Exhibit Panel #6: *La Marqueta* (Latin open market under the elevated trains at Park Avenue.) Photo Credit: Judith Freidenberg

Citas seleccionadas de entrevistas:
- "[Otro cambio en El Barrio es...] que quieren hacer un Seaport ahí."
- "Bueno, cerca de la Marqueta que es bueno pero casi está destruído también porque cobran mucho dinero y han dejado los puestos."
- "Tengo 42 años en El Barrio pero no paraba en casa, entonces no sé como están las cosas. Pero siempre he mantenido la moral y la seriedad. Ya tú ves, conozco a todo el mundo aquí. Si tú eres una persona decente que no te metes con nadie...[no te pasa nada malo]"

Selected quotes from interviews:
- "[Another change in *El Barrio* is] that they want to open a Seaport there."
- "Well, near the Marqueta (open market under the elevated trains) it is good but it is almost destroyed as well because they charged too much and they had to leave their booths."
- "I have lived in El Barrio for forty-two years but I did not stay at home much so I do not know how things are. I have always maintained morals and seriousness. You see, I know everybody here. If you are a decent person who does not get involved with anyone...[nothing bad happens to you]."

Figure 2. (Growing Old in *El Barrio*–Exhibit Panel #5): Boarded-up buildings on Third Ave. Photo Credit: Edmundo Morales

Citas seleccionadas de entrevistas:
- "El proyecto municipal ahora mismo está todos los meses subiendo. ¿Cuándo tú has visto una persona mayor en un proyecto de la ciudad pagando $ 500, $ 400?"
- "Estos son edificios vacíos...lo que quieren es que la gente se mude para ellos arreglarlos y pedir $500 para arriba."
- "No se sabe a dónde vá a parar El Barrio."

Selected quotes from interviews:
- "The [cost of] city housing is going up now. When have you seen that an elderly person in a city project is asked to pay up to $500, $400?"
- "These are empty buildings...what they want is to fix them and ask $500 and more."
- "Nobody knows where *El Barrio* will wind up."

Figure 3. (Growing Old in *El Barrio* - Exhibit Panel #8) Medical office at 103rd Street. Photo Credit: Judith Freidenberg

Citas seleccionadas de entrevistas:
- "A los viejos es que cojen porque no pueden correr."
- "...que como uno tiene que estar encerrado...porque no se atreve a salir; porque hay gente muy mala por ahí, [por] la droga."
- "De la juventud perdida...los crímenes, el abuso...que hoy siendo yo una persona mayor también que sufre la situación...(en El Barrio)."

Selected quotes from interviews:
- "They get the elderly because they cannot run."
- "...Since one has to live locked up, one does not dare go out because there are very mean people out there [because of] drugs."
- "The youth is lost; there are crimes; there is abuse...Today as an elderly person I too suffer from the situation in (El Barrio)."

anthropologists enable their informants to express their voices to diverse sectors of society, including policymakers? Who are those sectors? Where can they best be reached? In order to contribute to public awareness of the social issues related to growing old Latino in Harlem, I chose to share and debate the findings in a space open to the public. A museum interested in the community provided the medium to display policy ethnography on walls.

General publics are best reached when findings are presented in a documentary fashion, that is, with the least intermediation from anthropological interpretation. Visual, as different from oral, means of communication are effective ways of reaching out in a direct fashion. The space of a museum, allowing the viewer to stroll at her own pace, and to choose the order in which to view displayed material, is ideal for reaching out to general publics. I also designed this exhibit to encourage the participation of diverse audiences in identifying issues that affect their life circumstances, and in suggesting strategies for change.

In 1992, I was invited by the Museum of the City of New York to curate an exhibit based on my anthropological fieldwork. The Museum is situated at the edge of East Harlem, yet it faces Fifth Avenue, a symbol in and by itself of the class stratification of the city, and of its changing social ecology. The Museum of the City of New York is a private, not-for-profit, educational agency established in 1923 to collect, preserve, and present original cultural materials related to the history of New York City. By acquiring collections that illustrate the historical experience of New York City, the Museum contributes to a better understanding of a common past and a civ-

Figure 4. Guests at the opening reception for "Growing Old in Spanish Harlem," Museum of the City of New York, 1992, viewing Artifact Niche. (Photo Credit: Michel Craig)

ilizing sense of place, time, and self that has proven vital to the welfare and advancement of all communities. "Growing Old in Spanish Harlem" intended to add a contribution to the Museum's mission to place issues of contemporary interest and relevance in a context accessible to broad audiences (FIGS. 4 and 5).

The Museum has an annual attendance of over 200,000 people. This audience is drawn from the diverse social, ethnic, and economic strata of the metropolitan New York area. It includes approximately 40,000 school children from all grade levels, organized adult tours and walk-in visitation by adolescents, adults, and family groups.

"Growing Old in Spanish Harlem" was featured in the New York City Community Gallery, supported by Philip Morris Companies Inc., between September 12 and November 5, 1992. The Museum hosted a celebration to mark the opening of the exhibition featuring a performance by members of "Los Pleneros de la 21", a dance band specializing in the traditional Puerto Rican song styles of the *bomba* and *plena*. There were refreshments, and the event was free with admission contribution.

The exhibit consisted of three sections. The first two—entitled "Growing Old" and "Growing Old in El Barrio"—contained the photographs and excerpts from the oral interviews with the visual instrument.

Figure 5. Docent, Museum of the City of New York, giving a guided tour of the exhibit "Growing old in Spanish Harlem," 1992. (Photo Credit: Judith Freidenberg)

A third section contained artifacts from the homes of some of the respondents, including an altar, a family photograph, and other items that reflect the hope and faith that elderly Latinos perceive to be central to coping with daily life in El Barrio. An accompanying video provided a context for understanding the world of the elderly subjects.

In curating the exhibit, I had to collaborate with museum staff, and develop insights on how to re-present data for a general audience. How to display research findings in a way that the population, rather than the anthropologist, spoke directly to the viewer? As a fieldworker, I attempted to disappear behind the photos. In presenting the analysis and interpretation of the findings, I attempted to disappear behind the informants, whose voices are themselves directly addressing the public from the museum walls. For example, although I had analyzed the informants' responses to the visual instrument, we decided not to use categories in the display panels when we realized that a category, for example "housing," evoked different cognitive representations for the study population and those of us mounting the exhibit. For those who were homebound, housing meant isolation; for those who were afraid to venture into the streets, the deteriorating housing in the area connoted fear of personal attack; for those who lived in poorly heated apartments, housing meant sickness. Instead, it is the informants' own words which appear on the walls. In the presence of these personal testimonies, each individual who comes to see the exhibit can make her or his categorizations or interpretations.

Care was also taken to ensure that the viewer encounters a diversity of opinions, a chorus rather than a "representative voice." Thus, at least two quotations from interviews responding to a visual stimulus were selected, and those that were chosen represented different opinions. For example, next to a photograph of an elderly man sitting with arms crossed, a museum label reproduces two different views of the aging process, as expressed in the following two interview quotes:

- He is thinking...about having a good life and prospering. Even if you are old you can think about the future; the future does not end until you die.
- What will happen to us tomorrow, to us who are alone, old and sick?

The informants' presence was also an important consideration in deciding how to feature the two languages: after meetings with museum staff, I persuaded them that since the language of interview was Spanish, that language should be displayed first in the panels. In addition, since being bilingual did not necessarily make my translations reliable to the speech of the study population (I am Argentinian), I validated each of my translations with key informants.

The exhibition thus examined the experience of growing old among elderly Latinos in East Harlem using a combination of visual ethnographic techniques for data collection and presentation: photography, written text, artifact display, and film. These ethnographic techniques bring the viewer into close intimacy with the message communicated by the study population, and it has the manifest object of inviting participation and response. How was this accomplished?

DEBATING ANTHROPOLOGICAL DATA ON SOCIAL ISSUES: CONVERSATIONS AT A MUSEUM

How can we create a multi-class structure where audiences engage in critical thinking about the policy implications of the issues presented? The traditional purpose of research is to reach specialized audiences by verbal or written means. Yet this short-circuits the opportunity to raise questions for discussion and debate, which is central to the policy process. I experimented with debating anthropological knowledge on social issues by using a structure that allows the least intermediation from the anthropologist: four forums were held where informants, researchers, service providers, policymakers, and the general public were convened at the museum's auditorium to discuss the social issues that, in their view, were generated by the exhibit.

Karp (1992) has reflected on the politics of displaying culture and has urged museums to engage viewers in conversations. I used the exhibit as a performance (Beeman, 1993), engaging the participation of audiences to probe deeper into the meaning of the cultural materials displayed. The exhibit thus facilitated conversations among the elderly informants and other residents of Harlem, the health and social service providers who serve them, the public policymakers who influence public programs that affect the elderly, the academic community, and the general public. While the exhibit was on display, these diverse groups were gathered to discuss specific issues that concerned the target population—such as poverty, housing, violence, access to services—, some generic issues affecting us all—such as aging, social connections, residence in a multicultural society, ethnicity and social class—, as well as ways to address change. The diversity of viewpoints that emerged illustrated, in practical terms, Ames's view of the interpretative junction of contemporary museums:

> Museum policy can no longer make undisputed claims for the privileges of neutrality and universality. Representation is a political act. Sponsorship is a political act. Curation is a political act. Working in a museum is a political act. (Ames 1991:13)

Two of the forums coordinated by informants in collaboration with me and the Museum's Education Department (Fig. 6) were public programs that represented the view from El Barrio's residents. The first one, entitled "A Poetry Reading," was organized by an East Harlem poet on behalf of

Los Envejecientes Del Este De Harlem
Presentan Sus Preocupaciones
En Un Foro De La Comunidad
Unase a nosotros el Jueves, 24 De Setiembre
de 2 a 5 pm
Para expresar sus preocupaciones
en referencia a
La Vivienda
La Atencion De La Salud
El Acceso A Los Servicios
El Seguro Social

Hemos invitada a representantes
de la agencias del gobierno
y la prensa para que escuchen
sus preocupaciones

Poetry Reading

En Commemoracion de nuestra herencia cultural
la edad de oro en accion se complace en presentar
"Lectura de Poemas Originales de las Poetisas"
Sra. Encarnacion Ramirez y la Sra. Susana Matos Martinez.
con la cooperacion de Don Luis Perez, y la Sra. Daisy Martinez
como pianistas, el Sr. Carlos Jose Rodriguez,
Sr. Otilio Diaz y la cooperacion especial de la
Doctora Freidenberg.

Saturday, October 17
2:00 pm
Free with admission contribution

Museum of City of New York
103rd Street at Fifth Avenue
For more information please call (212) 534-1672

FIGURE 6. Flyers for the forums coordinated by informants (with my collaboration). The text appeared in English on the other side.

an organization of poets-in-residence, "The Golden Age in Action." Through the medium of poetry and song, the issues of aging, facing poverty, living in El Barrio, being a Latino immigrant, holding religious and spiritual beliefs, were shared with the public. The outcome of this forum was that the audience arrived at a consensus regarding the meaning of being aged. It was pointed out that being aged was construed in our culture as being inactive and uninterested in social activities, a notion with which the audience disagreed. It was also pointed out that agencies that serviced the elderly programmed activities to entertain the seniors, but that the residents' creativity, that reflected their active construction of self rather than their role as passive service recipients, was often left untapped.

A second forum, entitled "East Harlem Elderly Speak Out," as quoted in the flyer (drafted by informants), was organized by two key informants who were long-term activists in East Harlem. This forum was unique in that the policy issues to be discussed with public servants at community, city, and state levels—housing, access to health care, and other entitlements—were selected by the informants who coordinated the event.

The two other forums were conceived as specialized conventions of specialists and thus were not open to the public. The third forum, "Developing Culturally Sensitive Research Programs for Minority Communities," presented the view of providers of social and health care services about how to incorporate the population's view of issues. The Department of Community Relations, Mount Sinai Hospital organized a panel presentation of modalities of providing culturally sensitive programs, that resulted in a dialogue between researchers, providers of social and health care services in East Harlem, and public officials who formulate policies that affect minority communities. Some of the issues discussed at that panel of providers and researchers included: Does researcher accountability differ when there is disparity between the ethnic, cultural, and social background of the researcher and the study population? Should we develop institutional policies to protect populations, in addition to individuals, with whom we conduct research and who we service?

The last forum presented the view of urban ethnographers of East Harlem since the 1950s, and provided the background for the present volume.

In addition to these specialized groups, the viewers were asked to react to the issues generated by the exhibit. I attempted to capture the diversity of museum audiences by inviting viewers to record their impressions of the exhibit and issues it generated in a special book where age, residence, country of birth, and sex were asked. The 350 written responses collected show that reflecting on the life circumstances of the population portrayed inspires viewers to reflect on their own, and that social class, gender, age, ethnicity, and other markers of social articulation to the larger society affect such opinions.

What are the implications of engaging audiences in conversations to advocate change in low-income urban enclaves? What was the impact of the forums described for people and policies? In the two public events, access to the museum staff and auditorium meant that the informants' voices, and those they embodied, were amplified for other sectors of society. The effect was empowering: the informants designed the program, invited the audience, selected the format of presentation, prepared press releases and fliers, announced the program, and were in charge of the event. They counted on full institutional support to use public space as an arena to meet those who could address their needs. In evaluations of the event with Museum staff and myself after the events, the informant-organizers said this approach, in which *they* invited policymakers and providers to debate needs as they defined them, and holding these conversations in their turf, was more powerful than when they operated within an imposed structure, as when they were asked to testify at public hearings and just made presentations. The Museum staff was also very encouraged with the enthusiastic response evoked, and continues to communicate with people and organizations in East Harlem. The third forum, organized by the Department of Community Relations of Mount Sinai Hospital, was the first time, in the ten years of my tenure there, that regulating the conduct of research with the East Harlem population came up. The consensus reached on that occasion of having the Department oversee future research in that area was a step toward influencing researchers to assume responsibility for both individuals and the populations of which they are a part, and of reminding the research institution that it has an ethical commitment to the population geographically surrounding it. Finally, the last forum engaged researchers in a reflection of how studying these communities can contribute to addressing change. The fact that their deliberations have resulted in the present publication is a tribute to the legitimacy of thinking about the import of our work for social change, and not solely about the academic value of our work.

This experience has confirmed that culture is not frozen in time, and that the function of a museum goes beyond the presentation of culture. If viewers are engaged, culture is, in the process of being communicated, constantly being created and re-created.

POLICY ETHNOGRAPHY

In the project described in this paper, the goal was to bring to light both the historical and contemporary issues affecting immigrant aging populations in East Harlem. I used a public space as both a medium of communication, as well as a meeting ground to engage diverse sectors of society in dialogue. This paradigm I call policy ethnography: the process of producing anthropological knowledge on public policy issues, translating ethnographic findings to the public in ways that debate on such issues is stimulated, and using the data created with a variety of respondents to formulate new research problems. Let me now turn to the impact of this paradigm for social science and policy making.

What impact do our audiences have in deepening the understandings of social science research, and providing feedback? The experience described here shows the value of policy ethnography to social scientists, particularly those who use visual media in research and to museologists who use popular input in exhibits to reflect contemporary social experience. My experience is that by displaying and discussing data collected, new data are produced and the understanding of old data is enhanced. The perspective of "others"—researchers, providers, policy planners, government officials—on the issues that affect daily life, might not coincide with that of persons who constitute their target populations. We have much to learn from reflecting on the discrepancies between informants' constructions of social experience and interpretative views of those experiences by others. This approach offers new ways for anthropologists to listen to informants, for museum people to talk to viewers, and for grassroots people to talk to policy makers.

What are the implications of this kind of work for policy formulation? In my experience, community interventions and provider programs have a much better chance of succeeding if designed on the basis of research on the needs of clients, as perceived by them and not solely the researcher. In addition to what we normally call the target population, there are multiple actors and populations involved in program planning and implementation, (such as funding agencies, researchers, service providers, administrators at program sites). These power networks construct and debate the social issues in the process of interacting around a specific action. Very often we think of the policy implications of our data, yet conceptualize both our data and the policy that is influenced by it as closed systems and as outcomes. I strongly believe that one should think of various arenas in which our research is discussed as feeding into the collective framing of policy issues. In thinking of ourselves as contributing to policy, as a process not as an outcome, we can most effectively relate research finding and policy discourse. In this particular experiment, what was focused on was the impact of environment and of aging on immigrants to East Harlem as well as on positive social action necessary to begin dealing with some of the fears and realities of that aging population.

Conveying personal issues elicited from informants to museum audiences and public forums amplified individual voices and translated experience into information for formulating responsive public policy. This paper provides a testimony of how anthropological research can inform social policy throughout the process of producing, disseminating and debating findings. The methods chosen to construct such knowledge—oral elicitation, visual documentation and projection, museum display, discussion forums—help audiences sharpen their perspectives on social issues, and contribute to the process of policy formulation.

FIGURES 7 and 8. Esta exhibición fue preparada para el Museo de la Ciudad de Nueva York y se presentó de septiembre de 1992 a enero de 1993, En Mexico, se presenta bajo el patrocinio del Comité Organizador del XIII CICAE (Congreso Internacional de Ciencias Anthropológicas y Etnológicas), la AAGE (Asociación de Antropología y Gerontología, USA) y la IUAES (Comisíon para el Envejecimiento, Internacional). [This exhibit was prepared for the Museum of the City of New York where it was on view from September 1992 to January 1993. In Mexico, it is presented under the sponsorship of the Organizing Committee of the XIII ICAES (International Congress of Anthropological and Ethnological Sciences), AAGE (Association for Anthropology and Gerontology, USA) and IAUES (Commission on Aging and the Aged, International.)] Photo Credit: Judith Freidenberg

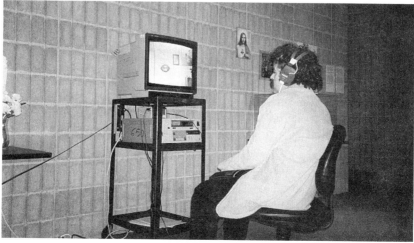

The issue of how this process of constructing policy-relevant knowledge and having various sectors of society communicating about social issues affects more sensitive social policies and a more useful anthropology is one that I am currently reflecting upon, but I believe this is a good start. One, because it compels consideration of knowledge-building as both producing and communicating to a variety of audiences. Two, because it shows that knowledge building is an open-ended activity: by sharing data with varied publics, anthropologists learn much about how to interpret data gathered and gain suggestions for future collection. A circular, feedback process of knowledge building has much to offer a self-reflective anthropology grounded in the political economy of the issues it studies.

Anthropologists usually present findings to policymakers based on their interpretation of data. This paper advocates an extension of the traditional role of the anthropologist to that of mediator and translator of messages that stem from dialogues between diverse publics and audiences. The role of translator involves: 1) Amplifying the voices of study populations to the larger society; 2) Paying attention to the language of communication: rethinking the medium chosen to convey a message so that communication occurs efficiently. For example, findings can be debated with an audience and translated in written form for consumption by policy makers; 3) Creating spaces for communication between different interlocutors, in both a real and a symbolic sense, for the discussion of topics that are relevant to national culture, so that various sectors of society engage in the discussion; 4) Promoting the participation of the study populations; 5) Engaging the response of policy makers, who are aware that they need to hear messages from consumers. The approach proposed in this paper can aid in solving social problems, by suggesting processes that providers and policymakers should address at the stage of project formulation.

ACKNOWLEDGMENTS

The research on the elderly Latino was supported in part by grants from the National Institute on Aging (1-R21-AGO-702701), the Social Science Research Council (Committee for Research on the Causes and Consequences of Puerto Rican Povery), and the Mount Sinai Medical Center.

[Postscript: This exhibition was also shown in July of 1993 in Mexico City and at the Graduate Center of the City University of New York (May through October 1994) (Figs. 7 and 8)]

REFERENCES

AMES, M.
1991 Biculturalism in exhibitions. *Museum Anthropology* 15 (2):7–15.
BEEMAN, WILLIAM
1993 The anthropology of theatre and spectacle. *Annual Reviews of Anthropology* 119 (22):369–393.
COLLIER, JOHN AND MALCOLM COLLIER
1986 *Visual Anthropology. Photography as a Research Method.* Albuquerque: University of New Mexico Press
FREIDENBERG, JUDITH
1993 Growing old in Spanish Harlem: Museums as multicultural settings. Society for Applied Anthropology, San Antonio, April.
FREIDENBERG, JUDITH, MICHAEL MULVIHILL, AND LOUIS CARABALLO
1993 From ethnography to survey: Some methodological issues in research on health seeking in East Harlem. *Human Organization* Vol. 52 (2):151–161.
KARP, IVAN, CHRISTINE MULLEN KREAMER, AND STEPHEN LEVINE
1992 *Museums and Communities: Debating Public Culture.* Washington, DC: Smithsonian Institution Press
ROGLER, LLOYD
1989 The meaning of culturally sensitive research in mental health. *American Journal of Psychiatry* 146:296–303.

A Retrospective on Two and a Half Decades of East Harlem Research

ANNA LOU DEHAVENON

Department of Community Medicine
Mount Sinai School of Medicine (CUNY)
1150 Fifth Avenue, Suite 5B
New York, New York 10128

This essay describes research carried out in East Harlem where I began Ph.D. dissertation fieldwork in 1971 (Dehavenon 1978). After 1979, the research was the basis for annual reports with recommendations to ameliorate the causes and conditions of hunger and homelessness in New York City (Action Research Project on Hunger, Homelessness, and Family Health 1989, 1990, 1991, 1992, 1993, 1994; Dehavenon 1979, 1980, 1981, 1982, 1983, 1984, 1985, 1986, 1987a, 1987b, 1988). This essay also describes how the results of nearly 25 years of research contributed to positive changes for participants in welfare programs.

While in 1984 the research was extended to include comparable neighborhoods and socio-cultural settings in Brooklyn and the Bronx,[1] East Harlem remained the primary focus. The continuity in this work was clearly facilitated by my permanent residence within the geographic boundaries of East Harlem and by funding from private foundations since 1984.[2]

I. THE FIRST PHASE, 1971–1976
A VIDEOANALYSIS OF PATTERNS OF FAMILY AUTHORITY IN FOUR LOW-INCOME URBAN HOMES

Between 1971 and 1976, I worked with a team of anthropologists, graduate students of anthropology, physicians, and medical students to develop a new cultural materialist methodology for the cross-cultural study of fam-

---

[1] The agencies collaborating in the research are the Citizens Advice Bureau in the South Bronx, the Family Centers of the Archdiocese of Brooklyn in Bedford Stuyvesant, Bushwick, and North Brooklyn, the Little Sisters of the Assumption Family Health Center and St. Cecilia's Parish Services in East Harlem, and the Entitlements Clinic of West Harlem.

[2] These include the Foundation for child Development, the Edna McConnell Clark Foundation, J.P. Morgan & Co. Incorporated, the New York Community Trust, and the Olive Bridge Fund.

ily life based on videotapes recorded in the home.[3] The four families who consented to participate in the research signed a legal contract with the project that awarded them control over the presence of videocameras in their homes and the recording and viewing of the videotapes. Three of the four families lived in East Harlem.

The Role of Family Health Adviser in the Videotape Research of Family Life

Dr. Charles M. Goodrich, then of the Department of Community Medicine of the Mount Sinai School of Medicine, volunteered to collaborate with the project. He wanted to investigate how the observation and micro analysis of family behavior videotaped in the home could be used to improve the health care of families as social units rather than as congeries of individuals. He helped us gain access to the sample of 400 families (matched for low income, family size, and the urban birth of at least one parent) from which the four research families were randomly selected.

Dr. Goodrich volunteered as health adviser to each of the families, free of charge, for as long as they contacted him for help. Before the camera installation in each home, he explained to the family that his role was to respond to their requests for help with health problems that affected the family as a group. Subsequently, he helped all four families manage a variety of health and medical problems when the cameras were in their homes and thereafter. For example, 19 years after the cameras were removed from her home, one of the mothers contacted him for the first time for help in a severe diabetic crisis.[4]

The Installation of the Video Cameras in One East Harlem Family

In August 1973, the video equipment was installed in the home of the last of the four families in the research project on family authority. Plans were for the research team to stay four weeks, in a rented apartment next door to the one in which the family lived in a housing project which is only a short walk from the site of the workshop that led to this volume. For the

---

[3] Patterns of Authority and Superordination in Four Urban Domiciles" (NSF GS 2916). Principal Investigator, Marvin Harris; Field Director, Anna Lou Dehavenon. Department of Anthropology, Columbia University.

[4] In the 1950s, Dr. Goodrich was a young medical resident in Dr. Beatrice Berle's clinic on 100th Street that was mentioned in Joan Mencher's earlier presentation. Dr. Goodrich provided a link for the later work on hunger and homelessness with the Little Sisters of the Assumption Family Health Services on 115th Street. In the early 1970s, the sisters were also experimenting with a family health care model based on home visits in East Harlem.

first three weeks, our goal was to 24 hours a day monitor and log all the behaviors of family members that occurred in the public areas of the apartment. Assuming that over time the members of the family would become less sensitive to the presence of the cameras, our second goal was to video-record all their verbal and nonverbal behaviors during the installation's fourth, final week.

After the team had monitored the family for two weeks, the mother phoned to say that her college-age daughter would be home for the weekend. This young woman was the only member of the family with whom the research team did not meet before signing the legal agreement with the rest of the family. Earlier, her mother had told me that she had some questions about her family's participation in the research and was planning to go to law school. As a precaution against not being able to collect the data if the family decided to unplug the cameras during the daughter's visit (as was their legal right), the team videotaped the third week with the intention of rerecording the fourth week on the same videotapes if the family left the cameras alone. Fortunately, we did so and therefore had recorded our research data when the young woman entered the apartment and asked her mother to disconnect the cameras.

The cultural materialist perspective employed in this research distinguished between two approaches to data collection (Dehavenon 1978; 1995a). The first approach was based on concepts and distinctions meaningful to the informants. Its use depended on the observation and coding of family members' semantic categories incorporated in the verbal requests they made of one another for action, information, and attention. The second approach was based on concepts and distinctions meaningful to the community of scientific observers. Its use depended on the observation and coding of family members' nonverbal behaviors incorporated in their preparation, distribution, and consumption of calories.

Patterns of family food behavior were thus a focus of the research on family authority. This focus was based on the assumption that food was a scarce resource in these households and that how individual family members controlled and consumed calories and proteins would reveal the patterns of relative authority among them.

The United States was in recession in 1973, and New York City was in fiscal crisis. By mid-August, the inflation that followed the Mideast oil embargo had increased the prices of food and other essentials substantially. Just before the video cameras were installed in his home, the father of the fourth family lost his job. In August, we observed him "comparison shop" for a week before buying a turkey for ten dollars. His sister had given him the money to buy food for the family. Later, we observed how he prepared the turkey and how the family consumed it throughout the entire next week. These and other observations of daily life in the home provided rich empirical data on the material constraints experienced by low income families during a long period of economic recession.

Founding the East Harlem Interfaith Welfare Committee

Through my association with the Little Sisters of the Assumption Family Health Services, I participated in early 1974 in a meditation group on the social movements of Cesar Chavez, Mohandas Gandhi, and Martin Luther King, Jr. The group was led by Reverend Norman C. Eddy of East Harlem Interfaith (EHI). Representatives of other religion-based agencies who worked with East Harlem families also participated. We reflected together regularly for six weeks on the lives of these men within the context of the impact on low-income families of recent unemployment and cutbacks in social and community development programs. We then decided to organize the EHI Welfare Committee (EHIWC).[5]

II. THE SECOND PHASE (1974–TODAY)
RESEARCH ON THE CAUSES OF HUNGER CONDITIONS AND HOMELESSNESS IN EAST HARLEM, BROOKLYN, AND THE BRONX

Studying Family Food Emergencies with the EHI Welfare Committee

The EHI Welfare Committee was a coalition of religion-based, voluntary agencies that provided families with social services in East Harlem. These services included welfare advocacy. My role was to design the committee's research, analyze the data the agencies collected using brief questionnaires that documented the problems of affected client families, and draft the policy-relevant recommendations suggested by the research results. A cultural materialist approach derived from the methodology developed in the video-tape study of family life (Dehavenon 1978, 1995a) was used in the design of the questionnaires. Informants were only asked about those aspects of their life histories that if they had been recorded on videotape could be directly observed and documented by the observer without interacting with them verbally.

At the committee's monthly meetings between 1974 and 1987, the member agencies reported on the problems of families who sought their help. When more than one reported the same new problem, the committee would decide whether or not to undertake to document it systematically in a larger sample of families.

Families on welfare in New York State receive two bi-weekly grants: one for "food and other" and one for rent. They also receive a monthly food

---

[5] When EHI's mission changed in 1988, the research relocated to the Community Food Resource Center as the Action Research Project on Hunger, Homelessness, and Family Health. The project continued to produce annual reports with recommendations on poverty issues based on data collected within the calendar year of their release.

stamp supplement that is not intended to meet all of a family's nutritional needs.

Between 1974 and 1979, the committee's research findings were the basis for a number of policy changes at city and state levels of government. In response to the results of a study carried out in August 1974 after budget cuts forced the closing of one welfare center in East Harlem, the city increased the number of workers (especially of Spanish-speaking workers) at another center where families had been camping overnight on the sidewalk for services the next day. In 1977 in response to another research study, members of state legislature decided not to decrease the welfare rent payment as they had previously considered doing.

Later at the committee's monthly meeting in January 1979, several of the agencies reported that a number of the families who came to them for help the month before did not have food. Further inquiry showed that the city had stopped giving emergency food stamps to those who ran out before their next welfare checks arrived.

A preliminary analysis of these "food emergencies" in a small sample of families showed that most were in families who were recipients, new applicants, or re-applicants for welfare. The committee knew that welfare payments are not indexed to changes in the cost of living. They hypothesized that the food emergencies in families on welfare were a symptom of the impact of inflation on the purchasing power of the "food and other" grant which had increased only 15 percent since 1969 when budgets were first set by family size. The committee's agencies decided to undertake to document and analyze these emergencies as one indicator of the need for a rise in the "food and other" grant. The agencies defined a food emergency operationally as existing when one of them used its own criteria to determine that a family had run out of food—or was in imminent danger of doing so—and then provided them with a small nonperishable food supply to eat in the home. The agency worker explained the purpose of the food emergency study to the family before completing a two-page questionnaire with those who consented to participate.

The analysis of the food emergency data collected in 1979 revealed three principal causes of hunger: 1) families ran out of food and money for food before their next welfare check or food stamps arrived; 2) welfare cases were closed for administrative reasons unrelated to financial need, leaving families with no income—a practice known as "churning" because families had to re-apply to reinstate their payments (see Dehavenon 1989, 1990); 3) families were forced to use their food money to pay the rent because the welfare shelter payment did not cover it. Thus, as early as 1979, the committee documented families forced to choose between paying for food or rent to avoid homelessness.

The committee discovered early on that public officials were more responsive to their research findings after they and their constituents learned about them through the media. An important aspect of the committee's work soon became the release of its reports to representatives of the media before sending them to the administrators and legislators of welfare programs at the three levels of government. The committee's first report on family food emergencies in 1979 was covered widely in the local and national media. Contributions began pouring into EHI from people all over the country who were shocked to learn that such hunger conditions existed in the United States.

Later the committee's 1979, 1980, and 1981 reports on the causes of family food emergencies were circulated widely as evidence of the need to increase New York State's "food and other" grant. After a New York Times editorial in March 1981 cited the committee's findings as evidence of the need for such an increase, the state legislature voted a 15 percent rise. The committee's reports were generally credited with having sensitized church leaders, public officials, and the general public to the need for the rise.

The families in what became the committee's annual studies of food emergencies typically reported being highly vulnerable to the adverse consequences of inadequate income. For example, in 1987 two-thirds of the households in the committee's study of 1,905 food emergencies included children under 18 years of age. The families reported an unusually high incidence of medical problems, and one-fifth reported a pregnancy. Almost a third did not live in their own apartments. Of this subgroup of homeless families, less than two-fifths reported having a regular source of income.

Twice again in the 1980s, advocates used the findings in the committee's annual reports to successfully pressure the governor to raise the welfare shelter grant by 15 percent. Still, the grant was on average only half what New York City families needed to rent apartments in the private market in the 1990s. This disparity between the welfare shelter payment and the rent costs is the primary cause of homelessness today among New York City families who are poor enough to be on welfare. This is the only form of publicly entitled income that is not indexed to the cost of living, and nationally welfare's purchasing power has declined by almost half since 1970. The persistent discrepancy between the cost of living and the low level of minimum wage and welfare payments remains the primary cause of hunger conditions and homelessness throughout the United States.

III. THE THIRD PHASE (1986–TODAY) RESEARCH ON FAMILY HOMELESSNESS IN NEW YORK CITY'S EMERGENCY ASSISTANCE UNITS IN THE BRONX, BROOKLYN, AND MANHATTAN

Churning, Family Homelessness, and Effecting Changes in City Policy

During the 1980s, it was not difficult to imagine what was happening to the people who were falling through the "safety net." Since 1979 the committee's annual reports had documented the devastating impact of the churning of eligible families on and off welfare (Dehavenon 1989, 1990). Each year the research showed that the closing of cases for administrative reasons unrelated to family need was the second most frequent cause of family food emergencies. However, between 1979 and 1987, the city consistently ignored this finding and denied that churning was a problem. For many poor families administrative closings were a fact of life. In 1987, approximately 83 percent of the food emergency families reported experiencing an administrative closing at least once in the preceding twelve months. More than a third experienced more than one such closing during the same period. As a result, families usually lost their sole means of support. In the 1987 report, almost all those whose cases were closed lost their welfare payments. More than two-thirds lost their food stamps, and more than one-third also lost their Medicaid benefit.

Typically, families with closed cases sought to have them reinstated. The committee's 1987 report showed that most families with closed cases tried to contact their welfare centers to reopen them. Usually they endured a lengthy interruption of payments. Most reported losing them for over two weeks; more than half lost them for over a month; and one-sixth lost them for more than three months. Of all the families who were interacting with the welfare system, more than two-thirds reported food emergencies that lasted over a week, and one-quarter reported emergencies of a month's duration or longer. On average, families with welfare cases closed administratively reported food emergencies that lasted 30 days.

The long interruption in welfare payments often pushed desperate families "to the wall." Many reported having to beg, borrow, or steal to survive. The vast majority tried to borrow money to buy food, most often from friends, relatives, and neighbors. Less frequently, they borrowed from landlords, grocers, and local loan sharks.

To pursue the issue of churning further, I first undertook participant observation in the Emergency Assistance Units (EAUs) in July 1986 as a monitor for the Coalition for the Homeless. The EAUs are the city's after-hours welfare centers where homeless families with children wait for emergency shelter placements for the night. These families have nowhere else to go when they become homeless at night, or, as is very often the case, when their regular centers fail to place them during the day. The EAU research was carried out at the EAUs in the Bronx, Brooklyn, and Manhattan—the same boroughs where the agencies documented family food emergencies and the city's rates of poverty and welfare participation are highest. Initially, the EAU research was based on the assumption that families without permanent addresses would have greater difficulty keeping their welfare cases open than families who had them. Thus, the EAU research was not first undertaken to study family homelessness per se, but to observe the frequency in which the cases of homeless families on welfare were closed for administrative reasons.

The city's reasons for closing cases were: 1) a family's failing to keep an eligibility appointment because they did not receive the notice; 2) a family's failing to return a questionnaire on time; or 3) the system's classifying a family as "whereabouts unknown" after a single piece of mail was returned from their most recent address. The research data showed that cases were often closed because of a computer or worker error. Indeed, the first EAU report (Dehavenon 1987a) revealed that the cases of half the homeless families already on welfare were closed at the interview stage. As a result, they were not only rendered homeless but exposed to the high risk of chronic hunger and poor health.

The research methodology required staying at the EAUs until the precise time when the families I interviewed earlier in the evening secured a shelter placement. I also documented the length of the placement and the time they left the EAU. Monday, August 15, 1986, was the first time that it was necessary to stay all night to complete these observations. That night, I documented the number of families who were there throughout the night, as well as the numbers of observably pregnant women, other adults, newborns, infants, preschool, and school-age children who stayed all night because the city failed to find them shelter placements.

These observations were the basis for my affidavit in a motion to the Appellate Division submitted on August 16th in the lawsuit known as *McCain v. Koch*. This suit was first brought in 1983 by the Legal Aid Homeless Family Rights Project. Based on a May 1986 New York State Appellate Division decision that the State Constitution and social services laws required the state and city to provide shelter to destitute families with children, in July 1986 the State Supreme Court ordered the city to "provide lawful emergency housing to all eligible homeless families with children, such emergency housing not to include overnight accommodations at Emergency Assistance Units or Income Maintenance Centers." As a result of the August 16th motion in which my affidavit and data on families remaining at the EAU overnight was included, the Appellate division removed a stay of this order which the city had obtained by appealing the Supreme Court's July order.

The first EAU study revealed that the cases of half the homeless families already on welfare were closed at the time of the interview (Dehavenon 1987a). All these families reported being in food emergencies because they had no money for food.

The first study also illustrated what happens when families who are already on the verge of homelessness lose their welfare payments. Of those who were made homeless by losing their apartments, more than a third could not keep up with the rent because they had recently lost their welfare due to administrative closings. Similarly, the same high proportion of those who lost a "double up" in someone else's apartment within the prior month had their welfare terminated for administrative reasons.

Finally in 1988, the city implemented three of the committee's recommendations to reduce churning. The recommendations are found in the committee's annual reports each year beginning in 1984. As a result, in February 1988, the city began putting a reminder to recipients of their impending face-to-face eligibility re-certification appointments on the voucher they received with their regular payments. These were delivered through an electronic payments system rather than by mail. Later that year, the city stopped closing cases for the failure to return an eligibility questionnaire. In November, the city stopped closing cases for "whereabouts unknown," except after a letter was returned to the system and the family missed their next eligibility appointment. By 1989, the city estimated that these reforms had already reduced the number of administrative case closings by more than 3,000 per month. The median number of persons on a family welfare case is three. It can therefore be estimated that the reforms reduced the risk of hunger and homelessness every month for 9,000 or more persons. The city is now implementing a fourth of the committee's recommendations to further reduce churning by including the date and time of recipient appointments on the voucher they receive with their regular payments. This has already been done for work program appointments. Ongoing fieldwork at the one remaining EAU in the South Bronx in 1994, revealed almost no families with welfare cases closed for administrative reasons.

The Action Research Project and Other Aspects of Family Homelessness

As churning became a less frequent cause of hunger conditions and homelessness, the EAU research began looking more deeply at other aspects of family homelessness (Action Research Project on Hunger, Homelessness, and Family Health 1989, 1990; 1991; 1992; 1993; 1994). For example, the later annual reports revealed how the process of seeking emergency shelter directly challenged the maintenance of intact family life by separating spouses from spouses, parents from children, siblings from siblings, and all these from the members of their extended families. When the city refused to shelter the father with his family, he often stayed on at the EAU to help the mother with the children and to learn where they would be placed in shelter. In families who were short of food, fathers gave nutritional priority to mothers, and mothers gave the same priority to children.

Seeking emergency shelter was a particularly harsh experience for pregnant women and infants because of the instability of shelter placements, lack of sleep, and difficulty in maintaining clinic appointments and adequate nutrition. Epidemics of diarrhea and upper respiratory infections were recurrent in the EAUs. The schooling of older children was interrupted until the families were placed in stable shelter.

The Research Data and Support for the Legal Rights of Homeless
Families.

Each year the EAU research showed how the city failed to provide homeless families with social services as required by law. Most homeless families did not receive all the welfare payments and special grants to which they were entitled. Frequently, they were denied the required food and transportation grants and not sheltered in accordance with the law.

Findings from the 1990, 1991, 1992, and 1994, EAU reports were submitted in six more affidavits in the *McCain v. Dinkins* lawsuit. Court orders in the *McCain* litigation forbade placing families with pregnant women or infants under six months of age in shelters where they did not have their own rooms, sending them to multiple one-night placements, and denying them shelter by refusing to place them or by leaving them to stay overnight in an EAU.

Findings from the EAU research were also used in other arenas of public policy, for example: in expert witness testimony in two cases brought in the New York State Supreme Court on behalf of homeless and other low-income families by the Legal Aid Society; and in testimony before the General Welfare Committee of the New York City Council. My March 1991 testimony in *Jiggetts v. Perales,* a lawsuit which sought to raise public assistance shelter payments to fair market levels, included findings from the annual research reports from 1981 to 1991. These showed how the level of the welfare shelter grant routinely forced families into food emergencies when they used their food money to pay rents in excess of the grant to avoid homelessness. It also showed how the low grant level forced them to double-up in other people's apartments and then seek emergency shelter when they were evicted. Since 1990, rulings in the Jiggetts lawsuit on behalf of individual families in danger of being evicted from their own apartments for the nonpayment of rents in excess of the welfare shelter allowance enabled 14,000 to remain in their apartments. Under the Jiggetts order, New York State must continue to pay the actual amount of their rents to provide them stable housing.

On five days in October-November 1991, preliminary findings from the 1991 research report were the basis for extensive expert witness testimony in the *McCain v. Dinkins* contempt proceedings. These proceedings sought to find New York City and individual senior city officials in contempt of court for leaving homeless families to stay overnight in the EAUs. The findings in this testimony were based on direct observation and systematic interviews using questionnaires with 93 families who fell within the research sampling frame as they spent the night in the Manhattan EAU in July-August 1991. For the first time in November 1992, and four times again in 1993 and 1994, State Supreme Court Justice Helen E. Freedman found the city and its top officials in contempt of court.

Justice Freedman's first 1992 contempt ruling cited the project's expert witness testimony extensively. She also ruled that homeless families forced to stay overnight at the EAU were to receive $50 damages for the first night they were not placed by 8:00 a.m. and $100 if the city failed to place them by 12:00 noon the same day. Thereafter, the families were to receive an additional $100 for every 24-hour period, or portion thereof, they waited for the city to place them in shelter. By May 1994, the city estimated that 5,000 families who stayed overnight at the EAUs in 1991- 1992 would be paid fines of $3.5 million! Also as a result of Justice Freedman's first contempt finding, a number of top city officials were ordered to spend the night in one of the EAUs and remain there until all the families who waited with them were placed in shelter.

The cultural materialist distinction in this work between two approaches to the collection of research data was particularly significant in the context of the expert witness testimony in testimony in *McCain vs. Dinkins* (cf. p. 5). Had I not been certified as expert witness, my testimony would have been limited to reporting on only what I had personally observed directly, *e.g.*, on etic events such as the exact time each of the 93 informant families entered and left the EAU. Once certified, my testimony could also include research data collected using any of the other standard methods of my discipline, *i.e.*, interviews with informants using questionnaires to document their reports of relevant events that I did not observe directly. Thus the law of legal evidence maintains the same distinction as the cultural materialist approach in this work between information gathered from direct observation and information gathered from third-party reports. The law excludes the latter as "hearsay" unless it is presented in expert witness testimony.

The Homelessness of Doubled Up Families

Another salient finding of the EAU research was that many of the families seeking emergency shelter at the EAUs had never lived in apartments of their own. Instead, they lived doubled up in the apartments of relatives, friends, or in rented rooms. Many of those who did have apartments also stayed in double ups before coming to the EAU. Family homelessness is therefore defined operationally in this work as the lack of a stable shelter over which the family has legal control.

In 1992, the research project sharpened its focus on the experiences of doubled up homeless families in the analysis of the EAU data and that collected by the seven community-based agencies which participate in the research. The brief questionnaire they completed with families seeking help in food and housing emergencies was designed for use with families doubled up in the poorest areas of Harlem, Brooklyn, and the South Bronx.

The 1992, 1993 and 1994 reports compare overcrowding and other conditions in three sub-samples of doubled up families. Families in the first two still lived doubled up in the community. They included the "can stay" respondents who judged that they could stay permanently in the double up, and the "cannot stay" respondents who judged that they could not stay doubled up permanently. The third sub-sample was of families forced to leave double ups and seek emergency shelter at the EAUs.

The data analysis revealed a substantial difference in the levels of crowding in the three sub-samples. Crowding was least severe in the "can stay" double ups; more severe in the "cannot stay" double ups; and most severe in the double ups families left for the shelter system. The analysis also showed that the "can stays" were more likely than the "cannot stays" to pay rent to the primary tenant and have their own room. Often the rent was equal to the welfare shelter grant for the family's size. Families who did not pay rent were more likely to leave and come to the EAU.[6]

IV. THE FOURTH PHASE (1994 AND THE FUTURE)
A CHANGING NEIGHBORHOOD, COUNTRY, AND WORLD

The research on the causes and conditions of hunger and homelessness in East Harlem and New York City goes on in 1995. Twenty-three years of fieldwork are being extended through the present and into the future as I continue to witness the vast changes in East Harlem since 1971: 1) a substantial loss of habitable, privately-owned housing; 2) a population decrease of from 180,000 to 110,000 people that correlates with the housing loss; 3) the disappearance of anti-poverty programs and withdrawal of banking and other services; 4) the closing of welfare centers and parochial and public schools; and 5) the disease and violence associated with increasing poverty and the crack cocaine epidemic.

East Harlem's location on the upper eastside of Manhattan is a primary asset for the future development of New York City. Midtown is an easy commute, and East Harlem's housing is at a premium in times of economic growth. Many people would like to live in its large stock of relatively well-maintained public housing. (The waiting list for an apartment in the projects city wide is 200,000.) Although local real estate values escalated after 1980, there has been relatively little gentrification to date. The city sold many of the buildings seized through landlord tax default in the 1970s to speculators who now control many of the uninhabited buildings in which the apartments are "warehoused" while they wait for an upturn in the economy. Future development is unlikely to include more affordable housing for low-income people. For now, the city waits and the number of freshly painted murals increase steadily on the walls of the empty buildings where they memorialize the young who have died in drug-related violence.

In 1994, the new mayor cut the most successful program in providing homeless families with permanent housing severely (Kennedy 1994; *New*

---

[6] The Action Research Project's research on the single homelessness was carried out in a small pentecostal church in lower East Harlem beginning in 1982 (Dehavenon, 1992, 1993, 1995b)

York Times 1994). At the state level where tax revenues for 1994-1995 exceeded expectations, the governor's budget failed to include the significant increase in the welfare shelter payment that had been expected (Sack 1993).

At the federal level, the new administration's plan to end homelessness" recognized the problem as "far larger than commonly thought." It reflected substantial progress over the thinking of two previous administrations in recognizing poverty as a major factor in differentiating between two groups at risk of homelessness: the smaller "more visible" group of addicts and the mentally ill and the larger "more hidden" group of those who are chronically impoverished. It seeks to increase the U.S. Department of Housing and Urban Development's budget "to make up for past budget cuts" and to spend unspecified new sums on housing, mental health, and tax credit programs (DeParle 1994). The extent to which the plan can reduce homelessness depends largely on the congressional support it does or does not receive.

Slow economic growth, recession, and the globalization of labor and capital produced similar changes world wide during the 1980s, and there was a substantial increase in poverty and homelessness. The leading social democracies of Western Europe reduced their social programs which had been more generous than those in the United States since World War II. With the collapse of the Soviet experiment, the social programs in most central and eastern European nations were dismantled to fulfill the requirements of privatization and the international lending institutions. In most nations of the developing world the same requirements produced the same results. At home and abroad, the trends toward disinvestment in human capital and cultural resources held serious portent for a changing world in the 1990s.

Plans for future fieldwork include comparative research with Indian colleagues on urban poverty and homelessness in New Delhi and New York City. Future publications include the annual reports of the Action Research Project on Hunger, Homelessness, and Family Health on hunger conditions and homelessness in New York City, and an edited volume on homelessness in the United States.

REFERENCES

ACTION RESEARCH PROJECT ON HUNGER, HOMELESSNESS AND FAMILY HEALTH
  1989   The Tyranny of Indifference: a Study of Hunger, Homelessness, Poor Health, and Family Dismemberment in 818 New York City Households with Children in 1988-1989. New York City.
  1990   The Tyranny of Indifference: a Study of Hunger, Homelessness, Poor Health, and Family Dismemberment in 1,325 New York City Households with Children in 1989-1990. New York City.

1991   No Room at the Inn: an Interim Report with Recommendations on Homeless Families with Children Requesting Shelter at New York City's Emergency Assistance Units in 1991. New York City.

1992   Promises! Promises! the Failed Hopes of New York City's Homeless Families in 1992. New York City.

1993   Out of Sight! Out of Mind! or How New York City and New York State Tried to Abandon the City's Homeless Families in 1993. New York City.

1994   No Room At The Inn: How New York City Abandoned Homeless Families to Public Places in 1994. New York City.

DEHAVENON, ANNA LOU

1978   Superordinate Behavior in Urban Homes: A Video Analysis of Request-Compliance and Food Control Behavior in Two Black and Two White Families Living in New York City. Ph.D. Dissertation. Columbia University.

1979   Results of a Questionnaire on Welfare Clients' Food Emergencies in East Harlem: February 16, 1979 to March 19, 1979. New York City: East Harlem Interfaith.

1980   Hunger, Poverty, and Disease in East Harlem: Findings from a Questionnaire Survey of Food Emergencies in the Client Households of the Voluntary Agencies on the East Harlem Interfaith Welfare Committee: November 1, 1979 to March 1, 1980. New York City: East Harlem Interfaith.

1981   Hunger, Poverty and Disease in East Harlem in 1980: A Survey of Food Emergencies in the Client Households of the Six Voluntary Agencies on the East Harlem Interfaith Welfare Committee. New York City: East Harlem Interfaith.

1982   Hunger, Poverty, and Disease in East Harlem: A Study of the Food Emergencies in 723 Households with Children in 1981. New York City: East Harlem Interfaith.

1983   The Tyranny of Indifference and the Re-Institutionalization of Hunger, Homelessness, and Poor Health: A Study of the Causes and Conditions of Food Emergencies in 669 Households with Children in Manhattan, Brooklyn, and the Bronx in 1982. New York City: East Harlem Interfaith.

1984   The Tyranny of Indifference and the Re-Institutionalization of Hunger, Homelessness, and Poor Health: A Study of the Causes and Conditions of the Food Emergencies in 805 Households with Children in Manhattan, Brooklyn, and the Bronx in 1983. New York City: East Harlem Interfaith.

1985   The Tyranny of Indifference and the Re-Institutionalization of Hunger, Homelessness, and Poor Health: A Study of the Causes and Conditions of the Food Emergencies in 1,506 Households with Children In Manhattan, Brooklyn, and the Bronx in 1984. New York City: East Harlem Interfaith.

1986   The Tyranny of Indifference and the Re-Institutionalization of Hunger, Homelessness, and Poor Health: A Study of the Causes and Conditions of the Food Emergencies in 1,576 Households with Children In Manhattan, Brooklyn, and the Bronx in 1985.

1987a   Toward a Policy for the Amelioration and Prevention of Family Homelessness and Dissolution: New York City's After- Hours Emergency Assistance Units in 1986-1987. New York City: East Harlem Interfaith.

1987b   The Tyranny of Indifference and the Re-Institutionalization of Hunger, Homelessness, and Poor Health: A Study of the Causes and Conditions of the Food Emergencies in 1,708 Households with Children in Manhattan, Brooklyn, and the Bronx in 1986. New York City: East Harlem Interfaith.

1988   The Tyranny of Indifference and the Re-Institutionalization of Hunger, Homelessness, and Poor Health: a Study of the Causes and Conditions of the Food Emergencies in 1,905 Households with Children In Manhattan, Brooklyn, and the Bronx in 1987. New York City: East Harlem Interfaith.

1989   Administrative closings of public assistance cases: The rise of hunger and homelessness in New York City. *New York University Review of Law and Social Change,* Vol. **XVI**. No. 4.

1990   Charles Dickens meets Franz Kafka: The maladministration of New York City's public assistance programs. *New York University Review of Law and Social Change,* Vol. **XVII**. No. 2.

1992   The holy woman and the homeless men of East Harlem: A brief look at the underclass concept. In *Culture and Contradiction: Dialectics of Wealth, Power and Symbol.* Hermine De Soto, Ed. San Francisco: Mellen Research University Press.

1993   D'Abord on les nourrit, ensuite on les habille, et puis on les sauve: Le banquet de dimanche dans une eglise de East Harlem a New York. In *Ferveur Contemporain: Textes Anthropologiques Offerts a Jacques Gutwirth.* Yves Delaporte & Colette Petonnet, Eds. Paris: L'Harmattan.

1995a   The cultural materialist approach and the causes of hunger and home-lessness. In *Science, Materialism, and the Study of Culture.* Maxine Margolis & Martin Murphy, Eds. University of Florida Press. Forthcoming.

1995b   First You Feed Them, Then You Clothe Them, Then You Save Them: the Hungry and Homeless and the Sunday Feast at a Pentecostal Storefront Church in East Harlem. *In* Celebrations and Festivals in North American Ethnic Communitties. Genevieve Fabre & Ramon A. Gutierrez, Eds. Albuquerque: University of New Mexico Press. Forthcoming.

DePARLE, JASON
1994   Report to Clinton sees vast extent of homelessness. *New York Times,* February 17, p. A1.

KENNEDY, SHAWN
1994   Giuliani cuts cash awards to landlords for homeless. *New York Times,* March 16, p. B1.

NEW YORK TIMES
1994   A dangerous homeless policy. Editorial, March 17, p. A22.

SACK, KEVIN
1993   Plan weighed to increase rent subsidy: Cuomo is considering first raise since 1988. *New York Times,* December 13, p. B1.

Public Housing Projects as Successful Environments for Adolescent Development[a]

TERRY WILLIAMS

Department of Sociology
New School for Social Research
65 Fifth Avenue
New York, New York 10003

WILLIAM KORNBLUM

Doctoral Program in Sociology
City University of New York Graduate Center
33 West 42nd Street
New York, New York 10036

At a time of crisis for the nation's poor, with homelessness on the rise and public housing widely regarded as a problem rather than a solution, there is need for more knowledge about what makes public housing more or less successful. New York City's public housing is among the best available in any large American city (U.S. Dept. of Housing and Urban Development, 1988) This paper is in part about why this is so and how some New York City projects have become safer and more desirable environments for child development than others.

With the help of a 1989 planning grant from the MacArthur Foundation's Committee on Successful Adolescence, we established a field research and youth mentoring presence in four Harlem housing projects. The research we describe is on-going, but even on the basis of the ethnographic work to date we are able to reach a few important conclusions about what makes public housing environments more or less successful places to raise children.

Our overall research aim was to explore the conditions which lead to successful and less successful housing projects, measured by how well the children coming of age in them seem to be doing by conventional (and less conventional) standards of achievement. Our first practical requirement, however, was to select housing projects that would allow us to control key

[a] This research was made possible by a grant from the MacArthur Foundation and support from the Russell Sage Foundation.

demographic variables so that differences in outcomes for children and their families could be traced to specific communal and organizational features of the projects themselves. After reviewing the demographic characteristics of over twenty large, high rise projects in New York City we selected four projects for more intense participant observation research. Two of the four projects exhibit rather unusual levels of conventional adolescent success. These two projects are also relatively successful at coping with the drug and crime epidemic. The other two housing projects we selected match the first pair in almost all social background and demographic characteristics but do not score so well on adolescent achievement and crime outcomes. Their relative success notwithstanding, all four of these projects are more desirable environments in which to raise children than most public housing described in the existing social science literature. One year of field research in four massive housing projects is not a sufficient period to fully explore how communal organization in the projects supports positive outcomes for children and families, but we can begin in this paper to offer some explanations for the similarities and differences one observes. We also will discuss the methodological strengths and limitations of our research and discuss some of the directions of research and involvement in the community we intend to pursue. The neighborhoods surrounding each of the housing projects where our research is conducted are severely run-down. During the 1980s many of Harlem's neighborhoods, and especially those in the areas we discuss, have continued to lose population and to deteriorate. Violence associated with the drug trade and with alienated youth has worsened even over the period of our research. Rates of infant mortality, teen pregnancy, homicide, rape, and other indicators have increased over the decade of the 1980s, despite major gains made during the previous two decades of social interventions (NYC Dept. of Health, 1989). The larger neighborhoods which surround each of the projects are scarred by high rates of vacancy and building abandonment, high rates of crime, and health indicators that make these neighborhoods compare with those of the most impoverished nations of the world. In contrast to the neighborhoods which surround them, the four Harlem public housing we describe are enclaves of relative stability and security. Yet in describing these more or less successful public housing environments we can not minimize the real danger to adolescents in the areas served by public housing. The people who live in the neighborhoods we will describe are frustrated in their fight to protect the children from violence, addiction, disease, and death. The risk that their children will be enticed by street life are greater than they have been for many years. Nonetheless, our data simply do not support the reigning stereotypes of life in "drug infested" public housing jungles (Vergara 1989; Terry 1991). Housing projects in Harlem and elsewhere in New York City are embattled neighborhoods but they offer opportunities to establish bases of support and security against escalating violence and danger. Built at a time in our history when there was a more bipartisan vision of what it takes to achieve a livable city, the housing projects were intended to be way stations to social mobility. Instead, during extremely hard times for the city's working parents, they have become priceless but embattled centers of neighborhood strength and empowerment.

FOUR HOUSING PROJECTS IN HARLEM

The housing projects were selected (in cooperation with Thomas Cook and Richard Jessor, members of the MacArthur Committee on Successful Adolescence) to hold constant most demographic and physical variables (*e.g.,* building size) (Williams and Kornblum 1994). This selection increases the likelihood that differences among the projects with regard to adolescent outcomes like school performance and crime, for example, are due to intervening social processes rather than to differences in population characteristics (such as the distribution and age grouping of children and adolescents). TABLE 1 summarizes the characteristics of each of the four. The names of each have been changed and the locations are purposely left approximate.

Each is a high-rise project with roughly the same population and about equal proportions of children and adolescents, equivalent income distributions and similar proportions of single parent households. TABLE 1 indicates that two of the projects, Mission Hill Houses and Zion Hill Houses are predominantly populated by African Americans. Puerto Rican households predominate at Pepsi Market Apartments and Novarios Apartments, but in each of those is also a significant African American presence (46 percent in Pepsi Market and 36 percent at Novarios).

Built in the 1950s or early 1960s, most Harlem public housing buildings are clusters of high rise towers (not surprising given Manhattan land values) and like most New York City public housing the apartment buildings have interior elevators which stop at each floor. This is not the case, for example, in many of the high rise housing projects in Chicago where elevators run in shafts outside the building and tenants must wait outdoors for elevators which often skip floors. All of the Harlem projects have community centers and day care facilities associated with them as well as active tenant associations. Interior court yards with community gardens, playgrounds, and bench-lined walks make the projects more open than most commercial developments of the same scale. High rise apartments have the distinct disadvantage of rendering child surveillance much more difficult than is the case in lower buildings, but increasingly in Manhattan this is a problem faced by persons of all social classes in elevator buildings. Members of upper classes, however, routinely channel their adolescent children toward after-school activities of all kinds, something parents in housing projects often attempt with less success.

The most significant demographic changes in Harlem housing projects over the past fifteen years are increases in three-generation families and greater rates of occupancy by persons over 65 years of age. The relatively

TABLE 1. Selected Demographic and Behavioral Characteristics, Four Harlem Public Housing Projects, 1989

	Mission City Houses	Zion Hill Houses	Pepsi Market Apartments	Novarios Apartments
Location	W 141-144th Street	W 112-115 Street	E112-115 Street	E99-106 Street
No. Buildings	5	10	10	13
No. Stories	19/21	13/14	6/10/14	6/15
No. Apt. Units	1217	1379	1310	1246
Socio/Demographic				
Population	3125	3664	3376	3180
% Black	92.3	83.2	46.0	37.2
% PR	5.3	14.4	51.4	56.8
% White	0.4	0.4	0.9	2.7
% Other	0.2	2.0	1.7	3.3
Under 21	1215	1594	1392	1292
% total pop.	38.9	43.5	41.2	40.6
% < 4	13.5	15.7	21.3	14.0
4-5	8.0	8.0	8.0	8.4
6-9	18.2	16.0	16.7	17.3
10-13	17.0	18.1	17.0	22.0
14-17	24.5	23.3	24.0	23.5
18-20	19.2	19.0	19.0	15.5
% > 62 yrs.	19.1	13.6	14.1	15.6
% Female Head	29.3	38.5	36.7	33.6
Mean Years (residence)	15.9	20.7	20.4	19.4
Economic				
Average Income	$11,418	$11,085	$10,865	$10,618
% AFDC	22.9	27.3	34.3	31.2
Social Indicators				
% Dropout 1980	33.0	7.2	22.0	17.0
1983 % <grade	70.0	32.4	69.2	25.4
1988 % <grade[a]	51.0	39.4	45.0	29.0
Crime Rates				
1983	36.1	32.9	37.1	33.0
1984	50.1	28.6	48.6	40.1
1985	55.5	37.6	40.7	45.8
1986	56.5	49.9	39.2	44.8
1987	85.4	46.1	61.5	44.2
1988	81.0	52.4	50.9	50.6
All NY Projects 1988	46.0			
NYC 1988	98.2			

[a] Reading test for Sixth Graders, test and norms changed after 1987. Crime rates are for index crime complaints in the project per 1000 residents.

long length of residence in the four projects (TABLE 1 indicates an average of over 18 years) combined with average proportions of persons under 21 of 40% is a consequence of the aging of public housing households and the doubling up with grandmothers of adult children and their children. The residential stability of the projects also highlights the lack of private sector housing alternatives for poor families.

When Kenneth Clark and his associates drafted *Youth in the Ghetto* in 1964, they noted that Harlem public housing households were at the lower end of the economic scale and that in about one third there was "no husband present" and one third were "on welfare" (p.109). The figures presented in TABLE 1 for welfare households, single parent households, and household income suggest that a similar resident profile exists today, although projects with greater proportions of Puerto Rican households also tend to have somewhat more households receiving AFDC payments. The residents of the four Harlem housing projects tend to be poor, a requirement for acceptance into public housing, but the majority of households are those of working women and men and their children and other kin.

Housing Projects and Harlem's Working Poor

Recent data on occupation and earnings which can be mapped to the projects at the Census Block Group level are not yet available, but the 1980 census data presented in TABLE 2 corroborate what one still observes about the work of project residents. A large proportion of the project adults work or are seeking work. Most who do work are in jobs where they earn low or very modest incomes. The single largest category of employment is in services—especially in hospitals, nursing care facilities and commercial food services. Typically this is work which continues to qualify adults with minor children at home for supplemental welfare benefits. The same is true for craft and operative occupations, much is near minimum wage work or "off the books," non-union construction work. Puerto Rican women are typically employed as machine operators and food service workers. In comparison with African American women they tend to have somewhat less education and more difficulty with English and are thus less likely to find employment in the clerical labor force. These facts help explain the somewhat greater proportion of AFDC recipients among the Puerto Rican households in the projects and the lower labor force participation of Pepsi Market residents. That project is located in the heart of East Harlem's Puerto Rican "Barrio" and could be expected to exhibit employment trends which reflect those in the surrounding Puerto Rican community.

Public housing helps keep a labor force in the central city which staffs many of Manhattan's most thankless jobs. Hospital work (typically as orderlies, attendants or nurses aids) often requires the adults to work rotating shifts or steady evenings or nights. From the projects in the early mornings one sees a stream of women and men catching the early busses or trudging

TABLE 2. Occupation of Working Males and Females over Age 16, Four Harlem Housing Projects, 1980

	Mission City	Zion Hill	Pepsi Market	Novarios
	Number (%)	Number (%)	Number (%)	Number (%)
Executive	36 (4.0)	50 (5.5)	19 (2.8)	22 (2.4)
Professional	47 (5.1)	88 (9.6)	49 (2.8)	61 (6.5)
Technical	7 (0.7)	21 (2.3)	5 (0.7)	8 (0.8)
Sales	57 (6.2)	38 (4.2)	30 (4.4)	76 (8.2)
Admin. Asst .	198 (21.4)	186 (20.3)	104 (15.1)	261 (28 .0)
Pvt. Hshld.	40 (4.3)	46 (5.0)	10 (1.5)	14 (1.5)
Protective	25 (2.7)	32 (3.5)	29 (4.2)	21 (2.3)
Other Service	308 (33.3)	250 (27.3)	153 (22.2)	249 (26.7)
Craft	89 (9.6)	43 (4.7)	69 (10.0)	58 (6.2)
Operative	91 (9.8)	47 (5.1)	129 (18.7)	68 (7.3)
Transp.	11 (1.2)	34 (3.7)	50 (7.3)	29 (3.1)
Labor	16 (1.7)	81 (8.8)	42 (6.1)	65 (7.0)
TOTAL	925 (100.0)	916 (100.0)	689 (100.0)	932 (100.0)

SOURCE: 1980 U.S. Census of Population, Table 66.

to the subways for work that begins at 7:00 a.m. Since almost none of the factory work and little of the labor or construction work is done at Manhattan's heavily unionized job sites, the blue collar work often requires long subway rides to other boroughs and is frequently subject to seasonal layoffs.

The demands of jobs and commuting often mean that older children are expected to attend to younger ones. Adolescents usually find that at least one of their peers has an empty apartment where all can congregate after school. Younger parents always express a great deal of concern over the supervision of children and experience continual pressure to find informal arrangements and reliable babysitting. Public and church sponsored daycare services are widely available for the youngest children but there is inadequate after school and weekend supervision available. Although the settlement houses and community programs are making heroic efforts to meet these needs their resources are limited. In recent years all have been competing for a shrinking pool of dollars. In consequence, women in the projects who do not work outside the home and can take on responsibilities for childcare and for project activities are vital to the community. Their supply is not as ample as stereotypes about life in public housing might suggest. About 29 percent, on the average, of households in the four projects are receiving AFDC payments, a marked contrast to figures of over 80 percent for Chicago's Robert Taylor Homes or Cabrini Green, often cited as negative examples of welfare dependency in public housing ghettos (Wilson 1987).

Children and Schools

Each of the four Harlem projects has roughly equal proportions of children and teenagers. Each is home to at least 300 girls and boys between ages 10 and 18. With proportions of children and adolescents usually around forty percent of total population, housing projects like these are, for better or worse, highly active children's environments. The projects are lively centers of child development; investments in child-centered programs and facilities immediately reach hundreds of "at-risk" young people.

The projects differ in the school achievement of their children and in rates of crime (much of which is normally associated with juveniles and young adults). Indeed the projects were initially chosen to vary on these dimensions such that there would be one predominantly African American project with relatively positive outcomes and another with less positive outcomes with regard to schooling and crime. The same criteria were applied to the choice of projects with majority Puerto Rican residents. Thus TABLE 1 indicates that compared to the projects with which they are matched, Zion Hill and Novarios had lower rates of school dropouts (as indicated in the 1980 census) and lower percentages of children in the sixth grade reading below grade level.

The reading achievement variable is an "ecological" measure based on performance of children in the local primary school which serves mainly, but not exclusively, children from each project. Families with children in New York City schools are increasingly free to choose from a range of primary and secondary school alternatives and are not bound to send children to the nearest neighborhood school. This is especially true for the community school district in which all the projects but Mission City are located. Harlem's Community School District #2 is a leader in its support for alternative public schools, including the Central Park East schools under the direction of Principal Deborah Meier. The Central Park East schools are adjacent to one of the projects in this study and there are children there who do attend these and other alternative schools. But the majority of children in all the projects attend the schools which are more or less encircled by the projects. To know how parents in the projects learn about educational alternatives and to assess their attitudes about their children's education would require systematic survey sampling of households with school-age children. In addition, the New York City Schools now have a highly efficient data base on pupil school attendance and achievement with which one could in principle track all the students from each project. These considerable research efforts would enable one to move from ecological to individual level analysis, a condition which also applies to the measures we provide for crime in the four projects.

Crime and the Drug Epidemic

Zion Hill exhibits lower crime rates (as measured by New York City Housing Police figures on crime complaints per 1000 residents) than does Mission City with which it was matched. Novarios also shows a lower jump in crime complaints between 1986 and 1987 than did Pepsi Market Apartments. 1986–87 crime data were used to make the initial project selection, but when we obtained a longer series of crime data only Mission City, among the four, continued to stand out as a project with consistently higher crime rates. But this difference is also a reflection of the higher rates of housing abandonment around Mission City and its location further away from the center of social services in the Harlem community.

In comparison with the entire city, the overall rate of index crime complaints is far lower in public housing. TABLE 1 shows that for the entire city in 1988 there were slightly over 98 index crime complaints per 1000 persons while the corresponding rate for all city public housing was 46.0. This difference would be entirely counter-intuitive except that when one disaggregates the overall rate into complaints of crimes against persons (especially murder, rape, robbery, and aggravated assault) the rate for the entire city was 22.3 compared to 26.8 for public housing. The real difference in rates is explained by complaints of crimes against property for which the city rate was 75.9 while for public housing it was 19.1. Measured by crimes against persons, Public housing environments are slightly more dangerous than the city as a whole but there are few automobiles and luxury possessions there to attract high levels of property crime. The reader must be warned, however, that none of the rates for public housing use actual population figures in calculating risk or exposure. Denominators are official occupancy figures. No one knows how many persons are doubled up in the apartments. The Authority's citywide estimate is 100,000 but many system managers place the figure closer to 120,000 or 150,000 or more. In the aggregate this means that Public Housing crime rates are inflated and the situation is somewhat better than it would appear with regard, for example, to crimes against the person. Unfortunately the epidemic of adolescent violence and involvement in the drug industry gravely affects all the projects. A relatively small number of violent adolescents and young adults can terrorize entire neighborhoods. Successful and less successful projects may be equally threatened by gang violence and criminal victimization associated with the crack epidemic and the ever more widespread distribution of lethal handguns.

Increases in crime rates for the city and the Housing Authority projects since the crack epidemic began around 1983 are dramatic. Within Housing Authority projects rates of aggravated assault have increased 111.6 percent, murder and non-negligent manslaughter by 118.5 percent, and complaints of sales of heroin and cocaine by 370 percent. Between 1987 and 1988 complaints of possession of dangerous weapons increased by 30 percent in the authority and 10 percent in the city. Similar increases in these crimes have occurred in the four projects we are working in. Significantly, between 1984 and 1988 Novarios and Pepsi market Houses experienced almost a tripling in the number of complaints of sale of cocaine and heroin (from 0.5/1000 residents to 3.0) while at Mission City the rate increased from 1.0 to 5.2. At Zion Hill, remarkably, the rate went from 0.5 to 0.0. The fact that there were no recorded complaints of sale of cocaine and heroin at Zion Hill in 1988, in the midst of a severe drug epidemic, is perhaps the best indicator of the relative success of tenants and management there.

The Projects and the Race-Class Divide

Whatever differences in outcome or organization one discovers in these four projects it is worthwhile to note that all four are considered by personnel of the Housing Authority and professionals in the community to be tough, segregated areas where children and adolescents are significantly "at risk." They all have the reputation of being challenging managerial assignments and difficult environments because they exist within larger neighborhoods that are terribly run down and plagued by every form of urban blight. None are show places. Among community leaders with whom we spoke during the early selection process, Mission city and Pepsi Market were regarded as having worse reputations than Zion Hill and Novarios. Yet in the early 1970s Zion Hill had such a poor reputation for its management and tenant problems (despite the relative success of its adolescents) that many tenants there were extremely dissatisfied. By the mid-1980s emergency steps were taken to 'turn the project around.' New and more energetic managers were appointed, improvements were made in the physical environment, and the name of the project was changed. As is evident from the quantitative indicators, these measures continue to have positive effect and will become part of the story we return to in explaining more about adolescent outcomes.

To further situate the four projects in Manhattan's social ecology we prepared a series of spatial-demographic maps, two of which are reproduced in this paper (FIGS. 1 and 2). For each of Manhattan's Census Block Groups (groups of two or three blocks within Census Tracts) we calculated the Ricketts-Sawhill indicators for a neighborhood's "underclass" status. These indicators are percent female-headed households, percent households receiving AFDC payments, percent males over age sixteen who are out of the labor force, and percent children under eighteen who are out of school. If a Block Group scored more than one standard deviation from the city mean on each of these four indicators the number "4" is printed at exactly the geographic coordinates of that area. If three indicators are one standard deviation above the city mean the program prints a three and so on. Ricketts, Sawhill, Mincy and others consider underclass neighborhoods to

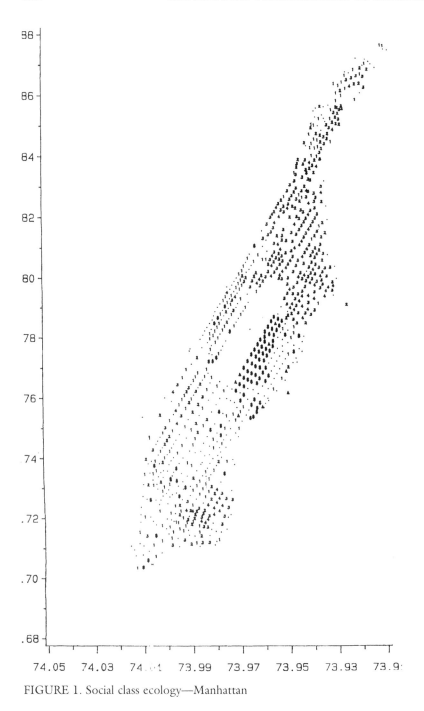

FIGURE 1. Social class ecology—Manhattan

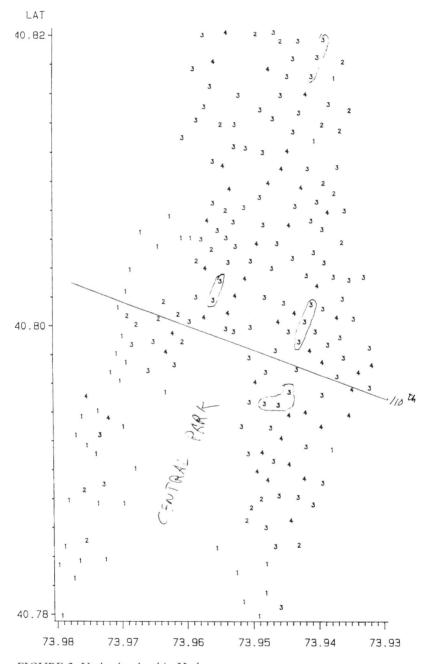

FIGURE 2. Underclass level in Harlem

be those which receive scores of four. Their research uses the Census Tract definition of a neighborhood. Use of the smaller Block Groups allow for more "fined grained" analysis of urban neighborhoods and allows one to compare the blocks in which our housing projects are located with the blocks surrounding the projects.

In addition to the four indicators of low neighborhood status, we calculated whether a Block Group fell within the top ten percent of household income for 1980. If it did so we printed a dollar sign at the geographic coordinates. Where a Manhattan block group would have had both a dollar sign indicating high income and one or more of the lower status indicators, our program places a "delta" at the appropriate coordinates. Where a block group scores neither high on income nor fulfills any of the low status criteria, our program prints a period (".") at the exact coordinates. The resulting map is a plot of what can be roughly considered to be the social class ecology of a city or part of a city, in this case of Manhattan.

These maps call attention to the fact that the housing projects do not satisfy ecological criteria for underclass areas. Yet as we have already noted with reference to housing abandonment and crime, the neighborhoods surrounding them usually do. More striking in the map of "Manhattan's Social Class Ecology" is the stark contrast between the East Side "gilded ghetto" and the neighborhoods to the North of Manhattan's 96th Street race-class divide. Few if any urban areas of the United States display as extensive and abrupt a gap between the "haves and have-nots." Below 96th Street apartments often sell for over $200,000 a room; above that divide one can buy an entire building with thirty or more families living in it for about the same amount. Below 96th Street are some of the nation's greatest cultural institutions, the Metropolitan Museum of Art, the Guggenheim, the Whitney, and many of its greatest scientific and educational institutions including Rockefeller University, Cornell-New York Hospital and others. Above 96th Street, in New York's Puerto Rican "Barrio" and in the more African American neighborhoods of Central and West Harlem the influences of race and relative poverty (and increasingly of immigration from Latin America) combine to limit investment and concentrate the ravages of alcohol, drugs and violence. The irony of public housing in this context is that were it not for this irreplaceable stock of low rent shelter, the rate of homelessness and building abandonment in the community would be even greater than it is. The great churches and venerable community institutions of Harlem would have even fewer stable households to attract. Yet given the continuing fear of investors about financing new construction in the ghetto, the projects are themselves a perceived obstacle to "redevelopment." But if Manhattan is to retain its minority working class, the public housing projects need to be viewed as assets of the community and the city . Their value should become more evident with a closer look at how the residents strive to keep them livable as places to raise children.

Challenges for Tenant Organizations and Management

The quality of local tenant organization and the conduct of everyday cooperation between tenants and project managers seems to account for the relative success of a project like Zion Hill or Novarios when compared with Mission City or Pepsi Market. This is the central finding of our field research to date . It suggests that efforts at tenant "empowerment" over the previous decades have had tangible results. But there are a number of related observations which qualify this very general point. First, neither tenant organization nor effective managerial operations seem sufficient as explanations of positive outcomes for project adolescents. Both are necessary but it is especially in the interaction between tenant councils and managers and leaders in larger community and city agencies that successful interventions are developed. Second, the relative success of the projects does not always produce visible results in the external environment of the projects or in positive adolescent outcomes. Teenagers circulate in a wider network of peer groups than those of the projects. The existence of a violent peer group in a project's vicinity, or negative changes in the climate of social control outside a project can, in the short run at least, outweigh the diligent efforts of tenants and managers. Third, tenant empowerment appears to increase the density of kinship attachments among tenants. We know from interviews with tenants that many have kin in their own projects, but more precise measurement of kin networks would require household sampling. We also know that the tenants' desire to populate their projects with kin and friends favors social control and positive outcomes for project adolescents but also works against the goal of more universal selection in public housing. A solution to this problem which would also benefit the surrounding community exists in the city's program of satellite housing and rehabilitation with ownership options. The remaining sections of this paper elaborate on these observations.

Projects by Day and Night

At some times of the afternoons the courtyards of Harlem public housing projects ring with the sounds of youth and neighborliness. One good time to watch the public life of a project is in the mid-afternoon as the children and teenagers are arriving home from school, and one can witness what Jane Jacobs might have called "the children's ballet in a public housing courtyard."

[Excerpt from field notes] Novarios, East Harlem. Wednesday, September 13, 1989, 2:30PM, seated on a bench near _____ Avenue and 100th Street.

A bright clear day, the children and teenagers are just returning from school. A line of third or fourth graders crosses the avenue with three adult monitors, women teacher's aids, who walk them past my bench into the courtyard where they are dismissed. In an instant the orderly line breaks into a joyous running jumble as the children dash in different directions toward their apartments. At least five women with carriages, and another dozen or more without strollers or carriages stand in small clusters near the crossing. There are many greetings and casual conversations going on, but all are watching the stream of children departing the school and gathering at the avenue crossing. There are smiles of greeting as the children zip by, and here and there a mother departs toward her apartment to join her children. When a line of smaller children crosses the avenue, women hurry toward the little ones. There are shy greetings and hugs as mothers steer these neophyte students away from their new classmates and toward their buildings.

Engrossed in watching the Novarios mothers greet their little ones, we are startled to realize that all around us are groups of children, ages about eight to ten or eleven. The section of the project court where we are seated has become a riot of children's play. Balls bounce everywhere, ropes swing, there are tag games galore and whistles and shouting. Boys and girls' groups are separate, of course. Most groups number about six or less. At some of the apartment entrances I notice older women, alone or in small groups who greet the arriving children and teens. Teen groups are gathering near the benches by the basketball courts. Racially all the groups appear to be unsegregated, that is one cannot recognize any patterns of separate Puerto Rican and black association either among the children or the parents.

Now the older kids are returning from junior high school and high school. Boys on bikes whiz by. Girls swing their bags and giggle at each other. From the entrances near our bench we count seven teenage boys who leave their buildings separately with smaller kids in tow. These seem to be the older brothers who have places to take the younger ones (perhaps to activities in the nearby settlement houses or community centers). Everywhere one looks there are children at play, and not far away there are adults watching, not only the mothers and grandmothers but many of the men of the project, especially the grounds workers and the older men who cluster in their usual corners of the courts.

On a school day afternoon there are few clues as to why children in and around these project neighborhoods are being shot or otherwise hurt in record numbers. If one watches carefully it is possible to spot a few clusters of teenagers which include some who are ready to steer customers toward a crack spot nearby. Or close by each of the projects one might spot a teenage and young adult crap game which attracts those drifting toward the faster track of street life. But these groups are small in number compared to the hundreds of children and teens who are playing at the same games of their contemporaries in any other American city neighborhood. During the day there is ample evidence of the work parents and older siblings put into the safety of their children. In each project one can spot the presence of tenant volunteers stationed outside the building entrances watching for suspicious characters. They watch at the doors, ready to lend a hand or to break up disputes and fights among the children.

From what one observes of children's supervision and the evidence of informal and formal watching after school there are no easily visible difference in the four projects. Inside the buildings, however, differences do appear with regard to how well each building and each floor is monitored. The most effective tenant councils, such as that of Zion Hill, are able to maintain the greatest extent of coverage and representation in all the project buildings and most of its 140 floors. This coverage translates into more effective, voluntary monitoring of the courtyards and interior commons areas.

Night imposes a social frontier in and around the projects. The problems of life in poor Communities and the effects of the current crisis on the housing project environments are far more evident at night. When the smaller children and their parents or siblings are home in the evening the project court yards and sometimes the hallways become the turf of teenagers and young adults. "Sometimes when I come home early in the morning " explains Kenya James, a young man from Pepsi Market, "I see people that's been out there all night. I mean these are not only kids, there are men and women that's out there too. I guess some are enticed with the drug game too. How are you going to stop kids from getting into it when, you know, when you got older people out there doing the same thing? It might be illegal as to law, but as to really law, it's not. It's separate." The conflicting moral systems of the larger society and the street is one of the troubling facts of their lives that teenagers and adults in the projects most often mention with a sense of both fear and bravado tinged, at times, with envy. Thus the same teenager from Pepsi Market observed that, "Some projects [names a middle income one nearby], that's a good one, you know because they have security. They have security guards. The intercoms are on the outside. It's like, it's almost like, if I didn't know any better I'd say, you know, its, those are for the better people. For people, we're not, like I'm not qualified to live in projects like that. And its just that some projects are better than others." Boys like Kenya with whom we speak in the projects yearn to escape their neighborhoods, by which they mean the public housing projects and the surrounding streets where, especially at night, they feel the ambiguity of values and suffer constant pressure to conform to conflicting codes of conduct.

Late at night the streets around the projects become (in this time of economic and social crisis) the turf of the addicted and the dealers, the prostitutes and tricks and drug coppers and cops. The majority of parents in the projects are straight, early risers who impose curfews and otherwise try to keep their children at home or in safe places. Above all they want to keep them out of the dark school yards and parks where the youth "mobs" gather to party. But this is extremely difficult. The kids know each other since early childhood They do not always see the dangers as being so immediate as do their parents. This is especially true of the most impressionable preadolescents and young teenagers who crave older teenage role models. Besides,"this is the big city, what good is it to stay shut up in the room?" complain the teenagers. Yet over and again we hear parents speak of how they resort to locking their teenage children at home in the evenings thus becoming their jailors. Effective tenant councils like that of Zion Hill can relieve this stress on parents somewhat by providing supervised community rooms for the teenagers to gather in at night. But even these most effective projects are limited in their repertoire by the tenants' lack of resources and time and ability to work with the teenagers.

Tenant Councils and Local Responsibility

Tenant Councils in New York public housing tend to be extremely active organizations. They meet once a month and more often as needed. Some have standing committees but others only form them when there is a crisis or special need. Representatives to the councils are the floor and building captains, ideally (but rarely ever in fact) one person for each floor in each building. Attendance is usually limited, even the most active Councils, to the usual dedicated minority. The best Tenant councils, such as the one at Zion Hill, maintain close contact with those who are not able to attend meetings regularly and in these successful Councils there is a wide spectrum of tenants (by age, gender, parental status, *etc.*) represented among the activists. Through the activities of the tenant councils the housing projects can become mobilized in a way almost unheard of in the surrounding neighborhoods, except those which have very active block associations. As Zion Hill's Manager says, "We consult with the tenants on every issue there is. They have to be on every decision. We are changing windows now; they have to have a say in choosing the type of frames and the color of the trim." Neighborhood block associations, in comparison to the tenant councils in the projects, are voluntary groups which struggle to represent a smaller population in the forum of community politics or in the community meetings of the Police Department. The tenant council of a major project, in contrast, has a direct link to the resources of the Housing Authority, itself a powerful city agency, as well as all the access a block association might have to other community institutions. The Tenant Councils also have some degree of influence over common resources within the project and these may be considerable. In this sense alone the housing project and its tenant council represent a node of organization in low income communities around which efforts to protect children and enhance their development can coalesce.

In the past year one tenant council in a large Central Harlem housing project, not one of the four included in this study, has maintained a rather successful rent strike in protest over policy differences with the Housing Authority. Other tenant associations, including all those in the projects where we conducted research, were actively involved (on an informal basis) in the mayoral primaries and general election, serving as local political organizations and attempting to mobilize a large vote to demonstrate organizational effectiveness. As a consequence of their larger political activities in some projects there is a tendency for the Council to become far more visible in its influence and demands than the project managers. Mr. J., the manager of Mission City projects says apologetically, "We [managers] come and go. The tenant president has the power to talk to tenants in getting me out of here [fired]. The days when the manager makes the final decisions about tenant life is no longer the case. I don't overstep my bounds, I don't run meetings. They [the tenants] establish the agenda." Division between management and tenant council leadership can undermine the legitimacy and effectiveness of local managers and in the long run weaken the ability of the project to marshall resources from the Authority and from other agencies of city government.

Creating Safe Niches in the Projects

To the outsider the projects appear to be looming, anonymous cityscapes. For project neighbors, however, their efforts at enhancing social control may impart a sense that the projects afford relatively safe niches for their children. This perception was well expressed by Mrs. V., a tenant and organizer of the tenant-run after school program at Pepsi Market Apartments:

> This particular development is very close knit. I mean you send your kids outside and you know you're going to have four or five people watching your child. And like with me, it's like all of the kids are here, I mean they know that I could tell their mother or grandmother, their aunt, their uncle, you know. So knowing that someone like that is looking over them it's—it makes them feel good because they run up the street and they are made to feel loved. There's somebody else out there hugging on them and kissing them other than their families. And that's primarily how I grew up. I was raised in these projects you know. Everybody was my mother.

On this comparative dimension of how well the projects actually succeed in creating safe niches for their children, Mission City and Zion Hill represent two ends of a continuum along which Novarios and Pepsi Market are positioned more in the center. Mission City, with the poorest outcomes for adolescent achievement, has the least success in creating safe niches for child development. Ironically, the project is reputed to have a strong Council directed by a veteran tenant organizer. Ms. B., the Mission City Council President is thought to be extremely powerful inside and outside the project. She is at the center of a network of other tenant organizers and community political activists, all from outside Mission City. Her advice is continually sought after by political candidates. She is a classical leader who can deliver gains to a constituency because of her ability to mobilize resources outside the neighborhood. Yet the tenant council she leads represents a project which seems to be doing worst in terms of adolescent outcomes. Part of the problem seems to be that while the tenant organization and their leader have the reputation for being forceful and unified, in fact this is not always the case. Mrs. B. is often opposed by some of the younger women in the project who think she and her supporters are not doing enough to mobilize the tenants in the more problematic buildings and are not doing enough to promote the creation of a safe niches for the children. There is grumbling at Mission City that the tenants and their organization are not doing enough to increase representation in the buildings where drug use is high and where breezeways and commons areas have become dominated by "the crack people."

One problem with tenant organization at Mission City is that there is presently an involvement gap between the older and the younger tenants. Ms. B.'s organization of tenant activists, which has maintained her in office for over fifteen years, tends to rely heavily on a "grandmother network" in Mission City. The organization has not worked to include a representative array of younger parents and female heads of households. On the other hand Ms. B. is such a strong personality and commands so much respect within the Authority and the community that on occasion she can personally countermand the desires of the Mission City manager. As noted earlier, the project manager seems to be intimidated by Ms. B. and the tenant council. In consequence there are delays and missed opportunities in developing programs and in starting efforts to increase local social control. Neither the tenant council nor the project management seem to get as much done in caring for the grounds, in maintaining apartments, or in mobilizing the efforts of local professionals on behalf of project tenants, as do the three others, and especially Zion Hill. Even more significantly, the buildings which are known to be dangerous because of loitering and drug use also tend to be buildings in which the tenant association has only token representation. While to the outside observers Mission City has the reputation for having a strong and effective tenant council, these problems prevent it from actually performing as well as others in our study.

As noted earlier, in the 1970s Zion Hill had an extremely poor reputation until steps were taken to "turn it around." One of those steps was to assign forceful, energetic managers who themselves had "been raised in the projects." This is a recruitment strategy which has become more common throughout the Housing Authority and seems to have had a positive effect in remedying the situation at Zion Hill. At this time the project is no showplace, but tenants and managers have a strong sense that it is "moving in the right direction." They are especially pleased about a multi-million dollar program of building refurbishment which will begin to be implemented this year and which will include tenant involvement in every phase. As Ms. J., the Project Manager explains it, "When I got here a few years ago I had to really assert myself and show the tenant council that I had my job to do and they had theirs. We were going to cooperate to get things done or I was not going to be with them for very long." Ms. J. believes it is critical that the tenant association have depth of active membership and be active in all the buildings, a managerial stance which does not appear in our observations and interviews to be so clearly operating in the other three projects.

Novarios and Pepsi Market Apartments also have active tenant association and competent managers. In both projects, however, there are buildings which are less organized than is desirable. Thus the tenant association president from Pepsi Market Apartments noted that, "We do have floor captains but we have not gone all out like we should to have floor captains. But they do work, it works to have somebody responsible for your floor. When someone new comes into your building its good to have someone in the building talk to them and say 'look, this is what we do, these are our rules and regulations, and you know we can help you.'" Differences we observe in the projects' tenant associations—either in their patterns of mobilization or in coverage of individual buildings—are not traceable to the mix of African American and Puerto Rican households in the four projects. The most salient differences among the four seem to be those which explain the degree of effective coordination of efforts between councils and managers and the success of efforts by the tenants and their formal organization to recruit trustworthy project neighbors.

Recruitment of Kin and Friends as Neighbors

The first line of defense for tenants of the housing projects is to seek some control over who becomes a tenant and who remains one. When Gerald Suttles (1969) studied neighborhoods of low-rise tenements (Chicago "three flats") and public housing he found that housing project neighbors often felt they lacked control over their surroundings and lacked the ability to express their own individual personalities and preferences through their physical environment. In this time of epidemic and violence these genuine complaints give way to more desperate feelings. Project tenants may feel safer inside their apartments than do the residents of surrounding neighborhoods, but they wish to make their projects more secure by increasing the density of people among their neighbors whom they know and can trust.

We continually hear tenants and managers speak of their longterm friends and kin who live in their buildings and elsewhere in the same projects. The residential stability of the projects itself is product of the tenants limited alternatives on the housing market and the fact that people do not wish to leave neighbors and kin with whom they have lived much of their adult lives. On entering any building in the four projects one is likely to be helped to find the desired apartment by a woman or man who has been living there a long time and who delights in showing newcomers that the building and the project are peopled by neighbors, not anonymous strangers. This phenomenon is not limited to those projects with better outcomes in our design, although as a quantitative trait there may be differences in the density of networks among the four.

The politics of the tenant selection process is a constant matter for debate and action in the Tenant Councils. In New York public housing, as elsewhere, tenant influence is most often exerted through the formal and informal activities of the managers and leaders of the Tenant Council. All the Tenant Councils endeavor to assist trustworthy tenants in their efforts to bring other segments of their extended families into the project. In addition, they may help families obtain larger apartments when children with children of their own seek to move in with parent-leaseholders. This pattern of tenant selection often conflicts with more universalistic criteria of selection and there are innumerable subtle ways in which bargaining and influence are brought to bear to arrive at compromises between the principles of kin selection and waiting-list primacy. As a result, every housing project is to some degree a neighborhood of kin folk and friends of long standing. Only apartment-to-apartment sample survey research might reveal the detailed ecology of kin and friendship networks which operate in a large housing project. Our hypothesis is that successful adolescent outcomes vary directly with the extensiveness of these kin and friendship networks and the manner in which their resource sharing contributes to the creation of safe niches for the project teenagers. We suspect this is true, but do not know from our research to date if Zion Hill, for example, has more extensive kin and friendship networks among the families with adolescent children than do the other projects.

There are stringent limits on the politics of kin selection. The Housing Authority must insist on its criteria of assignment to housing and there is only so much influence even the most effective tenant association can bring to bear on direct tenant selection. This is particularly true as waiting lists expand and the Authority comes under increasing pressure to admit the neediest families among the city's homeless. Faced with emergency situations in shelter, health, drugs, and gang violence all the projects are relative centers of calm in a storm of social crisis. But housing project neighbors and activists can also be overwhelmed by the demands placed on their resources of time and courage.

Zion Hill and the Limits of Local Initiative

During the initial months of our field research there were a number of tragedies involving children and teenagers from the projects and the surrounding Harlem blocks. These events highlight the strengths of effective tenant organization in response to crisis and they also point to the limits of local empowerment. Our field notes and the writing of the teenagers with whom we work define a frightening environment of violence through which most children somehow must pass on their way to successful development. One episode in particular demonstrates the strengths and limitations of housing neighborhoods when confronted with these dangers.

Two primary school-age children from Zion Hill were abducted from a nearby New York City managed playground in the spring of 1989. They have never been found. Despite all their efforts to control their environment and improve their housing project, Zion Hill's tenants felt terribly violated and demoralized by this sudden tragedy. A short time later two project teenagers suspected of involvement in the drug trade were assassinated in a neighboring project. Not long thereafter a jogger was raped in Central Park after a night of marauding by crews of teenagers, some of whom came from Zion Hill and other projects in this study (as well as from many other neighborhoods and middle-income projects). All the press attention centered on the Central Park rape, none on the other crimes. The leaders and activists at Zion Hill did not lose time complaining of the imbalance in reporting. They decided to act quickly and take more forceful steps to remove crack dealers from the streets adjacent to the project. They forced the police to arrest local dealers and forced other agencies of city government to inspect the buildings where crack dealing had been occurring. In one case they were successful in having an entire abandoned building directly across from the projects torn down entirely. Removal of this dangerous center of the drug industry hardly ended the risks to children in and around the Zion Hill project nor was it seen as a great victory of the tenant council and project manager. It could not, after all, bring the lost and dead children back. It was therefore, a victory that could only remind everyone involved that far more needed to be done than even the most effective tenants and managers could accomplish on their own.

CONCLUSION: ON PROJECTS AS STRATEGIC NEIGHBORHOODS

We have tried to show that it is possible to find housing projects which resemble one another on most physical and demographic dimensions and yet appear to differ in the success with which they provide adequate and safe environments for child development. Having located such differing projects, we have begun to explore some of the organizational features which distinguish the most successful among them. Relative success in exerting local social control emerges as the strongest explanation for the qualitative differences we describe. But we have also identified some of the limitations inherent in a focus on local empowerment at a time of macrosocial decline. While there are many more questions we intend to pursue in our research on teenagers and young adults in public housing environments, we wish to conclude this paper by posing only two of them. First, what are the strengths and weaknesses of these particular projects as strategic research sites for the study of successful adolescence in public housing? Second, what are some of the implications of our research to date for thinking about public housing in the United States.

The comparison between Zion Hill and Mission City appears from the quantitative indicators and from our field research to date to be rather marked and likely to hold through further investigation. Where Pepsi Market and Novarios fall on a continuum of adolescent success and local social control is less clear. Nor is it clear for any of the projects how well the ecological differences in outcome would predict quantitative indicators at the individual household level. Any decision about gathering household data, therefore, could be better informed by further demographic and ecological research which examines 1990 census data for the projects and which analyzes individual school records and vital statistics for project households. If these data show outcome differences continuing to hold (or that they have changed in important ways) it would suggest that there are indeed strategic comparisons that warrant more individual level data. Corroboration of the outcome differences that we believe do exist among these projects would also suggest new directions for our participant observation at the projects. Even if differences in outcomes for children and families prove not to hold in the directions we have them so far, we believe that together these four Harlem projects are strategic sites. We intend to continue our work in and around them because of their importance in the Harlem community and because of the balance they offer, even with their faults exposed, to the terribly distorted views which dominate most rhetoric about public housing in the United States.

Today in the United States there are about 3.5 million people living in 1.3 million public housing rental units administered by about 3,000 Public Housing Authorities. Two thirds of these housing units are administered by 134 large authorities which manage over 1,250 units each. Sixty three percent of all public housing units are occupied by families, and "76 percent of family households have a female head, 75 percent are minority, and 59 percent receive welfare payments" (U.S. Dept. of Housing & Urban Development 1988, p.8). In 1979 H.U.D. researchers found that approximately 7 percent of all public housing projects (containing about 180,000 or 15 percent of all units) were "troubled" either due to extreme physical deterioration or because of the kind of social ills which make projects like Robert Taylor such difficult places to raise children (Wilson 1987).

In France, to choose a Western industrial democracy not always cited as a marvel of social democratic policy, there are over 12 million people living in public housing of every description. There are also far more ways in which public sector housing can be planned and constructed than exist in the United States. The widespread belief in the United States that the public sector cannot build or manage decent housing must be in some degree an explanation for the U.S. failure to adequately house its poor and lower wage, working class citizens. Thus it is extremely useful to conduct research on projects in New York where there is a long and diverse record of experience with public housing.

About 600,000 adults and children now reside in the city's public housing, a population that would constitute the nation's nineteenth largest city. This population (about 20 percent of the nation's total) includes upwards of 120,000 persons who are "doubled" up in housing apartments. Were it not for the over 350 projects now in existence the city's homeless problem would be far worse even than it is. Among researchers at the federal Department of Housing and Urban Development New York City public housing has the reputation of being better designed and constructed and generally better managed than that of most other U.S. cities. Naturally there are housing critics from all ideological perspectives who dispute this claim. Some point out that it does not apply equally to all the city's projects. Others argue that relative success should not become a rationale for maintaining the patterns of racial and class segregation which public housing fostered. Still others are more interested in proving that public housing stimulates isolation and long-term dependencies. Lack of adequate research on life in public housing has only encouraged the din of debate and pronouncement. Indeed, Rachel G. Bratt concludes her extraordinarily useful assessment of the U.S. public housing record by noting that "a great deal more needs to be learned about what makes a problem housing authority. Research is needed on why some housing authorities have been successful, while others have failed. Similarly we know very little about why some projects in a given city are virtually trouble-free, while others, often only a few blocks away, are public disgraces" (Bratt 1989, p.85). To this point we would only add the observation that there is a great deal more to be learned about the role of public housing as bases of organization and activism in rebuilding the large community and city.

ACKNOWLEDGMENTS

The Authors wish to thank Richard Jessor, Thomas Cook, Katherine Newman, John Goering, Rosa Carillo, Huang Qi, James Beshers, Jose Figueroa, Margorie Innocent, and Alicia Smidt-Comacho.

REFERENCES

BRATT, RACHAEL G.
    1989   *Rebuilding a Low-Income Housing Policy* Philadelphia: Temple University Press.
CLARK, KENNETH
    1964   *Youth in the Ghetto*. New York: HARYOU.
NEW YORK CITY DEPARTMENT OF HEALTH
    1989   *Vital Statistics for New York City*.
TERRY, DON.
    1991   Project tenants see islands of safety wasting away. *New York Times*, February, 4 p. A1.

U.S. DEPARTMENT OF HOUSING AND URBAN DEVELOPMENT.
    1988   *Study of the Modernization Needs of the Public and Indian Housing Stock*. Cambridge, MA: Abt Associates, Inc., March.
VERGARA, CAMILO JOSE.
    1989   Hell in a very tall place. *The Atlantic Monthly*, September, pp. 72–78.
WILLIAMS, TERRY AND WILLIAM KORNBLUM,
    1994   *The Uptown Kids, Struggle and Hope in the Projects*. New York: Putnam.
WILSON, WILLIAM JULIUS.
    1987   *The Truly Disadvantaged*. Chicago: The University of Chicago Press.

"Mi Sacrificio Bien Pago"[1]
Puerto Rican Women on Welfare and Family Values

ROSA M. TORRUELLAS[†]

Language and Education Task Force
Center for Puerto Rican Studies
Hunter College
City University of New York
New York, New York 10021

INTRODUCTION

This paper aims to explore and to explode some deeply ingrained popular myths about poor women of color in general and Puerto Rican mothers on welfare in particular. It will examine how these women construct very powerful gender identities that challenge the uninformed representations of behavior upon which major negative stereotypes are built. And it will show the potential of ethnographic analysis in elaborating alternative understandings of the lived experience of poor and oppressed peoples in the United States.

This paper is based on an extensive study carried out by a team of researchers from the Centro de Estudios Puertorriqueños, with a group of 16 Puerto Rican women in *El Barrio,* East Harlem (Benmayor *et al.* 1992; Torruellas *et al.* 1990). I have known most of these women since 1985, when they enrolled in the El Barrio Popular Education Program, a community-based, Spanish literacy project that was created by the Centro, and which I had major responsibility for developing and directing.

I would like to share with you some of the knowledge we gained by doing life histories with these women. Although our intent was to better understand the dynamics of an educational empowerment process, including the relationship between personal and collective transformation, we chose not to circumscribe the life history interview questions to this particular topic. Instead, we wanted the women to structure their accounts as they saw fit, to let them speak about the issues *they* considered relevant in their lives.

---

[1] "My sacrifices paid off."
[†] Deceased.

And speak they did. The initial generating prompt on our part, "*Cuénteme la historia de su vida*" [Tell me your life story], resulted in an explosion of stories, anecdotes, reflections and discussions, about work, education, politics, life in Puerto Rico and in New York, the migration experience, traditional values, poverty, public assistance and *la familia* [THE FAMILY].

We were struck by the fact that the women's positive self-representations and identifications offered a stark contrast to the bleak portrayals of poor Puerto Rican women used in current poverty debates, and in the popular media. It is hard to believe that the hard-working, determined, responsible, resilient women whose stories we heard, are the supposedly lazy, unmotivated, parasitic, state-cheating welfare mothers both the news media and politicians are blaming for everything from the disintegration of traditional family values to the current economic recession (Chávez 1991). The fact that poverty is the most potent factor limiting the options and shaping the life choices of these and other women of color does not seem to be an issue in these debates. In fact, poverty has been turned from a systemic problem of social inequality into a personal issue of "dysfunctional" behavior.

There have been many attempts to assess the impact of various social and economic variables on poverty in the Puerto Rican community. These include the structural transformation which brought a decline in manufacturing sector jobs in the New York City economy since the 1960s (Torres and Bonilla 1993; discrimination in the labor market (Meléndez *et al.* 1991); the failure of the public schools to educate minority children (Aspira 1983); a pattern of circular migration between Puerto Rico and the United States (History Task Force 1979; *cf.* Bean and Tienda 1987); and selective migration of the poorest Puerto Ricans into New York City (Gurak and Falcón 1990).

All too often, however, explanations are based on cultural deficit models that attribute poverty to flaws in the character and behavior of Puerto Ricans. In fact, we are seeing a resurgence of the basic tenets of the culture of poverty theory, as proposed by Oscar Lewis in *La Vida* (1966), his classic study of "100 Puerto Rican families from four slums of San Juan and of their relatives in New York City" (xviii). In the prologue to the book, Lewis summarizes his approach:

> As an anthropologist I have tried to understand poverty and its associated traits as a culture or, more accurately, as a subculture with its own structure and rationale, as a way of life which is passed down from generation to generation along family lines (xiii).

Few social scientists today would claim adherence to this discredited theoretical framework, yet many are elaborating their studies of poverty upon the paradigm of the so called "underclass." The term, used by William J. Wilson (1987) to explain poverty in the Black community, refers to population groups affected by a host of social pathologies associated with inner-city life: high rates of joblessness, drugs, crime, female-headed households, and welfare dependency. Although Wilson attempted to link these social conditions to more structural factors, including the changing class structure of inner-city neighborhoods, the "underclass debate" has focused primarily on the anti-social behaviors that are said to be both the cause and the consequence of living in extreme poverty (Focus 1989). And while Wilson's research concentrated on poor urban African Americans, the term has been extended to other minority groups, including Puerto Ricans, who have been referred to as "the other underclass" (Lemann 1991).

By many measures, the women in this study would fit this categorization. They have little formal schooling, several of them having become literate only recently. They live on an income well below the poverty level. They have been away from the formal labor market for many years. Their primary or sole means of income is public assistance. And they are heads of household, most of them having raised their children on their own. A couple of years ago, a male Cuban journalist made the following remarks in a live television interview about Puerto Rican women who, like those in this study, were single mothers on welfare:

> . . . there is a grave family problem in the Puerto Rican ghettoes in the United States, where there are thousands of single mothers who are very young, who try to escape poverty through the welfare (system) or through new (male) companions that later leave (them) and leave other (new) children to aggravate the problem. With these conditions it is impossible to correctly raise and educate children that later will triumph in life. In conclusion, what is missing among the Puerto Ricans in the ghettoes in the United States are families, and that is the problem." [Carlos Montaner, translated transcript of live television interview on "*Portada*," Univisión, November 6, 1990].

The images that derive from these analyses are defeatist, weighty, fatalistic, providing little hope for even thinking the possibility of transformation. However, working with the Puerto Rican community in New York City has exposed me to a vitality and sense of purpose that belies the crushing portrayals that can only contribute to generate the oppressive conditions they purport to denounce.

I want to argue for constructing alternative ways of researching and explicating poverty that allow those more "intimate" understandings to surface. I want you to hear what the group of women we worked with had to say about being Puerto Rican, poor, female, being a mother, about raising children and being on welfare. These women's self-representation and gender identity seriously challenge the stereotyped assumptions upon which current poverty debates and welfare policy legislation rest. Allowing these "funds of knowledge" to guide the analysis results in a much richer and complex appreciation of the causes, consequences, and responses to poverty being elaborated by poor communities in their struggle to build a brighter future for themselves.

Y ASI PASÓ MI VIDA[2]: PRIORITIZING FAMILY

La familia [THE FAMILY] is one of the most significant sources of strength and emotional support for Puerto Rican women. A deep commitment to motherhood and to keeping the family together shape the decisions women make at particular points in their lives with regards to work, migration, marital status, and satisfaction of personal aspirations and needs. This became evident upon listening to the women's life histories. The self-constructed accounts, like their own lives, are organized around issues of domestic relations.

The life histories are as much personal narratives as they are historical accounts of a way of life in the rural Puerto Rico of the 1930s, '40s and '50s. From childhood, these women were socialized to assume major responsibility for family and home. The few of them who started school, were pulled out and enlisted to aid their parents in providing for the household. Cecilia González's story highlights the lack of social supports the women found for pursuing an education, as well as the pressures exerted by poverty on parents and children alike:

> I remember when I was in third grade, I had to work at a lady's house after school. . . . I remember when the lady sent for my mother and announced to her that she had to pull me out of school because I didn't have time to do my work well. . . . I looked at my mother like begging, "Don't pull me out of school" . . . . But since the situation was so difficult, the first thing my mother thought was, "Without her help . . . " My mother did not raise any objections. . . . She said, "All right, Lula, I'll pull her out of school". . . . I spent that night crying (Benmayor *et al.* 1992:69).

The decision not to send the girls to school responded to a large extent to the indigent conditions that characterized major segments of the Puerto Rican population at the time. As Mrs. González explains "*La situación estaba difícil, esa es la palabra. Eramos muchos. . . . Era una pobreza terrible.*" [Times were very rough, that's the truth. We were a large family. . . . And the poverty was terrible.] The development of agrarian capitalism after the 1898 U.S. invasion of Puerto Rico brought tremendous changes and upheavals to the insular economy during the first half of the century. Most of these women's families became part of the rural or urban proletariat, liv-

---

[2] "And that's how my life has been."

ing on well-below-subsistence wages. The whole family had to be put to work in order to survive.

But these economic determinants were also accompanied by ideological formulations that placed women's labor and future within the home. In this context, a formal education was not considered as necessary as practical socialization into female roles. Thus, domestic work, for wages or at home, became by definition these women's primary productive work from early on in their lives. Being directly linked to a gendered social division of labor, their identities as women and as workers merged and were forged upon a set of experiences and roles centered on the family.

As young adults, most of the women entered the formal labor market. The majority worked in the garment industry, a traditional source of employment for Puerto Rican women both on the Island and in the United States through the 1960s (Benmayor *et al.* 1988; Ortiz 1988). Others worked in candy, hair pin, belt, hat, yogurt cup, lamp, pocketbook, or any other of the numerous manufacturing factories that flourished during the economic expansion of the post war era. In effect, the women transferred the sewing, embroidering and other manual skills they had acquired doing domestic tasks at home into the new work setting.

The women's migration to New York during their youth was impelled by the same socioeconomic forces that sent more than a million Puerto Ricans to the United States from the late 1940s to the early 1960s (Bonilla and Campos 1986). Operation Bootstrap, the industrialization program aimed at developing an exports economy through heavy subsidies to U.S. capital, failed to produce enough jobs to substitute for those that were being lost in agriculture. Massive movements of people from rural to urban areas in Puerto Rico preceded the migration to the States.

At a personal level, the women's move to New York was motivated by the need and desire to find better employment opportunities and living conditions, or as they would put it, "*buscar ambiente*" [to find a better life]. In the words of Minerva Ríos:

> I was growing up and life was getting more expensive. So I said, "Well, I'm going to go to New York and at least I'll be able to help my family financially." So I did. My cousin sent me a ticket and I came (Benmayor *et al.* 1992:11).

And, she adds: "That's when hard times really began."

Being poor, these women grew up expecting having to work for the rest of their lives. And despite the fact that many of them have not held a waged job for years, and that their main or sole means of support is welfare, they would very strongly argue that they *have* worked hard all of their lives. Their accounts make clear that they feel deeply connected to "work," that they espouse a strong work ethic and that they view themselves as performing an invaluable social role, namely, that of taking care of and providing a nurturing environment for their children.

Upon marrying and becoming mothers, all but one of the women we interviewed left their paid jobs. They do not understand their decision to mean they turned their backs on work. On the contrary, they view their move as a continuation of the labor process they had been engaged in since childhood. Except this time, they focused their energy on developing and maintaining their new family. True to the American middle class ideal, they became housewives in nuclear households with a male bread-winner, even if temporarily.[3] Marriage and a male income allowed them to exercise an option—to stay home and raise their children themselves. However, this "choice" was also conditioned by a gender socialization based on a patriarchal ideology that ascribed decision-making and authority in the marriage to the man. Raquel Cossío recalled that: "*El nunca quiso que yo los diera a cuidar a nadie ni nada.*" [He (her husband) never wanted me to let anyone else take care of them (their children).]

In attempting to present the women's perspectives on the centrality of the family in their lives, I do not want to lose sight of the oppressive aspects of this institution. The picture of family life the women paint in their life histories is a complex one. Achievement stories are intermixed with stories of intense conflict. Raising children in a hostile social environment, with very scarce socioeconomic resources and other forms of support, placed severe stress on the women and the family as a whole. Moreover, most of these women experienced abuse or violence, during childhood or as adults. In several cases, the women could not take advantage of employment or educational options that became available, because of their spouse's whims. It is evident that these women's lives involve a continuous negotiation between the sustaining and the oppressive aspects of family life.

For many of the women shifts in marital status and income were the predominant reasons for their eventual turn to welfare.[4] In assuming the position as main provider for their families, they either had to find a job or

---

[3] As a middle class ideal, the notion of the nuclear family was also promoted in Puerto Rico, especially during the 1950s. Population control was one of the linchpins of "Operation Bootstrap," the industrialization plan for the island. Fully aware that this sort of economic "development" could not benefit the entire population, planners also put in place programs of female sterilization, ideological campaigns encouraging two-child nuclear families, and migration to the United States as strategic solutions. We should add that, in the U.S. context, the nuclear family was also an ideal espoused by the immigrant working class, as a symbol of progress.

[4] Historical research shows that this is not a recent development but has been true since colonial times (Abramovitz 1988). Today, households headed by single women are an increasingly common and permanent form of family structure in the United States. According to the 1980 Census, the percentage of female-headed families was 13.6 for non-Hispanic Whites, 40.6 for African Americans and 36.5 for Puerto Ricans (Bean and Tienda 1987:192). Data from the 1990 Census indicates that 16.5% of all families are headed by females and that the percentage for Puerto Ricans rose to 38.9% (Current Population Reports 1990:14-15). Yet, the nuclear family as a form of household organization remains a socially sanctioned ideal. Being

another source of income. Sometimes, the women tried to explore their options in the labor force once again, only to be faced head-on with the hard realities of a constricted labor market. For example, when her youngest child reached the age of sixteen, Mrs. González separated from her husband. She immediately looked for work. She found a job in a garment sweatshop, which turned out to be a "fly by night" operation and left her suddenly unemployed. She went on to a series of short-term factory jobs, the last of which she lost because of factory relocation. Through an agency, she was then employed as a homecare attendant for senior citizens. Since this paid so little, she was forced to work at night, cleaning offices. She recalls her experience:

> Any which way, things were tough. While I was working those two jobs, and since I've always suffered from asthma and allergies, I got very sick. I had to give up my jobs. I fought to get "disability," but I didn't get it. [Meanwhile] I would have to drag myself to work because I was very, very sick. They [her employers] were the ones who gave me a letter to apply for welfare (Benmayor *et al.* 1992:121).

For others, displacement from the labor market due to factory closings, or illness was the primary reason why they came to rely on welfare. Whichever circumstances accounted for the women's becoming welfare recipients, however, they do not see themselves as taking advantage of the system or, to use a popular image, "sponging off" the state. On the contrary, they view their being on welfare as a strategy that has allowed them to fulfill their most productive gender and social responsibility.

The women acknowledge, though, that prioritizing *la familia*, has placed a heavy toll on their personal lives. Most of them had to wait well into their adult lives to fulfill their long-deferred dream of getting an education. Most of them remained single at least until their children were older, not wanting, in their words to "*ponerle otro padre a mis hijos*" [give my children another father]. They admitted that they often felt lonely. However, they also explained that their time was very scarce for anything but the children. Mrs. de Jesús remembers the details of her life as her kids were growing up:

or becoming a single head of household carries with it a negative social connotation. As Abramovitz points out, even in colonial times a distinction was made between "worthy" female welfare recipients, *i.e.,* those who became household heads through widowhood or a husband's disability, and "unworthy" welfare recipients, *i.e.,* those females who became head of household through a divorce, having children out of wedlock, or remaining single. This distinction responds to and sustains the ideal of the nuclear family within a patriarchal structure. Although true for women of all groups, in the current context the stigma becomes more acutely felt by women of color because it is fed by prevailing attitudes toward race.

> . . . .my children occupied all of my time. I would take them to school, then go to pick them up. I would take them home, change their clothes, fix them some snack, and take them to the nearby park to play in the swings. . . . On weekends I would take them to the swimming pool. I always had some activity to keep them busy. We were always doing something. And every so often, on Saturday I would have a beer if someone from my family dropped by. *Y así pasó mi vida.* And that's how my life has been (Benmayor *et al.* 1992:91).

In addition, being on welfare exacted a price of indignity. In order to fulfill what they consider their duty *and* their right, *i.e.* providing for and raising responsible citizens, they have had to accommodate to minimum living standards. And, rather than receiving recognition and validation for their commitment to strong family values, which they would certainly get if they were white middle class, they have been relegated to the ranks of the "unworthy."

Still, we hear the women forging their gender and class in positive ways; speaking about *dignidad, respeto,* and *ayuda mutua* [dignity, respect, and mutual help], as cornerstones of a value system which still guides the consideration they give to and expect to receive from others. As difficult as their lives may have been or still are, they feel a great sense of accomplishment *"de haber echado pa'lante la familia"* [for helping the family get ahead]. In an essay aptly titled *"Mi sacrificio bien pago,"* [My sacrifices paid off], Esther Martínez captures the feeling many of the women share, and summarizes their assessment of the decisions they had to make throughout their lives:

> My children are now on their own and I feel good about the sacrifices I made for them, because they have shown their appreciation and have fulfilled my hopes that they would finish school and command better jobs than those their father and I had (Programa de Educación Popular de El Barrio 1988:153).

CONCLUSION

In trying to understand all of the elements that enter into the configuration of a Puerto Rican identity in the United States it is important to examine not only the affirmative cultural practices that give strength, but also those negative messages that have an impact on self-worth and contribute to oppression. The construction of identity rests upon the negotiation of these two opposed referents. I have already addressed the attacks levelled against Puerto Rican women and their families: dependent, lazy, lacking initiative, morality and so on. The status of Puerto Rican men in American society is no better: they are accused of being irresponsible, indolent, violent, unstable, *etcetera*. The portrayals of people of color on television, the most powerful medium for the dissemination of ideology at the popular level, reinforce the "otherness" and "dysfunctionality" of poor minority communities: rioting in Washington Heights, looting in Los Angeles, mass murdering of children in The Bronx. Even the advertisement for the TV series "Cops," shows policemen wrestling to the floor and practicing all kinds of different holds on "the criminals": African American and Latino men.

These messages have a tremendous impact at different levels. They turn the societal problems of poverty and racism into personal deviancy, deepening the distance between the poor (who exhibit this behavior) and the "mainstream" (who have to suffer its consequences). They shift attention away from searching for solutions that generate long-term social change, to implementing punitive measures to deal with some of the consequences of living in a system of inequality: put more cops on the street, build more jails. Finally, they undermine the confidence and self-esteem of those who see their lives portrayed in such negative terms. I am particularly concerned about Latino and African-American youth, who are still forging their identity, and who may not be able to draw on many of the sustaining cultural elements their parents may have used in the process of self-definition.

I would like to end by posing three basic questions that have guided the Centro's work in the Puerto Rican community for almost two decades, and that, in a sense, pertain to all of us who aim to carry out socially responsible research: What type of research initiatives do we develop to provide truly alternative understandings of poverty and oppression? How can we use this knowledge to influence effective policy making that capitalizes on the community's resources instead of focusing on its deficits? And, finally, how do we turn our findings into self-empowerment tools that the community itself can utilize in its struggle to build a more equitable society?

REFERENCES[5]

ABRAMOVITZ, MIMI
     1988   *Regulating the Lives of Women: Social Welfare Policy from Colonial Times to the Present.* Boston, MA: South End Press.
ASPIRA
     1983   *Racial and Ethnic High School Dropout Rates in New York City.* Summary Report. New York: ASPIRA.
BEAN, FRANK D. AND M. TIENDA
     1987   *The Hispanic Population of the United States.* The Population of the United States in the 1980s: A Census Monograph Series. New York: Russell Sage Foundation.
BENMAYOR, RINA, A. JUARBE, C. ALVAREZ, AND B. VAZQUEZ
     1988   Stories to live by: Continuity and change in three generations of Puerto Rican women. *Oral History Review* 16:2, Fall; and in *The Myths We Live By,* Paul Thompson and R. Samuels, Eds. London: Routledge.

[5] Rosa Torruellas died after completing and presenting this paper. I acknowledge, with deep appreciation, the dedication of Rina Benmayor, who completed the reference section of the paper. Judith Freidenberg

BENMAYOR, RINA, R. TORRUELLAS AND A. JUARBE
1992   *Responses to Poverty Among Puerto Rican Women: Identity. Community, and Cultural Citizenship.* Report to the Joint Committee for Public Policy Research on Contemporary Hispanic Issues of the Inter-University Program for Latino Research and The Social Science Research Council. New York: Centro de Estudios Puertorriqueños.

BONILLA, FRANK AND RICARDO CAMPOS
1986   *Industry & Idleness.* New York: History Migration Task Force, Centro de Estudios Puertorriqueños, Hunter College, City University of New York.

CHÁVEZ, LINDA
1991   *Out of the Barrio: Toward a New Politics of Hispanic Assimilation.* New York: Basic Books. *Current Population Report, 1990: 14–15.*

GARCÍA, JESÚS M. AND PATRICIA A. MONTGOMERY
1990   The Hispanic Population in the United States: March 1990. In *Current Population Reports: Population Characteristics.* U.S. Department of Commerce: Bureau of the Census, Series P-20, No. 449.

GURAK, DOUGLAS AND LOUIS FALCÓN
1990   The Puerto Rican family and poverty: Complex paths to poor out-comes. In *Puerto Ricans: Breaking Out of the Cycle of Poverty.* Washington, D.C.: National Puerto Rican Coalition.

FOCUS
1989   Special Issue: *Defining and Measuring the Underclass.* 12:1, Spring and Summer.

HISTORY TASK FORCE
1979   *Labor Migration Under Capitalism: The Puerto Rican Experience.* New York, London: Monthly Review Press.

LEMANN, NICHOLAS
1991   The other underclass. *The Atlantic Monthly,* December.

LEWIS, OSCAR
1966   *La Vida: A Puerto Rican Family in the Culture of Poverty—San Juan and New York.* New York: Random House.

MELENDEZ, EDWIN, CLARA RODRÍGUEZ, AND JANIS BARRY FIGUEROA, EDS.
1991   *His Panics in the Labor Force: Issues and Policies.* New York: Plenum Press.

ORTIZ, ALTAGRACIA
1985   Labor struggles of Puerto Rican women in the garment industry, New York City 1920–1960. *Cimarrón* I:3.

PROGRAMA DE EDUCACIÓN POPULAR DE EL BARRIO (Program of Popular Education of El Barrio)
1988   *Buscando un futuro mejor.* (Searching for a better future) New York: Programa de Educación Popular de El Barrio. Vol. 3.

RODRÍGUEZ, CLARA
1991   The effect of race on Puerto Rican wages, in *Hispanics in the Labor Force: Issues and Policies.* Edwin Meléndez, Clara Rodríguez, and Janis Barry Figueroa, Eds. New York: Plenum Press.

TORRES, ANDRÉS AND FRANK BONILLA
  1993   Regional, restructuring and Latino inequality: The New York
          Experience. In *Latinos In a Changing U.S. Economy: Comparative
          Perspectives on Growing Inequality*. Rebecca Morales and Frank Bonilla,
          Eds. California: Sage Publications.
TORRUELLAS, ROSA M., R. BENMAYOR, A. GORIS, AND A. JUARBE
  1990   Affirming cultural citizenship in the Puerto Rican community: The El
          Barrio Popular Education Program. In *Literacy As Praxis: Culture,
          Language and Pedagogy*, C.E. Walsh, Ed. Norwood, NJ: Ablex.
WILSON, WILLIAM JULIUS
  1987   *The Truly Disadvantaged: The Inner City, the Underclass and Public
          Policy*. Chicago: University of Chicago Press.

The Anthropology of Lower Income Urban Enclaves

DELMOS J. JONES

Department of Anthropology
Graduate School and University Center
City University of New York
New York, New York 10036

INTRODUCTION

The goal of this essay is to address some general concerns about the anthropology of lower income urban enclaves. I will describe some of the theoretical and conceptual inadequacies involved in the study of the poor and offer some suggestions that may improve our understanding of lower income urban enclaves. Two related issues need to be placed at the center of any analysis of lower income urban enclaves. One is capitalism itself, and the other is the social and economic complexity that accompanies it.

Poverty is not only a product of capitalism, as Oscar Lewis (1966) maintained, but capitalism continues to evolve and affect the poor. Lewis did note that poverty is a product of capitalism, but failed to note its continuing impact. What is missing from many discussions of the poor, including Lewis' critics, is that many poor people themselves act in conformity with capitalistic principles. Much of the literature views the life of the poor as being guided by a different set of principles, such as informal exchange (Stack 1974). I have argued elsewhere that the most problematic aspect of the poor is not just their poverty, but their desire to be better off (Jones 1993). Thus, capitalistic principles do not stop at the boundaries of lower income urban enclaves, but also influence how the poor interact with each other.

Aspects of the informal and underground economy are not alternatives to formal economic processes. Instead they are alternative ways of participating in the economy. They are not just strategies of survival, they are also strategies of accumulation. While there is considerable debate over the issue of social differentiation and economic inequality among peasants, there is little consideration of this topic among the poor.

The question must be asked, who profits from poverty and how? The answer should not exclude *some* of the poor themselves. It should also not exclude the professionals who work with the poor, or the social analysts who write about them.

In order to look at the manner in which capitalist forces continue to affect the poor, it is necessary to isolate distinctive aspects of the economic and social system that the poor people face everyday. These are easy to find. The first is employment, wages and the job market. The second has to do with principles of private property and property rights. Next is the institutional context of urban life. All of these are related to the conflict between use value and exchange value. Placing the forces of capitalism at the center of analysis allows us to distinguish between several different kinds of questions. The question as to why people are poor can be distinguished from the question of why some people are *persistently* poor.

Low wages are the primary cause of poverty (Klein and Rones 1989; Goldsmith 1982; Beeghley 1988). According to Goldsmith, "the forging of an impoverished proletariat, at work for low wages, on relief, or barely surviving on the edge of society, is the recognized counterpart of a spectacular achievement of industrial growth and capital accumulation" (Goldsmith 1982:38, see also Beeghley 1988:207).

Poverty is a product of economic processes, but these processes are somewhat neutral about *who* is poor. According to some estimates, only about three percent to five percent of the poor are persistently poor, while at least twenty-five percent of all Americans are poor for a year or more at some point in their lives. This poverty is due to divorce, death, illness, and unemployment. But while only three percent of the poor are persistently poor, sixty-two percent of this number is black (Klein and Rones 1989). It is impossible to look at this figure and not note the continuing significance of race and racism.

For the most part discussions of the poor are centered on the characteristics of the three percent to five percent of the persistently poor, and says little about twenty-five percent who are temporarily poor. While many questions remain about the intergenerational persistence of poverty within specific families, analysis should include the larger population of the poor.

A major characteristic of the poor is the constant struggle for survival; a struggle made necessary by economic scarcity and social neglect. The agencies and institutions of the society do not function well for the poor, and this is because people cannot afford the services they offer, are ineligible for them, or are suspicious of the institutions and the people that run them (Lewis 1961: xvii). According to Lewis, the poor develop *their own* social forms to solve problems not met by existing institutions and agencies (Lewis 1961: xvii). The issue of what the poor can and cannot do for themselves runs through much of the discussion about poverty. This matter cannot be discussed apart from the institutional context of urban society. This institutional context needs further formulation because it is the most critical aspect of urban life. It is the key not only to understanding the poor, but to understanding social life in the city more generally (Jones, Turner and Montbach 1992).

THE INSTITUTIONAL CONTEXT OF URBAN LIFE

Institutions and agencies of the city are responsible for what Warren (1969) calls "locality-relevant" functions. People who live in cities must still be born, pass through adolescence, marry and raise children, grow old, and die. An adequate material base is necessary in order for social life to be reproduced, including access to such simple necessities as food, shelter, and safety. A basic principle is that the delivery of social services by these institutions is an integral part of the material resource base upon which urban social life depends. This is why the institutional context of urban life is so critical. Increased unemployment, combined with cuts in social welfare and reduction in social services, means that it becomes very difficult for the social forms that develop among the poor to "serve a significant adaptive function" (Lewis 1966:3). That is, the poor cannot survive by their reliance on "their own" social forms.

The residents of lower income urban enclaves are helpless to exert any meaningful control over their immediate environment. This is because their environment is generally controlled by others, and it is also an important aspect of the system of profit. This is the basis of the conflict between use value and exchange value. The contradiction between use value and exchange value is characterized by Friedmann as a distinction between life space and economic space. Life space is bounded, territorial, named, and has sentiment attached to it. Economic space is abstract, discontinuous, open and unlimited. In a capitalist system, life space is constantly being transferred into economic space. "The capitalist city," writes Friedmann, "has no reverence for life. It bulldozes over neighborhoods to make way for businesses. It abandons entire regions, because profits are greater elsewhere. Deprived of their life space, people's lives are reduced to a purely economic dimension as workers and consumers—so long, at least, as there is work" (quoted in Bluestone and Harrison [1982:20]).

It is important to look at the social and economic evolution of the communities where the poor live. As is well known, these communities are older and more dilapidated. The physical conditions of these neighborhoods are often the source of health problems. They are often communities that have been used up and abandoned by others who have moved elsewhere for a better life. A considerable amount of the literature on the poor emphasizes their strength, their ability to survive despite the severe conditions under which they live. While much of this literature is designed to counter an approach that blames the poor for their own poverty, this position places more responsibility on the poor than they can possibly carry out. Moreover, it has resulted in a failure to look at the consequences of social life in poverty environments.

The earlier discussion of pathology suggested that racism and poverty were pathologies of capitalism. People who are forced to endure these conditions suffer from these conditions. The failure to address the consequences of existence in the midst of scarcity and institutional neglect have minimized the devastating and destructive consequences of poverty, imply-ing, in some cases that poverty is just another life style. There is an urgent need to articulate the consequences of poverty. The poor do not always sur-vive. Many of them are dying, and they are dying in different ways.

THE CONSEQUENCES OF POVERTY

There has been much debate against the idea of a culture of poverty, but I have argued elsewhere that the terms of this debate need to be reconsid-ered. While the existence of a "culture of poverty" can be argued, there is little doubt that poverty produces a secondary environment. Pinderhughes describes this as the victim system. This is a dynamic model that begins with conditions in the larger environment, such as limits to opportunity, and traces the impact of these conditions on individuals, families, and commu-nities (in Boyd-Franklin, 1989:11). When we take a close look at social life in lower income urban enclaves, we can easily see that poverty is not just another way of life. Poor mothers struggle to raise their children to be well-adjusted, productive, and successful adults with limited material resources (Drake and Cayton 1945; Belle 1988:220). Thus, they struggle on two fronts. They struggle to survive, and they struggle for a better future. The struggle for economic survival itself involves an intense and continuous effort that results in a great deal of stress (Bennett 1988:223–224). This is because they are frequently subjected to threatening and uncontrollable life events (Belle 1990). They are disproportionally exposed to crime and vio-lence, to the illness and death of children, to the imprisonment of husbands or children.

To be poor means that one is dependent on bureaucratic institutions such as the welfare system, Public Housing Authority, the health care sys-tem, and the courts. When the poor seek assistance from such systems, they often experience repeated failures. These failures do not reflect a lack of imagination or effort on their part, but suggest merely that a powerful insti-tution declined to respond. This institutional neglect was an important dimension of Lewis' culture of poverty. The institutions that deal with the poor frequently change their policies (Eden 1989), and this makes poverty a dynamic, not a static phenomenon. To survive, the poor must make repeated efforts and develop new strategies, and they experience repeated setbacks (see Belle, 1990:387).

The conditions under which the poor live affect health. A continuous crisis means that the problem remains unsolved, and this can be more dam-aging than periodic crises. The greater the stress, or problem, the more like-ly one is to become physically or mentally ill (Dennis 1977:319). Health and mental health problems are produced among the poor because effec-tive ". . . healthy, coping behavior might require an investment of time, energy, knowledge and money that is beyond the individual's or group's perceived or actual capacity . . . " (Paltiel 1988:195). The relationship between resources and effort is emphasized as an important dynamic. Poor people are more likely to contract diseases such as high blood pressure, heart disease, disease of the ear, disease of the kidney, rheumatism and arthritis, inflammatory diseases of the skin and eyes, infections, nervous and mental disease, digestive disease, metabolic disease, cancer, and diseases of resistance.

While social support networks can sometimes help the situation, the continuous nature of life crises means that the networks themselves often suffer from overload. According to Belle the "unemployed women with small networks were more likely to have high depressive symptom levels than unemployed women with larger networks" (1990:386). Because the condition of poverty is permanent and need is continuous, social support networks are placed under a great burden. Social networks can exact higher cost than they repay through the provision of supportive resources (Belle 1990:387).

LIFE IN LOWER INCOME URBAN ENCLAVES

My main argument in this paper is that the urban enclave as a physical and social entity deserves considerably more attention than it has received. I also argue that an adequate material base is necessary in order for community to exist, and urban populations are largely dependent upon large scale institutions to provide these, and that their provisions are conditioned by capitalist processes. The environment that urbanites relate to is a "built environment." The built environment includes physical structures and conceptual principles. Besides buildings, streets, telephone lines, sewer systems, *etc.*, it also refers to "spaces that are defined and bounded" (Lawrence and Low 1990:454). Definitions of space are present in terms of zoning ordinances, health and housing codes, and other regulations that place restrictions on the kinds of activities that can occur. This environment must be managed and maintained.

According to Harvey (1978:10) social life requires use value in the form of a built environment if it is to function effectively. Harvey argues that the separation between the place of work and the place of residence that accompanied the industrial revolution made it difficult to maintain and control the social conditions necessary for existence. Effort had to be expanded in two related settings. The first, located in the work place, is over the conditions of work and the wage rate that provides the purchasing power necessary to pay for consumption goods. The second, is fought in the place of residence against secondary forms of exploitation and appropriation represented by merchant capital, landed property, and the like. Harvey describes this as a fight over the cost and conditions of existence in the living place (1978:11). Thus, the ability to survive is dependent upon the ability to secure access to a particular bundle of resources in a reasonable health location (1978:31). Labor "in seeking to protect and enhance its standard of living, engages, in the living place, in a series of running battles over a variety of issues which relate to the creation, management, and use of the built environment" (1978:11) Examples of such struggles are over rent, pollution, site selection, all quality of life issues.

An urban neighborhood is not only a setting where social and cultural relationships occur, but represents both real and potential wealth and the background for success in life (Shepard 1975). Success in life is a motivation of all Americans, and in this respect urban neighborhoods are temporary settings through which some people pass on their way to greater achievement, including new and better neighborhoods. Given this as a motivation, it is necessary to look at the degree to which people are locked into their neighborhoods, at the means by which this is achieved, and the consequences of this situation. Cohen and Shinar's (1985) study of neighborhoods and friendship networks in three communities in Jerusalem illustrates this issue.

Cohen and Shinar (*ibid*) found that, in contrast to conventional wisdom, lack of attachment to place was most evident in residents of lower class neighborhoods. In addition, the longer the length of residence in the neighborhood, the lower the attachment to the neighborhood. They argued that this was so because those with the longest term residence were lower class, wanted to leave, were unable to leave the neighborhood, and felt trapped in it (1985:100). Cohen and Shinar relate attachment to neighborhood to a host of neighborhood context variables. These context variables refer to the "character" of the neighborhood, as expressed by accessibility and availability of existing (and desirable) facilities and services, by the composition of the population and its social behavior, by the quality and age of buildings, by rates of delinquency and crime, and so on (1985:99). These conditions are generally produced by forces external to the local community. I return here to the basic premise of this essay: poverty and poverty conditions are products of capitalist forces. Any suggestion that the poor can overcome these conditions through their own institutional forms, is politically naive and socially irresponsible.

The major issue here is the implication of the context variables discussed by Cohen and Shinar. I am stressing the inability of the poor to develop and maintain life space, as defined by Friedmann. The inability of the poor to develop and maintain adequate life space, and the transformation of life space into economic space has social and psychological implications.

Certain basic psychic and biological needs must be satisfied in order for humans to survive and have a healthy life. According to Lewin, a clear and firm "social ground" is necessary to the individual's security, direction, and identity (1943:16), and "if a person is not clear about his belongingness his life-space will show the characteristic of an unstable ground" (Lewin 1943:86, see also Erikson cited in Jacobson-Widding 1988:14). Lewin was, of course, talking about being well established in a group, but this may also be said of place. The issue that arises here is the relationships among social stability, personal and cultural identities, and place. A place possesses a history, and the relationship of people to a place is influenced by this history. Historical continuity and feeling of belonging are also related to place.

Studies of traditional cultures are implicitly and explicitly filled with references to the importance of place. The peak of place attachment, according to Relph is the home. "Home in its most profound form is an attachment to a particular setting, a particular environment. . . . " Home ". . . is the point of departure from which we orient ourselves and take possession of the world" (quoted in Cohen and Shinar 1985). Relph goes on to argue that a deep relationship with place is as necessary, and perhaps as unavoidable, as close relationships with people. Without it human existence is bereft of much of its significance. Loss of place could cause a social and personal identity crisis. What happens when people do not lose place, but lose the ability to exert control over it? According to Cohen and Shinar "in modern society there are phenomena of alienation and feelings of not belonging to society. Many people do not feel attached to a place; on the contrary, they feel that they are prisoners of their place without the ability to change the situation" (Cohen and Shinar 1985:7). Such feelings could evolve into a deep hatred of place and all of its elements; location, landscape, life experiences in that setting, and historical continuity.

SOCIAL COMPLEXITY AND THE STUDY OF LOWER INCOME URBAN ENCLAVES

I am stressing in this essay the idea of lower income urban enclaves as a part of the larger system. As such, it cannot be considered as separate from its context. A central methodological and theoretical concern in all the social sciences is the nature of the relationship between the unit of study and the wider society of which it is a part (Weaver and White 1972:116 Elkins 1974:7). Wolf was speaking of peasant villages, not urban enclaves, when he said that what goes on therein "cannot be explained in terms of that village alone, the explanation must include consideration both of the outside forces impinging on these villages and the reaction of the villages to these forces" (1966:1). To solve this problem, it is necessary to study the "internal" characteristics of a subunit, and its "external" environment as part of the same phenomenon (Elkins 1974:7)

Anthropology is still anchored in the local unit, and there remains the tendency to view these units as separate things. Even when the impact of the larger context is recognized, we fall far short of showing the interaction between the "internal" and the "external."

An important aspect of complex systems is that they are hierarchical. A related process is that with social evolution major functions shift away from the local level to levels higher in the hierarchy. Bargatzky (1987), in discussing the processes of expanding and evolving systems, describes "the principle of the selective neglect of certain details" as, the taking over by the supralocal system of specific functions that were once performed by local (or regional) systems, thus making these latter dependent on the center. This gives rise to a growing complexity of the center, with at the same time a reduction of the span of control of the local or regional systems (Claessen and Van de Velde 1987:14).

Whether we are dealing with families, communities, or subcultures, control over many essential functions is located in higher level institutions. Few would disagree that in urban society most essential functions that would constitute an important aspect of a traditional anthropological study—activities such as economic production, security, education, *etc.*—are functions of institutions that are external to the local group. Whether particular functions are effectively carried out by these institutions on behalf of a specific group, is often related to the social status of that group. Many of the concerns that poor people express, refer specifically to their treatment by urban institutions. Much of the knowledge that poor people pass on to each other and their children, is about the institutions that they have to deal with. Much of the medical knowledge that they share is not "folk" medicine, but "folk" information about the uses of modern medicine.

The agencies and institutions of the city are aspects of the relevant "environment" that urbanites interact with. This means that as a research strategy we must consider urban institutions and local groups as part of a single complex that combines to influence socialization patterns, social behavior, intergroup relations, and psychological states of mind.

Modern states are by their very nature composed of a variety of different kinds of social groups. This being the case, we must move beyond the point of focusing too much on this diversity as a significant social and political factor. "When a considerable number of people are brought together under a single government, common values and norms regarding important aspects of the social organization are hardly to be expected, for instance, as the interests of the constituent groups are bound to be at variance *almost by definition*" (Claessen 1987:14). If we assume that conflict of interest is an inherent aspect of complex systems, we should then be careful in how we treat incidents of conflict, and especially careful about how we use terms such as "resistance" and "empowerment."

Uniformity in complex systems is neither desirable nor possible. Thus, "a central government *cannot* control everything. . . . Hence, the central hierarchy has to ignore some details of movement at the lower level" (Bargatzky 1987:33). Indeed, a control hierarchy may grant some limited freedom at the local level because it does not matter much and "because the political power of these institutions is negligible, compared with the instruments of power that the state has at its disposal." Moreover, it is necessary to leave certain aspects of local units unintegrated and semi-autonomous, so that they can fulfill functions delegated to them by higher level institutions.

A hierarchy implies a descending order. The State must be able to operate at the local level. To do so it must have information about conditions in the local environment, and this requires mechanisms to transmit information upward and to receive instructions (or commands) from a higher level. This means that some form of local-level social viability is essential. Problems of control are not always produced by a limited degree of independence and autonomy at the local level, or by the persistence of traditional social forms. Instead, it may be the absence of *a certain degree* of independence and autonomy that produces problems for the State. Thus, where local constituent units do not exist, they are created, and this is the case whether we are speaking of colonial administration creating chieftainships where none existed, or city governments creating local organizations in hard-to-reach areas of the city (Jones, Montbach and Turner 1982; Jones and Tumelty 1986; Jones 1987).

The above does not mean that we should not study the activities of individuals and local groups. To the contrary, we should study them from a different perspective. The activities that local groups engage in, such as organizing political protest, earning a living, finding shelter, getting an education, obtaining medical treatment, must be studied in considerably more detail than they now are if we are to understand social life in lower income urban enclaves. These must be studied in their institutional and economic context.

In order for individuals and groups to interact with any environment they must have information about it. The urban environment, as already noted, is composed of a host of important institutions and agencies that urban residents must rely on for essential goods and services. In any social situation, information is required to make decisions about what action to take, how to take it, and when to take it. All of this is readily apparent when one pays attention to the content of conversation. I have observed elsewhere,

> If one sits and listens to their [poor people's] conversations, one hears a preoccupation with housing and landlords, judges and courts, hospitals and doctors, schools and teachers, social workers and welfare, etc. These represent major 'domains' in the people's own view of their material, social and psychological world (Jones 1977:455).

Activities within the household must be organized among its members in coordination with the rules and schedules of institutions and agencies that families must deal with. This can become complex and elaborate in households with children of different ages, involved in different activities, and households where both parents must work or in households composed of a single parent.

I am proposing an ethnography of everyday life, modeled after traditional ethnographies, and one that describes the different kinds of information that different classes of urban dwellers must possess to survive in cities. It is possible to describe the process of obtaining housing in terms of *all* the activities and all the institutions (telephone company, gas and electric utilities, real estate agencies, banks and their lending policies, the local housing authorities, *etc.*), which must be dealt with. Spradley (1972) may be correct that members of subgroups assign different values to their interactions with institutions, but institutions also place values on their interaction with different types of subgroups and treat them accordingly. Thus, residents of lower income urban enclaves are often required to pay a deposit to get a telephone installed; their desire to buy a home is often blocked by the unwillingness of banks to lend them money, a process known as "redlining." The decisions by these institutions mean that members of this population have been classified in a certain manner and singled out for special treatment. The policies of urban institutions often determine the forms local units assume, as Susser has shown for families (Susser 1993).

The relationship between the locality and the agencies and institutions of government have been characterized in terms of dependency (Jones, Turner and Montbach 1992). While tensions and conflicts of interest obviously exist between the local level and higher level institutions and agencies, this is not a relationship that is characterized solely, or even primarily, by opposition. On the one hand, residents in an area of New York City may mobilize against the city's proposals to place dump sites in their neighborhood, while simultaneously pressuring the city to expand the sewer system, pave the streets, improve transportation to the area, provide better police protection, expand the housing stock, and keep the streets cleaner. Political mobilization to maintain and preserve life space is the major subject of Castells' *The City and the Grassroots* (1983).

CONCLUSIONS

The major theme of this essay has been to emphasize the relationship between poverty and capitalism and to stress the need to consider the complexity of that relationship. This complexity includes the relationship between the poor and the larger society as well as among the poor themselves. The whole issue of poverty and capitalism must be considered in the context of Baron's claim that the very existence of racism and poverty operates to maintain capitalism (Baron 1976:190), and Reich's contention that the status of poor blacks "is deeply rooted in the current economic institutions of America, and is likely to survive as long as they do" (Reich 1976:224). If this is the case, and I believe it to be so, we ought to be careful that the nature of our research does not add support to the mystification of poverty. Vincent's (1993) discussion of the concept of the "residuum" that was used to explain the poverty of the Irish in England in the nineteenth century is pertinent here. Vincent shows that this older concept is similar to the current views of "underclass," and argues that there is a "perduring contradiction in capitalism whereby the requirements of the economy run counter to those of civil ideology." The concept of the "underclass," she writes, "thus becomes largely one of mystification, containment, and management." I also argue that the characterization of the poor as culturally different, whether it is couched in terms of a culture of poverty or of a different "authentic" culture, is also part of the mystification process (Jones 1993). Those who describe the poor as guided by a set of principles different from the rest of the society, reinforce the idea that they do not want, do not need, or do not deserve what others have, especially if it makes them similar to the middle class. Yet the desire for a better life is endemic among the poor, and this desire for success is the source of the tension between the poor and the larger system. How is that tension managed? Given the nature of capitalism, any significant increase in the living standards of the poor is impossible without drastic changes in the system of distribution. Thus, it could be assumed that the more poor people want to share in the wealth of the system, the greater the tension, and increased tension is threatening to the stability of the social system (see Buckley 1963:493). Any approach to the study of lower income enclaves that does not attempt to expose these tensions and contradictions can be suspected of contributing to the mystification, containment, and management of the poor.

REFERENCES

BARGATZKY, T.
  1987   Upward evolution, suprasystem dominance and the mature state. In *Early State Dynamics*. H. S. M. Claessen and P. van de Velde, Eds. Leiden New York: E. J. Brill.
BARON, H. M.
  1976   The demand for Black labor. In *Racial Conflict, Discrimination, and Power: Historical and Contemporary Studies*. William Barclay, Krishna Kumar, and Ruth P. Simms, Eds. New York: AMS Press.
BEEGHLEY, LEONARD
  1988   Individual and structural explanations of poverty. *Population Research and Policy Review* 7(3):201–222.
BELLE, DEBORAH
  1990   Poverty and Women's Mental Health. *American Psychologist* 45:385–389.
BENNETT, MAISHA, B.
  1988   Afro-American women, poverty and mental health: A social essay. In *Women Health, and Poverty*. A special issue of *Women and Health*, 12:213–228. Parales, Casar A. and Lauren S. Young, Eds. New York: The Hawworth Press.
BLUESTONE, BARRY AND BENNETT HARRISON
  1982   *The Deindustrialization of America: Plant Closing Community Abandonment, and the Dismantling of Basic Industry*. New York: Basic Books.
BOYD-FRANKLIN, NANCY
  1989   *Black Families in Therapy: A Multisystems Approach*. New York, London: The Guilford Press.

BUCKLEY, WALTER
  1968   Society as a complex adaptive system. In *Modern Systems Research for the Behavioral Scientist: A Sourcebook,* Walter Buckley Chicago: Aldine Publishing Company. pp. 490–513
CALHOUN, CRAIG
  1991   Indirect relationships and imagined communities: Large-scale social integration and the transformation of everyday life. In *Social Theory for a Changing Society,* Pierre Bourdieu and James S. Coleman, Eds. Boulder, San Francisco, Oxford: Westview Press (Russell Sage Foundation)
CASTELLS, MANUEL
  1983   *The City and the Grassroots.* Berkeley and Los Angeles: University of California Press.
CLAESSEN, H. S. M. AND P. VAN DE VELDE
  1987   Introduction. In *Early State Dynamics.* Leiden, New York: E. J. Brill.
COHEN, Y. S. AND AMMNON SHINAR
  1985   Neighborhood and friendship networks. University of Chicago Department of Geography Research Paper No. 215
COLEMAN, JAMES S.
  1991   Prologue: Constructed social organization. In *Social Theory for a Changing Society,* Pierre Bordieu and James S. Coleman, Eds. Boulder, San Francisco, Oxford: Westview Press. (Russell Sage Foundation)
DENNIS, RUTH E.
  1977   Social stress and mortality among nonwhite males. *Phylon* **38**:315–328.
DRAKE, ST. CLAIR AND HORACE R. CAYTON
  1945   *Black Metropolis: The Study of Negro Life in a Northern City.* New York: Harcourt, Brace & World, Inc.
EDIN, KATHRYN JO
  1989   *There's a lot of Month Left at the End of the Money: How Welfare Recipients in Chicago Make Ends Meet.* Ph. D. Dissertation, Northwestern University.
ELKINS, STEPHEN L.
  1974   Comparative urban politics and interorganizational behavior. *Comparative Urban Research* :5–28
FORDE, C. D.
  1963   *Habitat, Economy and Society: A Geographical Introduction to Ethnology.* New York: E. P. Dutton.
FRIEDMANN, JOHN
  1982   Life Space and Economic Space: Contradictions in Regional Development. M.S. UCLA 1981.20
GOLDSMITH, W. W.
  1982   Poverty and profit in urban growth and decline. In *Race, Poverty, and the Urban Underclass.* Clements Cottingham, Ed. Lexington, MA: D. C. Heath and Company. pp. 25–60
HARRIES-JONES, PETER
  1991   Sustainable anthropology: Ecology and anthropology in the future. In *Contemporary Futures: Perspectives from Social Anthropology,* Sandra Wallman, Ed. ASA Monograph 30. London and New York. Routledge. pp. 157–171

HARVEY, DAVID
    1978   Labor, capital, and class struggle around the built environment in
            advanced capitalist societies. In *Urbanization and Conflict in Market
            Societies.* Kevin R. Cox, Ed. Chicago: Maaroufa Press, Inc. pp. 9–37.
HARVEY, DAVED
    1985   *Consciousness and the Urban Experience.* Oxford: Oxford University
            Press
HUNTER, A.
    1979   The urban neighborhood: Its analytical and social context. *Urban
            Affairs Quarterly* 14 (3):267–288.
JACOBSON-WIDDING, ANITA
    1983   Introduction. In *Identity: Personal and Socio-Cultural,* Anita Jacobson-
            Widding, Ed. Highland Heights, NJ. Humanities Press, Inc.
JONES, DELMOS J.
    1968   The multivillage community: Village segmentation and coalescence in
            northern Thailand. *Behavioral Science Notes* 3:149–174.
    1971   Village autonomy, cultural status, and self perception. *Anthropological
            Quarterly* 44:1–11.
    1977   Social complexity and the institutionalization of cultural diversity.
            Reviews in Anthropology 5:451–462
    1987   The Community and Organizations in the Community. In
            Anthropology in the United States, Leith Mullings, Ed. New York:
            Columbia University Press.
    1993   The culture of achievement among the poor: The case of mothers and
            children in a Headstart program. *Critique of Anthropology, A Journal
            for the Critical Reconstruction of Anthropology* 13(3):247–266.
JONES, DELMOS J., JOAN MONTBACH, AND JOAN TURNER
    1982   Are local organizations local? *Social Policy* 13(2):42–45
JONES, DELMOS J. AND SUSANNE TUMELTY
    1986   Are there really 10,000 block associations in New York City? *Social
            Policy.* Fall, 1986
JONES, DELMOS J., JOAN TURNER, AND JOAN MONTBACH
    1992   Declining social services and the threat to social reproduction: An
            urban dilemma. *City and Society* 6:99–114
KLEIN, B. W. AND P. L. RONES
    1989   A profile of the working poor. *Monthly Labor Review.* 112:3–13.
LAWRENCE, D. L. AND S. LOW
    1990   The built environment and spatial form *Annual Reviews in
            Anthropology.* Alen Beals, Ed. Palo Alto, CA: Annual Reviews, Inc.
LEEDS, ANTHONA
    1964   Brazilian careers and social structure: An evolutionary model and case
            history. *American Anthropologist* 66:1321–47
LEWIN, KURT
    1948   *Resolving Social Conflict: Selected Papers on Group Dynamics.* New
            York. Harper and Brothers
LEWIS, OSCAR
    1961   *The Children of Sanchez.* New York: Random House
    1966   The Culture of Poverty. *Scientific American* 215, 4:19–25

1975   Urbanization without breakdown: A case study. In *City Ways: A Selective Reader in Urban Anthropology.* John Friedl and Noel J. Chrisman, Eds. New York: Thomas Y. Crowell.

MEGGERS, BETTY J.
1954   Environmental limitations on the development of culture. *American Anthropologist* **56**:801–824

PALTIEL, FREDA L.
1988   Is being poor a mental health hazard? In *Women Health, and Poverty.* Casar A. Parales and Lauren S. Young, Eds. A special issue of *Women and Health.* **12**:189–211 New York: The Hawworth Press.

PARK, ROBERT
1915   The City: Suggestion for the investigation of human Behavior in the City Environment. *American Journal of Sociology* **20**:577–612

PINDERHUGHES, ELAINE
1989   *Understanding Race, Ethnicity, and Power: The Key to Efficacy in Clinical Practice.* Free Press: Collier Macmillan.

REICH, MICHAEL
1976   The economics of racism. In *Racial Conflict, Discrimination, and Power: Historical and Contemporary Studies.* William Barclay, Krishna Kumar and Ruth P. Simms, Eds. pp. 124–130. New York: AMS Press.

RELPH, E. L.
1976   *Place & Placelessness.* London: Pion.

SANDERS, PETER
1981   *Social Theory and the Urban Question.* London: Hutchinson University Library

SHEPARD, BRUCE
1975   Metropolitan political decentralization: A test of the life-style value model. *Urban Affairs Quarterly* **10**(3):296–313.

SPRADELEY, JAMES
1972   Adaptive strategies of urban nomads: The ethno-science of tramp culture. In *The Anthropology of Urban Environments,* Thomas Weaver and Douglas White, Eds. The Society for Applied Anthropology Monograph Series:Monograph Number II, pp. 21–38

STACK, CAROL
1974   *All Our Kin: Strategies for Survival in a Black Community.* New York: Harper & Row.

SUSSER, IDA
1993   Creating family forms: The exclusion of men and teenage boys from families in the New York City shelter system, 1987–92.*Critique of Anthropology, A Journal for the Critical Reconstruction of Anthropology* **133**(3). 267–283.

VINCENT, JOAN
1993   Framing the underclass. *Critique of Anthropology, A Journal for the Critical Reconstruction of Anthropology* **133**: 215–230

WARREN, ROLAND L.
1969   Politics and the ghetto system. In *Politics and the Ghettos,* Roland L. Warren, Ed. New York: Atherton Press. pp. 11–30.

WEAVER, THOMAS AND DOUGLAS WHITE
1972   *The Anthropology of Urban Environments.* The Society for Applied Anthropology Monograph Series: Monograph Number II.

WELLMAN, BARRY, PETER J. CARRINGTON AND ALAN HALL
    1988   Networks as personal communities. In *Social Structures: A Network Approach*. Barry Wellman and S. D. Berkowitz, Eds., New York: Cambridge University Press. pp 130–184
WOLF, ERIC
    1966   *Peasants*. Englewood Cliffs, NJ: Prentice-Hall.

Anthropology of Stranger and Native

JUNE NASH

Department of Anthropology
City College of the City University of New York
137th Street and Convent Avenue
New York, New York 10031

The papers given at the workshop on "The Anthropology of Lower-Income Urban Enclaves: The case of East Harlem" raise the issue of the relationship between anthropologists and informants in this postmodern world. Now that we as anthropologists have been deprived of the authoritative voice we once enjoyed in writing our field work, we are left to invent what our relationship with our subjects will be. Postmodernism is, if anything, the condition of awareness of multiple voices and identities. Whether we come as a stranger—the preferred persona of unreconstructed authoritative texts—or native, a humble and elusive identity lost sometime between our first exam and defense of thesis in graduate school, we now feel obliged to make the relationship explicit.

For the most part, reflexive inquiry into our relationship with subjects has been individualistic—viz Rosaldo discovering his own pain and anger transmuted into that of his headhunting hosts, or Crapanzano introspectively querying his own self-doubts as he interviews Tuhami. At a recent American Anthropological Association meeting I went to a story was circulating as to how postmodern anthropologists relate to their informants, and it concluded with a quote from an apochryphal anthropologist interviewing "the native," "OK, that's enough about your problems. Let me tell you about mine."

One way to find an exit from the solipsistic inquiry is to draw from our origins in the quest for illuminating the many varieties of human expression. The unusual feature about this workshop in these times is the concentration on the problems the anthropologists learn about in the field as they approach it with the spirit of discovery. We are brought full circle to the earlier years in the discipline when the excitement centered on how you conceive of problems from the perspective of the people you are studying. At the same time, all of the papers have engaged in a reflexive and dialogical engagement with their subjects more typical of the postmodern encounter. And if the people they study are more likely than not immigrants who have recently arrived in this country, then we have indeed reversed the authoritative equation as we the anthropologists become the native and they the stranger, with our role often that of informing our subjects what this culture is all about as we gain entry into their perspective on what they experience in this strange environment. The reciprocal exchange of information between the stranger/informant and the native/anthropologist maintains rapport in relationships that might otherwise become one-sided.

Another unusual feature of this workshop is the sensitivity shown by rapporteurs not only to the needs of their informant collaborators but also to their mutual interests in decoding their environment. In the dialogue in which they participated, the informants became part of a constructive interaction in which both are contributing their knowledge from within, as identified with the subject, and without, as analyst. Neither is totally stranger or native. I undertook field work in Pittsfield, Massachusetts, in an attempt to capture the essence of being in my own culture in order to compare it with my other experiences in field work in Guatemala, Bolivia, and Mexico. After about three months of fieldwork, I was really feeling at home working in a town much like the one I grew up in. In fact the main manufacturing plant, Sylvania Electric Company, employed electrical workers on assembly line, which was my first job while still in high school during World War II. It was, in fact, the incentive for my going to college so I wouldn't spend the rest of my life on an assembly line. So I was feeling like a real native in the culture one day, when a woman who was a first generation Italian—she was two years old when she arrived in this country—looked at me reflectively and said, "I don't know what it is about you, June, but there is something very foreign about you." It proved to me the impossibility of being a true native regardless of one's birth and upbringing. By virtue of the socialization in academic culture itself, we lose the identity with our roots as we move into the middle class and to other more cosmopolitan setting. Her comment proved to me the unlikelihood of my gaining greater rapport or more profound insight into the meaning system by virtue of studying people in "my own" culture.

The advantages of the role of the stranger used to be extolled in the social sciences when I was a student of anthropology in Chicago in the 1950s. My professors, Sol Tax and Robert Redfield, suggested that it was a way of distancing oneself from a situation in part to gain objectivity. Yet they were also aware of the advantages to be gained from the inner view, as their correspondence (Rubenstein 1991) reveals, allowing greater access. The exercise of the kind of self-awareness implied by being a stranger springs from many sources rather than just national or territorial birth. I now realize that it must rest on broader ontological bases in the construction of the self as a social scientist than simply coming from distant lands.

I think most of the presenters were very aware of these distinctions as they carried out fieldwork, sometimes with people very like themselves. The fact that they were close to the subject matter and to the subjects gives a special awareness that promotes the reciprocity in the field work. These researchers evidently gave back to the people an enhancement of their self-awareness that makes them better able to assess their life conditions. This reciprocity has provided them with an entry into the research and ways of understanding that enhances the final product. Rosa Torruellas obviously communicated this in her research for her article, "'Mi Sacrificio Bien Pago': Puerto Rican Women on Welfare and Family Values" (this volume) as did Pedro Pedraza and Jorge Ayala. But empathy is not lacking in William Kornblum's contribution to the socialization study he did with Terry Williams in East Harlem, revealing once again the many ways that the stranger/native boundary can be erased.

One of the real discoveries is the nature of stereotypes and how they affect the way in which people act out their lives. Pedro Pedraza's presentation shows how research that has the objective of overcoming stereotypes can heighten the awareness to their existence among people who confront them in their lives. By working in intervention research as he has done, one can begin to discuss in terms of "emic" and "etic" the distinctions that Judith Freidenberg brought out. With the insights Freidenberg provides us, we can expand this distinction to consider several layers of inner understandings as well as outer perceptions, with the knowledge that these layers are related to the levels of sensitivity and rapprochement that we reach through the dialogical encounter. The presentations have made me ever more aware that the "etic" pose itself is a scientific stereotype that we have constructed in our interface with the subject. Possibly anthropologists are less guilty of this than other social science disciplines since our methodology and perspective mitigate its adoption. We are as a consequence, less likely to take extreme positions characteristic of either emic or etic approaches as we expand our empathetic as well as analytical skills in the field work process.

Research into poverty in the United States reminds us of the growing gap between the stereotype of the United States as a rich nation and the reality. Just before this conference opened the newspapers announced that Miami has opened up its slum barrios, or "cinturón de miseria," to allow people to build their shacks just as they are allowed to in Latin American megalopolises and to inhabit the dwellings that are a permanent exhibition of the real impoverishment of our society. New York City is now accepting the relative permanence of inhabitants in the shanty town next to the FDR drive, and other cities will undoubtedly follow suit as the ranks of the homeless grow and become a permanent fixture in our society. The fact that Oxfam has now put the United States on its list of recipients for food should make us very conscious of how our country is being turned into a third world, and that the trichotomy of first, second, and third world is fading.

Although the financial difficulties and the scarcity of jobs facing intellectuals is not as harsh as for those who face homelessness, they may be affecting the way in which we cast the problems we research. Funding agencies, which have always existed as a shadowy partner to the research undertaking, now become a potential ally along with informants in shaping the research. We have always pretended to distance ourselves from the funding agencies so we wouldn't be influenced by them. But a new level of interaction is suggested by those who have worked in the Taller.

Rosa Torruellas' paper carries out many of the points I have mentioned in showing how research can be a means of empowerment for the people, allowing the women informants to shape the discourse, fulfilling many of the objectives that those in the cultural critique of ethnology say should be our objectives in overcoming the problems they address but too often fail to put into practice. The personal biographies then show a different image than those that spring from stereotypes. We cannot deny that such preconceptions exist, since we never quite overcome them. Allowing the kind of collaborative research in which the subject enters in and defines the goals is one of the most important ways in which to learn about how they themselves perceive the categories in which they find themselves and how they escape them. Stereotypes about women, about poor people, about welfare mothers in particular can demean people's self-conception. The work of the Center of Puerto Rican Studies has indicated the political field in which welfare recipients becomes a different and positive source for certain movements when the claims that have been made about a society become shared. Frances Fox Piven and Richard Cloward (1977) have shown this dramatically in their studies of the structural setting of welfare. But the Center has added a new dimension with the narratives of welfare recipients. By taking part in the discourse, they alter the assumptions about what giving and taking involve. I am waiting for somebody to redo Mauss's *The Gift*, putting welfare within a frame of redistributive politics and the way in which that can shift a power base in society.

Myths about the "other" proliferate in the absence of this kind of collaborative research. The paper by Williams and Kornblum (this volume) on public housing reminded me of a book, *Seven Myths about Public Housing*, that I read in preparation for my first professional job, that of a researcher for a public housing agency in Boston. One of the most prevalent myths was that the poor who inhabit housing projects have so little acquaintance with indoor plumbing that they use their bathtubs to store coal. The myth was debunked by pointing to the use of automatically controlled central heating, but even these considerations are lost on those who persist in blaming the victims for their own poverty. Whoever deals with research on the poor must, like Williams, eliminate the tangle of myths and distortions that grow like weeds in the soil fertilized by public spending.

The research we have been hearing about is successfully demystifying and debunking myths about the poor. It is easy to fall into romanticizing the subject as we try to rescue them from the stereotypes. Although there, is less of that exhibited here than among the Mayanists with whom I find myself associating more often than with poverty specialists in conferences, it is a tendency we must be constantly aware of. The degree to which the subjects enter into the design of the research mitigates the essentializing or romanticizing, which by definition lies outside the framework in which they operate. No one is more adept at this than Philippe Bourgois, who has looked at the mean side of the streets on the far upper east side of New York (see chapter in this volume), the often criminal strategies engaged in by its inhabitants without losing sight of the context that generates it. His work on drug sellers indicates a new beginning for culture and personality studies. Informed by studies in the construction of gender, he plumbs the motivational basis for the risky ventures in drug trafficking by which men in this area restore their sense of manhood, rescuing it from the feminized low-paid job market that is their only venue to legal employment.

Judith Freidenberg's edited volume based on this stimulating workshop provides a prototype for thinking our way beyond the epistemiological quandaries posed by postmodern ethnography. In response to those who pose anthropology as a subjective narrative akin to literature (Marcus and Fischer 1986; Clifford and Marcus 1986; Clifford 1988), as well as those who claim the wave of the future is writing by the former subjects of research (Sanjek 1990), the contributors to this book remind us of what the enterprise of ethnography is about. They succeed in writing good ethnography without losing the subjective perspectives that are highlighted in narratives or the objective analyses contained in their interpretations. These strangers and natives within ethnography bring us new insights into what poverty and cultural marginalization mean.

REFERENCES

CLIFFORD, JAMES
　　1988　　*The Predicament of Culture: Twentieth Century Ethnography, Literature, and Art.* Cambridge, MA: Harvard University Press.
CLIFFORD, JAMES AND GEORGE E. MARCUS, EDS.
　　1986　　*Writing Culture: The Poetics and Politics of Ethnography.* Berkeley: University of California Press.
MARCUS, GEORGE E. AND MICHAEL N.J. FISCHER
　　1986　　*Anthropology as Culture Critique: An Experimental Moment in the Human Sciences.* Chicago: University of Chicago Press.
PIVEN, FRANCES FOX AND RICHARD A. CLOWARD
　　1977　　*Poor People's Movements.* New York: Pantheon Books.
RUBINSTEIN, ROBERT A., ED.
　　1991　　*The Correspondence of Robert Redfield and Sol Tax.* Boulder, CO: Westview Press.
SANJEK, ROGER, ED.
　　1990　　*Fieldnotes: The Making of Anthropology.* Ithaca, NY: Cornell University Press.

Some Comments on the Anthropology of Lower Income Urban Enclaves

Dominican Newcomers in the City

NINNA NYBERG SØRENSEN

Centre for Development Research
Gammel Kongevej 5
DK - 1610 Copenhagen V, Denmark

Puerto Ricans have been migrating to the United States in significant numbers since the beginning of this century. As participants in one of the first
great airborne migrations in which two islands—Puerto Rico and
Manhattan—became intimately interconnected, Puerto Rican migrants,
Puerto Rican settlements in New York City and Puerto Rican discourses on
cultural identity, provide researchers interested in the same processes
among other groups of 'newer' New Yorkers an excellent opportunity for
studying the dynamics of 20th century migration. I am therefore very
grateful to Judith Freidenberg for inviting me to participate in this event,
and to all the participants who have shared their knowledge of the Puerto
Rican migration experience with me during the workshop.

Before I turn to commenting upon the workshop—from the perspective
of being a Danish anthropologist working with Dominican immigrants in
New York City—I will outline my background in Danish
anthropology/cultural sociology very briefly.

Unlike Danish anthropology, American anthropology has a long tradition of urban ethnic minority studies.[1] The Danish lack of interest (until
recently) in this branch of urban anthropology seems rather strange, if one
considers the fact that one of the founders of American urban studies,
Robert Park from the University of Chicago, was trained very close to
Denmark: at the University of Berlin in 1900 (Schwartz 1989). However,
notions of urban melting pots (imagined or not) in which peoples, cultures,
and races were assumed to create new breeds of urban labor forces and
future citizens did not seem relevant to a small Scandinavian country which
regarded itself as rather homogeneous in terms of demography as well as

---

[1] I find it expedient to delimit ethnic minority studies from other urban studies
as *e.g.* urban aesthetics, youth culture, urban everyday life, and sexual minorities, in
which Danish scholars have taken a great interest.

geography. When immigrants began to enter Denmark in the late 1960s they were considered guests and were until recently called guestworkers, not immigrants. The vast majority of Danish researchers concerned with ethnic enclaves in urban centers therefore conducted their studies abroad.

During the 1970s and 1980s researchers and students at the Institute of Cultural Sociology at the University of Copenhagen began to carry out studies among immigrants in Denmark and to question whether the "guests" were actually birds of passage or if they were rather becoming groups of new Danes, who contributed to creating new multi-cultural urban enclaves in Danish society. (See for example Schwartz 1985; Horst 1991). Many of us, however, continued to seek our theoretical inspiration abroad: Flemming Røgilds in England and South Africa (see Røgilds 1988, 1989), I myself in the Caribbean and New York City (see Sørensen 1991, 1993). At the Institute of Anthropology, Ann-Belinda Steen (1993) brought urban anthropology back to Denmark by studying Tamil refugee experiences in England and Denmark, respectively, and Røgilds—among others —has lately taken up the study of second generation immigrant youths in Denmark and the emerging multi-cultural and multiracial bridges built between Danish and "ethnic" youngsters. However, cities of the United States and their ethnically and racially diverse inhabitants continue to be a great challenge to Danish researchers, who live in a country in which the foreign-born inhabitants still constitute less than three percent of the population.[2] New York City, the USA's still preeminent (though declining) destination for immigrants, offers the Danish researcher an outstanding opportunity to examine the condition under which newcomers cope not only with North American society but also with a locality in which more than 28 percent of the population is foreign born.

I have myself been working with Dominican migration since 1985. First, I did a study of women's everyday lives in a tobacco-producing area in one of the northern provinces of the country and of the internal migration of some of these women to one of the 25 Free Trade Zones established in the Dominican Republic since 1969. During my fieldwork I often met the "American Dream" in frequent references made to *Nueva York* and all the

---

[2] In 1990, the number of foreigners amounted to about 2.9 percent of the total population in Denmark. Out of this group, approximately one third came from the Nordic countries, other European Community countries and other western indus- trialized societies, leaving us with less than two-thirds of immigrants and refugees originating in Third World countries, the non-European part of the Mediterranean and the Middle East. Among the immigrants the main places of origin are Turkey, Yugoslavia, Pakistan and Morocco; among the refugees Iran, Palestine and Lebanon, Sri Lanka and Vietnam are the primary sending countries (Horst 1991). At the moment of writing, refugees from the former Yugoslavia constitute the main group of new arrivals.

opportunities out of reach only because of the unjust boundaries of life—boundaries that actually could be crossed and had been by many relatives, neighbors and friends. I became very curious as I learned that thousands of Dominicans actually resided in New York City and I soon learned that I had to move a lot if I wanted to talk to Dominicans. Because they do. Consequently, so did I.

DOMINICANS IN NEW YORK CITY

The size of the New York–based Dominican community has been debated for a long time. Estimates range from approximately 200,000 to 1,000,000, with the lower estimates being put forth by, among others. Larson and Sullivan (1987) and the higher estimates being forwarded by the Dominican community in New York City. We may allow for a "boastful" exaggeration in the Dominican estimate, but Larson and Sullivan's estimates are nevertheless open to criticism in as far as the transnational character of the United States-bound Dominican migration is left unconsidered. One could argue that the "problem" of double-counting not is a problem but a necessity when dealing with trans-migrants. If one moves into Washington Heights—as I did in 1991–92—one will experience a large and thriving Dominican community with a high level of back-and-forth movers. The numbers of Dominicans moving into New York City is so pronounced that slightly more than one out of every six recent immigrants to the city is Dominican. Out of these, approximately 50 percent moved into Manhattan's Upper West Side (Dept. of City Planning 1992).

Compared to Puerto Rico's long term involvement in United States–bound migration, the Dominican exodus is of a more recent date. Dominican international migration took off in the early 1960s. Though almost exclusively described as a traditional labor migrant population, Dominicans in New York City also consisted of a notable group of political exiles. These people began to leave the Dominican Republic during the Trujillo dictatorship (1930–61), but the majority left in the turbulent years following his assassination in 1961, during the Dominican revolution and the subsequent U.S. military intervention in 1965. These exiles, however, did not achieve refugee status. I mention this because I find it important to draw attention to the context in which displaced persons are categorized as either citizens, refugees, and immigrants in the host society. Though Spanish language, Catholicism, mixed racial background, and several contemporary every day life conditions unite Dominicans with their Puerto Rican (and Cuban) island-neighbors in New York City neighborhoods, their different statuses remain a dividing principle. Such divisions are not always visible on an overarching structural level. By focusing on everyday life experiences, the complex relational ways in which difference is constructed becomes too glaring to be overlooked.

If Dominican women, for example, accuse their Puerto Rican fellow women of being *putas*,[3] what is then at stake? Dominican prejudice and ethnic self-sufficiency or severe differences in access to the promised land due to different migrant status? I find it hard to overlook the fact, that Puerto Rican women—because of their status as citizens—are very "attractive" to Dominican men in search of a visa, although other factors may be important as well. On the other hand, a noticeable amount of Dominican-Puerto Rican intermarriage indicates that social bonds are drawn in New York City. Moreover, many of my female Dominican informants saw marriage to Puerto Rican men as having a liberating potential: "Puerto Rican men are not as *machista* as Dominican men, they are more relaxed," as a younger Dominican student put it. Last, but not least, Dominican and Puerto Rican women have organized collective actions against *machismo*, through social movements rooted in specific neighborhoods in the city. In other words, a complexity of factors tend to separate *and* unite Dominican New Yorkers from/with other migrant groups in the city.

Today Dominicans can be found all over New York City: in the Bronx, in Brooklyn, in Queens, and on Lower East Side and Upper West Side of Manhattan. The largest concentration of Dominicans is north west of Harlem, in Washington Heights, Inwood and Hamilton Heights, three adjoining areas stretching from Harlem and all the way up to the Bronx, which Dominicans call Washington Heights (or Quisqueya Heights if they want to emphasize their—portable—roots).

Dominican bodegas, liqueur stores, *botanicas* (herb shops selling religious and spiritual articles), restaurants, gipsy cabs, and travel agencies brighten up the streets. *Ida y vuelta, ida y vuelta* (departure and return–round-trip) flashes from the neon signs covering the entrances to the travel agencies, reminding passers-by of the transnational character of Dominican migration. Most neighborhoods show Caribbean forms of living. Children playing on the streets, men playing cards and dominos on brought-out tables and women chatting on the stairways. A few neighborhoods, especially around the subway stop at 145th Street, have a bad reputation for drug dealing and street violence. These are "tough" areas, and even among some Dominicans residing here considered off limit, dangerous, boundary areas. "Please remove coins, pencils, hairpins, nails, and bullets from clothes before filling in machines" a poster told where I did my laundry. On the other hand, these neighborhoods are familiar residential areas for others: "This is a bad neighborhood, even though it used to be a lot worse. Go up 163 Street—that's hell!", as one of my Dominican roommates reminded me several times, indicating that the place you reside is never as bad as its reputation for its residents and that the real danger emerges when you enter someone else's territory. I guess Dominican New Yorkers are neither more nor less involved in drug-dealing than other

---

[3] *Puta* = Prostitute, in this context.

minority groups in the City. Like Puerto Rican immigrants, Dominicans have been subjected to accusations of crime, violence, sexual promiscuity and so on, media pictures that create good growing conditions for all sorts of prejudice. Ironically, the accusations of drug-dealing may show up being a basis for ethnic organization in Washington Heights. When a Dominican youngster under suspicion of illegal weapon and drug possession was shot down on the street in the summer 1992, a storm of protests arose from several layers of the New York based Dominican community. These protests became during autumn 1992 the basis on which claims for community houses, stronger political representation, and more Dominican police officers, were based.

CONCEPTUALIZING URBAN LOWER INCOME ETHNIC ENCLAVES

Whereas anthropologists have realized that "culture" may as well be studied in urban settings as in the "traditional village," a tendency to study urban enclaves as "islands"—as localized bounded entities—prevailed for a long time. However, such studies have in the past years become subject to a great deal of anthropological criticism. James Clifford (1992) has convincingly argued that the common notions of culture have been biased toward rooting rather than travel, that culture has been defined through boundaries and that human beings have mistakenly been regarded as immobile. But human beings can no longer—if ever—be regarded as naturally rooted in particular areas, nor can they be seen as necessarily confined to a settled life, be it in rural villages or urban lower income ethnic enclaves. Displacement, relocation, and mobility seem to be equally important factors in human life.

Notions of locality, place, positionality, and space have been central to the latest debate on cultural and ethnic identity. Space and the spatial have increasingly been integrated in analyses concerning the making of history, and time and temporality have increasingly been integrated into geography (Gupta & Ferguson 1992, Massey 1992, Malkki 1992). It has become clear that the world cannot be understood as international in the sense of being made up of independent, separate nations with solid boundaries. Instead it has become a transnational, inter-dependent system where national boundaries are increasingly permeable[4] and where all that anthropologists thought was solid melts into air. This, on the other hand, does not mean that spe-

[4] The extent to which national boundaries are permeable to different groups of people varies. The actual international embargo laid on Haiti and the presence of U.S. Marines in the Caribbean sea surrounding Haiti serves at least two purposes: controlling the embargo and keeping Haitian people in place. The global, transnational world is intentionally denied to the poor. Nevertheless, people manage to cross borders despite restrictive immigration policies and border patrols.

cific localities have lost their importance. Such places may receive greater significance for their inhabitants because they are not viewed as natural conditions of life, but rather as places invested with cultural significance as local communities are carved out of hierarchically organized space (Gupta and Ferguson 1992).

Thus, I suggest that we approach urban ethnic enclaves not as discrete entities, but rather as hierarchically organized urban spaces. Rather than seeing the inhabitants as an undifferentiated group of uprooted islanders we should look at the multiple relations people sustain, construct, and reconstruct in their managing of everyday life. In the case of deterritorialized nations such as Puerto Rico and the Dominican Republic—where notable amounts of citizens live parts of their lives abroad—we should pay attention to the ways in which communities continuously are imagined, invented, and constructed.

In the creating of common grounds of life in internationalized societies, people are faced with powerful forces that works towards differentiating them. Cultural differences are constantly constructed in hierarchical processes—and are almost always strongly articulated in matters related to sexuality and culturally defined gendered orders. My example of the interconnection between immigration policy (differentiating people as citizens, refugees, documented and undocumented migrants) and the gendered notions people construct of each other is not just a curiosity but a serious suggestion for analyzing social relations within and among low income ethnic enclaves in urban settings.

REFERENCES

CLIFFORD, JAMES
 1992 Traveling cultures. In *Cultural Studies. L.* Grossberg, C. Nelson and P. Treichler, Eds. New York: Routledge.
DEPARTMENT OF CITY PLANNING
 1992 *The Newest New Yorkers: An Analysis of Immigration into New York City during the 1980s.* New York: Department of City Planning's Population Division.
GUPTA, AKHIL AND JAMES FERGUSON
 1992 Beyond 'culture': Space, identity, and the Politics of Difference. *Cultural Anthropology* 7 (No. 1):6–23.
HORST, CHRISTIAN
 1991 Social integration of immigrant families in Denmark. *European Journal of Intercultural Studies* 2 (No. 4):33–47.
LARSON, ERIC M. AND TERESA A. SULLIVAN
 1987 "Conventional numbers" in immigration research: The case of the missing Dominicans. *International Migration Review*, xxi (No. 4):1475–1497.

MALKKI, LIISA
1992   National Geographic: The rooting of peoples and the territorialization of national identity among scholars and refugees. *Cultural Anthropology* 7 (No. 1):24–44.
MASSEY, DOREEN
1992   Politics and space time. *New Left Review* **196**:65–84.
RØGILDS, FLEMMING
1988   *Rytme, Racisme og Nye Rødder* (Rhythm, Racism and New Roots). Copenhagen: Politisk Revy.
RØGILDS, FLEMMING, ED.
1989   *Every Cloud has a Silver Lining.* Copenhagen: Academic Publishers.
SCHWARTZ, JONATHAN MATTHEW
1985   *Reluctant Hosts: Denmarks Perception of Guest Workers.* Copenhagen: Academic Publishers.
1989   *In Defense of Homesickness: Nine Essays on Identity and Locality.* Copenhagen: Cultural-sociological Writings No. 26, Academic Publishers.
STEEN, ANN-BELINDA
1993   *Varieties of the Tamil Refugee Experience in Denmark and England.* Copenhagen: Minority Studies & the Danish Centre for Human Rights.
SØRENSEN, NINNA NYBERG
1991   Crossing Boundaries—Migration and Gender in the Dominican Republic. In *Gender, Culture, and Power.* Kristi Anne Stølen, Ed. Oslo: (SUM) University of Oslo.
1993   Ethnicity and gender: A crucial relation. In *Ethnicity and Nationalism: Formation of Identity and Dynamics of Conflict in the 1990s.* Helena Lindholm *et al.*, Eds. Göteborg: Nordic Network of Ethnic Studies.

Slums, Ghettos, and Other Conundrums in the Anthropology of Lower Income Urban Enclaves

M. PATRICIA FERNÁNDEZ KELLY

*Institute of Policy Studies
and Department of Sociology
The Johns Hopkins University
Wyman Park Building #546
Baltimore, Maryland 21218*

INTRODUCTION

To the extent that it assumes uniformity of experience on the part of the impoverished, the term *lower income enclave* can be deceptive: it encompasses both the immigrant slum and the African-American ghetto, not to mention a constellation of proletarian neighborhoods throughout the world in varying degrees of prosperity or deprivation. Most of those cases share in common the spatial concentration of economically vulnerable populations. Nevertheless, their resource base, composition, degree of atomization, density, and capacity for organization and mobilization can differ markedly. Immigrants have experienced penury in many countries as a necessary condition in the slow ascent towards economic success. Their journey has entailed a movement *away* from slums and shanty-towns—a vastly different trajectory than that of ghetto dwellers for whom concentration in impoverished neighborhoods constitutes the concluding episode in a tale of truncated social and economic mobility.

In this paper, I first provide a brief outline of the main forces that have led to the clustering of working-class populations in urban spaces for the last two centuries. That cursory account is meant to act as a reminder of the range of experience concealed behind the rubric *lower income urban enclaves*. I give attention to Mexico's *maquiladora* program because it has stimulated female migration and the concentration of working women in cities along the United States-Mexico border. The case makes plain the role of industrial hiring strategies that target specific groups—in this case women—leading to the clustering of distinct populations in particular urban spaces.

That introductory sketch is followed by a more detailed description of the ways in which migration, ethnicity and race have shaped the American city. Although those three factors have had a long lasting effect on U.S. metropolitan areas, economic globalization and industrial restructuring have transformed the experience of both immigrants and racial minorities. One way to approach the subject is by noting that the two groups are connected: immigrants of the past have become the racial and ethnic minorities of the present. The opposite is also true: impoverished minorities have roots in an immigrant past. A question yet to be answered is whether recently arrived immigrants will be able to find avenues leading to occupational mobility or whether they will see their hopes crushed by economic restructuring. This is tantamount to asking whether, for them, the slum will be a temporary stopover or the ghetto a final destination.

INDUSTRIAL PRODUCTION AND THE FORMATION OF LOWER INCOME URBAN ENCLAVES

The history of industrial capitalism mirrors the effects of segregative and desegregative forces that have resulted in the concentration and dispersion of populations depending on their position within the larger productive system (Frisbie and Kasarda 1988, p. 630). In Europe the emergence of modern cities, since the late eighteenth century, coincided with the displacement of the peasantry, steady flows of rural-urban migration, and the growth of proletarian clusters around new places of employment in metropolitan areas. The arrival of new immigrants caused with varying degrees of rapidity, the exodus of more affluent populations from their original areas of residence. Urban space was thus repeatedly segmented along social class lines. While this phenomenon was evident in the European context—especially in major industrial powers like England—it was even more striking in the United States where racial divides and uninterrupted domestic and international migration have left a durable imprint.

In Latin America, as well, processes of modernization associated with the mechanization of agriculture led to the displacement of rural populations and the proliferation of working-class neighborhoods within or in the vicinity of urban centers. Known under various names in the relevant literature—*conventillos, fabelas, colonias, barrios, poblaciones, zonas marginadas*—those urban areas often grew around squatter settlements and shanty-towns where residents undertook the construction of their own homes and exerted pressure upon national governments for the eventual provision of public services. During the first half of the twentieth century, those proletarian neighborhoods formed through illicit occupation, tenacious settlement, and turbulent interaction with state authorities provided the grist for industry and the constituencies upon which populist states gained legitimacy. Argentina, Brazil and Mexico are examples of that early trend.

Starting in the late 1960s, the globalization of the economy generated new pressures resulting in demographic reconcentration and dispersion. Seeking to retain a competitive edge in world markets by lowering production costs, firms in advanced industrial nations seized opportunities for investment in less developed countries, mainly in Asia and Latin America. The availability of computer technology and low-cost transportation, among other factors, enabled them to coordinate manufacturing operations in distant geographical areas where the cost of labor was comparatively low and protective legislation almost non-existent (Fernández Kelly 1989; see also Nash and Fernández Kelly 1983, Portes and Walton 1981, Storper 1985). In the United States and England the effect of this trend was *deindustrialization,* that is, an epidemic of plant-closings and extensive worker dislocation during the 1970s and 1980s (Bluestone and Harrison 1982). However, in areas like the U.S.-Mexico border, the same process,resulted in the consolidation of the largest experiment in export-processing industrialization—the well-known *maquiladora* program. Although the program has experienced several permutations since it was established in the late 1960s, it continues to promote the employment of a predominantly young and female work-force. During the early years of their existence, *maquiladoras* hired a large number of women, most of them between the ages of 16 and 25, in garment and electronics assembly. Since 1983, a new sector of auto-transport equipment plants created opportunities for men but, as the century draws to an end, 75% of nearly 420,000 *maquiladora* workers are still women.

The recruiting strategies of firms along the U.S.-Mexico border have had consequences for the patterns of urban settlement. Assembly workers first employed in Ciudad Juárez, a major focus of *maquiladora* activity, were girls who had grown up in the city after their families migrated, displaced by the increasing mechanization of agriculture in their hometowns (Fernández Kelly 1983). More recently, maquiladoras have acted as a magnet attracting individuals whose families are left behind. Two effects of this process are worth mentioning: One is the concentration of predominantly female immigrants in marginal working-class neighborhoods and the growth in the number of female-headed households in those residential areas. Another is the widespread multiplication of women as main providers rather than supplementary wage-earners for their families. This shift in gender roles is similar in importance to that which accompanied the emergence of the family wage, men as *bread-winners* and women as housewives during the early stages of the industrial revolution. Although the Mexican case is impressive for its magnitude, it is echoed in Asia and the Caribbean Basin where similar processes of export-oriented industrialization have taken place.

The sketch above condenses a familiar pattern consisting of the concomitant concentration and deconcentration of working-class populations following particular types of investment and disinvestment. In the remainder of this paper, I give attention to the way in which the American city has been shaped by ethnic and racial demarcations.

URBAN DESIGN AND THE POLITICS OF RACE AND ETHNICITY

Two great sagas—international migration and racial polarization—have left their indelible mark in American cities. Praises to the forbearance and determination of an immigrant ancestry are deeply ingrained in the American lore. At the same time, immigrants have almost always been seen as social contaminants, the purveyors of disease, ignorance, and dubious morality (Portes and Rumbaut 1990 p. 99). Few and far between have been the instances when foreigners have not been received with suspicion and hostility by those who had claimed this land at an earlier date. A consistent pattern in U.S. metropolitan areas has been the departure of older, mostly white, populations after every arrival of immigrant and racial minorities.

Although many immigrants have spontaneously moved to this country driven by hopes for a better life, active recruitment played a major role in the beginning. As a budding economic power, the United States experienced rising labor demands in the nineteenth century, but its emerging opportunities were not well known abroad. Employers, therefore, had to mobilize to attract labor. Business delegates were sent to Mexico, Ireland, southern Italy, and the Austro-Hungarian empire to enlighten potential workers about the favorable terms available in the eastern canal companies and the western railroads. At the turn of the century, Central and Eastern Europeans were actively enlisted for work in the Midwest following the development of capital-intensive industries in that region—first steel and then auto manufacturing. Several decades before, labor recruitment by the Hudson and other canal companies moved contingents of Irish and Italian workers towards the routes followed by canal construction. In the West, Chinese workers traveled inland after mass recruitment by the railway companies. The Union Pacific and the Central Pacific also recruited Mexicans. About the same time, Finnish workers made their appearance in northern Wisconsin, Minnesota, and the Michigan Peninsula, hired by the copper mines and timber companies (Portes and Rumbaut 1990, p.13)

Geographical proximity to their points of origin influenced the settlement patterns of early immigrants. That explains why the majority of European immigrants gathered along the mid-and north-Atlantic Seaboard, Asians clustered in California and other Pacific states, and Mexican immigration concentrated in the Southwest. The importance of geographical propinquity was most vividly manifested by immigrant communities established right by the waterfront, in port cities of both coasts. The "Little Italies" nestled along the harbor in Boston, New York, Philadelphia, and Baltimore or San Francisco's "Chinatown" remain as evidence of immigrant flows that, having reached U.S. shores would venture no farther (Portes and Rumbaut 1990, p. 29) Clusters of foreigners of varying nationalities dotted urban landscapes throughout the latter part of the nineteenth century.

By the early 1900s, the United States was receiving unprecedented numbers of immigrants per year; foreigners represented up to 21 percent of the American labor force and close to half of the urban population. In contrast to picturesque appraisals written many years later, reports of the time evince a persistent alarm over living conditions in immigrant settlements. As "slum" and "foreign colony" became interchangeable terms, a perception grew that immigrants, especially those from Southern and Eastern Europe, had "hereditary peculiarities" that threatened the fabric of American institutions. Even at that early stage, government agencies invested personnel and resources to investigate the social pathologies contained in immigrant neighborhoods. A major report issued in 1894 by the Department of Labor compared Baltimore, Chicago, New York, and Philadelphia and defined slum as "an area of dirty back streets, especially when inhabited by a squalid and criminal population" (Wright 1894, p. 3). The rawness of its phrasing notwithstanding, that description eerily evokes contemporary accounts of the black ghetto in the inner city.

An illustration of the conditions and changes endured by the immigrant slum is found in Upton, a West Baltimore area that grew in the late eighteenth century as a result of European migration. Irish, German, Polish and Bohemian waves first, and then Eastern European Jews, coexisted in Upton with manumitted slaves in a manner akin to that which characterized the slums of other developing cities. Many residents were unskilled manual workers and domestic servants employed in expanding commercial districts and wealthy homes (Olson 1980, p. 121) Following a national pattern, this working class neighborhood emerged in relative proximity to more affluent residential areas.

The early nineteenth century witnessed increases in the rates of homicide and pauperism in Upton. Observers noted a rise of disease, filth, and crowded living conditions. Epidemics of smallpox, diphtheria and measles were common by 1821 when a noted physician characterized a section in Upton as "A nest of houses tenanted by *negroes* and divided by an alley [where] disease and death have year after year luxuriously rioted among the miserable and abandoned victims who have there nestled together" (Dr. G. S. Townsend as quoted in Griffith 1833, p. 288; see also Scharf 1874). By the 1860s, local government sought to make provision for the protection of "unfortunate helpless maniacs" who were appearing on the streets of West Baltimore. There was a great increase of idle and wandering poor, chiefly women with children and without husbands, and old men destitute, helpless, and without work. Historical accounts also mention multitudes of arrivals, especially Irish who flocked to the area, worn-out *negroes,* and infant beggars (Olson 1980, pp. 53-54).

In West Baltimore as in other urban areas, European immigrants followed a well-known trajectory: they lived poorly and worked tirelessly; they saved hoping to move to better places. They viewed the slum and the sordid tenements as temporary calamities to be endured in the search for a good life. For the majority, economic advancement meant relocating to other, more prosperous, neighborhoods. Social reconfigurations were mirrored by spatial rearrangements. However, moving to better neighborhoods was out of reach for African Americans who were shunned as a result of strict racial demarcations. As immigrants moved to more attractive locations, permanent enclosure, on the basis of color and race, became Upton's trademark. West Baltimore epitomizes a common phenomenon: the transformation of immigrant slums into black ghettos (see Philpott 1978 for an excellent account of this phenomenon).

The gradual integration of immigrants and their children into American society paralleled the expansion of metropolitan areas and the tendency towards suburbanization. As upwardly mobile populations fled to more attractive residential areas in suburban rings, a new class of real estate brokers and developers grew. Larger demographic and economic changes further contributed to the dispersion of older populations. In particular, the industrial expansion in the North created an increased demand for labor which, at the time of World War I, began to be filled by black immigrants from the rural South where cotton agriculture was declining. The impact of black northward migration was profound. In 1910, almost 90 percent of blacks were living in the South, but sixty years later, little more than half remained there. Streams of southern blacks to the North and West reached epic proportions from 1940 to 1970, with almost 1.5 million blacks leaving in each of these three decades (Marger 1994). Moreover, this migration was almost wholly to the cities, making blacks an increasingly urbanized population.

African Americans arrived in cities like Chicago, New York, Boston and Philadelphia with expectations of upward mobility identical to those of older European immigrants and under conditions which early students of ethnicity regarded as optimum for assimilation.[1] For that reason, they posed a threat to white workers in the North, and the violence and intimidation that had characterized southern race relations became a national phenomenon. Competition for work and housing, and growing impatience among blacks, translated into an increase in the frequency and severity of black-white hostilities (see, for example Tuttle 1970).

At the same time, despite the barriers of discrimination, many blacks rose to middle class status and, like other Americans, they sought to move to more attractive residential areas. Ironically, this opened opportunities for real estate speculators willing to profit from the rising aspirations of blacks

---

[1] See, for example, Burgess, 1925, pp. 47–62. Those early expectations for the assimilation of African-Americans did not materialize. What has been most striking about urban black ghettos is their persistence over time. Although other ethnic groups have clustered in *barrios* and slums, their eventual integration into desegregated neighborhoods has been much higher (see Massey and Denton 1987).

and the prejudice of whites. Profits to be made in buying homes from Jewish and other white owners at below market prices and reselling them to blacks for exorbitant sums ignited the practice of blockbusting.[2] Real estate agents began placing middle class families in previously all-white neighborhoods triggering panic about potential losses in property values. In the process, all-white areas were quickly transformed into all-black areas and, often, into extensions of older ghettos. Blacks invariably paid more for the housing than the former residents, enabling realtors to boost their commissions. Such practices yielded substantial fortunes in every major American city.

Although significant, *blockbusting* was only one of several factors maintaining residential segregation. Government policies, for example, created much of the framework necessary to perpetuate it. Since the 1930s, the federal government had encouraged home ownership among middle- and working-class people through the establishment of the Federal Housing Administration (FHA) and other housing-related agencies. Their purpose was to provide low-cost financing by providing government-backed mortgage insurance. From the outset, the FHA discouraged integration by refusing to guarantee loans for homes that were not in racially homogeneous areas (Feagin and Feagin 1978). Although this policy was altered in 1962—when non-discriminatory pledges were required from loan applicants—it laid the basis for persistent residential segregation.

Banks and other lending institutions contributed to the same system by *redlining*, that is, designating certain areas within which real estate loans would not be made. Zoning regulations were established specifying the types of housing that could be built in particular neighborhoods; these were designed to exclude low-income, mainly black, units. Restrictive covenants, and other similar agreements, were also used to bar blacks and other minorities from white residential areas. Until the Civil Rights Act of 1968 prohibited discrimination in housing, such covenants were widely applied and even supported by law until 1948.[3]

The result of these formal and informal policies was the consolidation of a dual housing market in the United States: one predominantly white and the other mostly black. Driven by forces that were largely economic (like the search for financial gain) but also social (like racial prejudice), the real estate industry, banks and lending institutions, and government agencies played a role in the maintenance of a system which has had far reaching

---

[2] A chilling account of these practices, as manifested in Boston, is provided in Levine and Harmon 1992; see also Philpott 1978 and Olson 1980.

[3] A counterpart of these developments consisted of the recalcitrant tendency to locate publicly subsidized housing projects in impoverished, mostly African-American, neighborhoods. The infamous *projects* contributed to further concentrate poverty in the inner city. For an eloquent illustration of this process in Chicago's Governor Henry Horner Homes—"The Hornets"—see Kotlowitz 1992.

consequences. For example, redlining in black neighborhoods had a major negative repercussion on public school financing which has historically depended on taxation based on property values. The exodus of affluent populations and the concentration of impoverished groups in central cities created serious financial problems for local governments which were doubly exacerbated, in recent years, by the loss of manufacturing jobs (see Wilson 1987, pp. 95-104). Deteriorated and boarded-up housing units, high vacancy rates and a paucity of business activity in black neighborhoods are among the visible manifestations of institutional arrangements that have persisted for most of the twentieth century.

Finally, and perhaps most insidiously, residential segregation, has resulted in the truncation of social ties upon which processes of successful incorporation into the larger society depend. A substantial number of African-American children continue to grow up in urban environments as highly segregated as those that existed more than thirty years ago, before the beginning of the Civil Rights Movement. Largely for that reason, their experience differs markedly from that of youngsters living in more affluent neighborhoods (Wilson 1987, pp. 60-62). Thus, the most disturbing effect of residential segregation may have been the shrinkage of experience created by insularity, confinement and the dearth of resources of superior quality available to new generations (Fernández Kelly 1994). Although other immigrant groups have endured harsh treatment in their journey towards assimilation, African-Americans stand alone as an illustration of stubborn exclusion even in the face of governmental efforts to promote incorporation.

Immigration and racial polarization—the two great American dramas— have left a durable mark upon cities in the United States. The chronicle of immigration contains complex sub-processes such as the dynamics of attraction/repulsion evident in the coexistence of immigrant recruitment and stigmatization that paralleled the formation of urban slums at the turn-of-the-century. The same is true about racial divisions: legislative attempts to promote inclusion have continuously clashed with a collective will to maintain rigid demarcations. In both cases race and ethnicity have reflected larger processes of class domination and subordination. The assimilation of older immigrant groups entailed their ascent in the social and occupational ladders but also their actual movement away from the slum. The perpetuation of poverty among African-Americans has been mirrored by the hardening contours of the urban ghetto (Massey 1993a and 1993b).

DIVIDED FATES: IMMIGRANTS AND RACIAL MINORITIES IN THE NEW AMERICAN METROPOLIS

Starting in the mid-1960s a major shift towards economic globalization was made possible by revolutionary changes in technology. The invention and refinement of the semiconductor, as well as the design of affordable computers of manageable size and increased capacity for the storage and transmission of information, recast the options of consumers and producers; workers and employers (see Siegel 1984; see also Shurkin). The dazzling array of high-tech innovation also had a visible impact upon cities in the United States and abroad. A major effect of computer technology has been the creation of international communication and production networks that have greatly diminished the constraints imposed by geographical distance and linked urban spaces in ways never seen before (see Bradshaw and Freeman 1984; see also Glassmeier, Markusen and Hall 1983 and Castells 1985).

Although technological development does not occur independently from economic, cultural, and political processes, high-tech innovations have been of such magnitude as to mark the beginning of a new stage in capitalist development. The application of advanced technology to production propelled a shift from manufacturing to services and information-based industries. Automation and the abandonment of traditional factories resulted in reductions in the number of unionized jobs and the outmigration of people from older manufacturing cities. At the same time, high-tech and white-collar service sectors grew rapidly. Vast increases in communications capacity stimulated a corporate strategy of interregional and international production regardless of the social and economic consequences for local areas. Government contributed to this process by providing support for capital growth in the form of defense spending and reduced social expenditures throughout the 1970s and, especially, during the 1980s (see Castells 1985).

High-technology industries have promoted new spatial patterns of production. In the United States, old industrial centers, ports and depots, have been replaced by pools of technical and scientific workers, centers of defense spending, sources of innovative venture capital, and strategic nodes in a communication network. In the same vein, changing technology has altered the locational behavior of industry and encouraged the growth of new regions. Older sites constituted by an assortment of physical places have been infiltrated, and in some cases replaced, by intangible spaces formed by flows of information.[4] This, in turn, is constituting a new hierarchy of functions and power accessible in varying degree to social groups differentiated by class, race, ethnicity and gender.

The electronics industry, which has been part and parcel of these processes, embodies some of the critical changes undergone by the broader economy over the last three decades. The export of jobs to less developed countries, low rates of unionization, and the combination of automation in the United States with labor-intensive operations abroad, are all features of

---

[4] The notion of a new intangible spaces created by communication flows is more than a metaphor. One of the major developments in 1993 was the emergence of the *information superhighway* connecting individuals and institutions vying for access to the most advanced scientific, financial, and technical data.

electronics manufacture. In New York's Manhattan, an early clustering of large, vertically integrated corporations gave way during the late 1970s and early 1980s to a multiplicity of small companies in its periphery, including neighboring counties in New Jersey. Restructuring encompassed shifts in the spatial distribution of firms of various types and a movement towards specialized activities which in many cases resemble a new form of artisanal production. Many of the new entrepreneurs in the New York metropolitan area are individuals previously associated with larger, vertically integrated, firms which pioneered development in the electronics industry. Those new entrepreneurs are especially skilled in areas such as design and tend to sub-contract for a variety of firms while at the same time "putting-out" part of the production process to smaller, often unregulated—or informal—estab-lishments and home workers. Thus, the lowest echelon of the industry is characterized by the presence of industrial home workers many of whom are women (Fernández Kelly 1993).

In Southern California, where the largest number of electronics firms was contained during the 1980s, variations of the same critical features are apparent. There, electronics firms have resorted to a series of strategies to retain a competitive edge, including an explicit avoidance of unionized work forces, a move away from vertically integrated operations, reductions in plant size, and a shift toward subcontracting. Subcontracting, in partic-ular, has spurred the demand for Hispanic workers most of whom are women and many of whom are foreign born. High-tech firms have favored locations in sprawling suburban conglomerates and fostered the employ-ment of immigrants and refugees, while at the same time providing few opportunities for native-born minorities, especially African Americans.

A distinct effect of the rise of *global* or *informational* cities in the United States has been the growth in the demand for professional workers with high levels of education and endowed with symbolic skills. About one-third of the jobs created by the new economy require specialized knowledge (Reich 1991). Engineers, lawyers, communications experts, computer designers, software developers and related consultants of all kinds have tended to converge in large cities characterized by their integral location within the new world economy—New York, Los Angeles, Boston, Chicago—and, to a lesser extent, in smaller cities like Baltimore and Atlanta. Many of those specialists have entered the economy as members of two-earner households, thus representing highly lucrative prospects for real estate markets and related sectors of production and consumption.

The concentration of professionals in pivotal metropolitan areas has had a dual effect. First, it has spurred processes of *gentrification* encompassing the renovation of declining neighborhoods, with the consequent rise in property values, and the displacement of older and/or low-income popula-tions. At the same time, local governments trying to attract high-technolo-gy industries, as well as tourism, have provided tax incentives to developers engaged in urban revitalization projects. Old industrial areas in Baltimore, Pittsburgh and even Detroit have been transformed into showcases of customized entertainment and associated services. Revitalizing efforts have, in most cases, bifurcated the urban space into a glittering stratum, traversed by affluent citizens and tourists, and a less conspicuous layer of rotting infrastructure inhabited by impoverished populations.

Second, the new technocratic class has also invigorated the demand for a variety of labor-intensive activities ranging from domestic service, to restaurants and customized furniture and apparel. This has created interstices for the employment of recent waves of immigrants, primarily from Asia, Latin American and the Caribbean, many of whom are undocumented (for excellent descriptions of this process see Sassen 1988 and 1992). New *panethnic* formations constituted by the combination of immigrant businesses and workers sharing a common language but stratified in terms of social class, race and national origin have emerged in places like Los Angeles, Washington and, especially, New York.

Jackson Heights, in the borough of Queens is an apt illustration of this phenomenon. Noticeable in that area, along Roosevelt Avenue, is a vibrant cluster of mostly Colombian and some Dominican businesses thriving in what once was a predominantly Irish neighborhood. With few exceptions, commercial establishments bear fresh-paint traces of their recent establishment. Several miniature malls merge Korean and Colombian businesses, most of which hire Mexicans as low-skilled workers. In the lateral streets, industrial home work—mainly in garment manufacture—flourishes in a multitude of modest apartments and lofts. Also attesting to the vitality of a burgeoning unregulated economy, a myriad street merchants sell cheap goods and food alongside formal restaurants offering delicacies from Ecuador, Mexico, and the Dominican Republic. The external perception is that Jackson Heights is a *Hispanic* residential area, but from within, high levels of heterogeneity in terms of race, nationality and class are noticeable. Paradoxically, the age of advanced technology has not expunged older forms of labor supply; it has merely transformed them.

The concentration of immigrants in particular locations within or in the proximity of global cities depends on the characteristics of labor demand but also on the existence of transnational social networks formed by individuals who comfortably cross borders from specific points in areas of origin to specific points in areas of destination. At least for the time being, many of those immigrants appear less interested in assimilating to the larger society than in acquiring the means to maintain their status and visibility in their sending communities. The advantages of low-cost transportation that have enabled investors to relocate manufacturing operations to the less developed world have also facilitated the emergence of a new type of immigrant who sees cities in the United States as attractive places for employment but not necessarily permanent residence. Transnational labor markets appear to be one of the less obvious, albeit profoundly significant, consequences of globalization (see Sassen 1994).

A relatively short ride away from Roosevelt Avenue, in Washington Heights, a flourishing cluster of Dominican businesses merges almost imperceptibly with Harlem, the most notorious black area in New York. From an external vantage point, the two neighborhoods consolidate into a single black ghetto. From within, heterogeneity is again readily apparent. In contrast with the vitality of Washington heights, Harlem bears all the traces of despair associated with the presence of an urban *underclass*—abandoned houses, unemployed men dealing drugs in street corners, violence, high numbers of female-headed households dependent on public assistance, and numerous births out-of-wedlock to adolescents. Dominicans share residential spaces and schools with these, most vulnerable, populations. Outside their modest homes, Dominican children mingle with and mimic the fashions, style and mode of speech of impoverished African Americans. This raises questions about the extent to which assimilation, among these new immigrants, will mean *becoming black Americans* with the consequent extension of stigma, isolation and dismemberment from the larger society.[5] The options of new immigrants in the restructured economy may well divide depending on spatial locations and the concomitant access to differential social networks and economic resources.

Narratives focusing on the new *informational* or *global* city have focused on the awe-inspiring transformations brought about by computers. Nevertheless, there is another side to the same story: the application of advanced technology is part and parcel of processes that have stiffened social polarization and altered the prospects of both immigrants and native-born Americans. That bifurcation is being echoed every day in the reconstitution of urban spaces. The same city inhabited by the purveyors of symbolic skills is populated by less prominent, but more numerous, groups some of whom are providing muscle for the new economy and others who languish without purpose or function in the occupational ladder.

CONCLUSIONS

Since its inception, as part of the historical developments that brought about the Industrial Revolution in the nineteenth century, the modern city has been shaped by concentrations of people differentiated in terms of race, ethnicity, social class and—as the case of the U.S.-Mexico border shows—even gender. This has afforded the modern city a split identity; at the same time a place of progress and cultural innovation, and a field where the nightmares of modernization are played out without respite. In the collective mind, the city has always been constructed as a place of difference where impoverished populations seek survival. What has changed is the extent to which long-lived social and economic processes threaten to create

---

[5] Similar questions may be asked about Haitians clustered on the fringes of Liberty City, one of two ghettos in Miami, and about Mexicans and Central Americans in South Central Los Angeles (see Portes 1994).

a permanent division between those who are part of a revitalized capitalist enterprise and those who are now, for all practical purposes, evicted from the system of production.

Beyond its shimmering patina of computers, automated teller machines, video games and *information super highways,* the global city surges as the visible expression of new forms of incorporation of professionals and immigrants and the exclusion of native-born racial and ethnic minorities. Therein lies the paradox of continued immigration nourishing the ranks of the post-industrial working class, in coexistence with the agony that suffocates the urban ghetto.

REFERENCES

BLUESTONE, BARRY AND BENNETT HARRISON
    1982   *The Deindustrialization of America: Plant Closings, Community Abandonment, and the Dismantling of Basic Industry.* New York: Basic Books.

BRADSHAW, T. K. AND M. FREEMAN
    1984   The future of the electronics industry in California communities. Institute of Governmental Studies, University of California.

BURGESS, ERNEST W.
    1925   The growth of the city: An introduction to a research project. In *The City,* Robert Park, Ernest Burgess, and Roderick D. McKenzie, Eds. Chicago: University of Chicago Press.

CASTELLS, MANUEL
    1985   Towards the informational city, high technology, economic change and spatial structure: Some exploratory hypotheses. Working paper no. 430. Institute of Urban and Regional Development, University of California at Berkeley.
    1985   High technology, economic restructuring, and the urban-regional process in the United States. In *High Technology, Space, and Society,* Manuel Castells, Ed. Beverly Hills, CA: Sage Publications.

FEAGIN, JOE R. AND CLAIRECE BOOHER FEAGIN
    1978   *Discrimination American Style: Institutional Racism and Sexism.* Englewood Cliffs, NJ: Prentice-Hall.

FERNÁNDEZ KELLY, M. PATRICIA
    1982   *For We Are Sold, Me and My People: Women and Industry in Mexico's Frontier.* Albany: State University of New York Press.
    1989   International development and industrial restructuring: The case of garment and electronics industries in Southern California. In *Instability and Change in the World Economy,* Arthur MacEwan and William K. Tabb, Eds. New York: Monthly Review Press.
    1993   Labor force recomposition and industrial restructuring in electronics: Implications for free trade. *Hofstra Labor Law Journal* **10** (2) Spring: 644.
    1994   Social and cultural capital in the urban ghetto: Implications for economic sociology. In *The Economic Sociology of Immigration: Essays in Networks, Ethnicity, and Entrepreneurship.* New York: Russell Sage Foundation Press.

FRISBIE, W. PARKER AND JOHN D. KASARDA
  1988   Spatial processes. In *Handbook of Sociology,* Neil J. Smelser, Ed. Newbury Park, CA: Sage Publications.
GLASSMEIER, A., A.R. MARKUSEN, AND P. HALL
  1983   Defining high technology industries. Working paper no. 407. Institute of Urban and Regional Development, University of California at Berkeley.
GRIFFITH, W. THOMAS
  1833   *Annals of Baltimore.* Baltimore: W. Woody.
KOTLOWITZ, ALEX
  1992   *There Are No Children Here: The Story of Two Boys Growing up in the Other America.* New York: Doubleday.
LEVINE, HILLEL AND LAWRENCE HARMON
  1992   *The Death of an American Jewish Community: A Tragedy of Good Intentions.* New York: The Free Press.
MARGER, MARTIN N.
  1994   *Race and Ethnic Relations: American and Global Perspectives.* Belmont, CA: Wadsworth.
MASSEY, DOUGLAS S. AND NANCY A. DENTON
  1987   Trends in the residential segregation of Blacks, Hispanics, and Asians: 1970 - 1980. *American Sociological Review* **52**: 802-825.
MASSEY, DOUGLAS
  1993   *American Apartheid: Segregation and the Making of the Underclass.* Cambridge, MA: Harvard University Press.
  1993   Black Migration, Segregation, and the Spatial Concentration of Poverty. Working Paper. Population Research Center, The University of Chicago (Mimeo).
NASH, JUNE AND M. PATRICIA FERNÁNDEZ KELLY, EDS.
  1983   *Women, Men, and the International Division of Labor.* Albany: State University of New York Press.
OLSON, SHERRY H.
  1980   *Baltimore: The Building of an American City.* Baltimore: Johns Hopkins University Press.
PHILPOTT, THOMAS LEE
  1978   *The Slum and the Ghetto: Neighborhood Deterioration and Middle-Class Reform. Chicago, 1880 -1930.* New York: Oxford University Press.
PORTES, ALEJANDRO
  1989   Latin American urbanization during the years of the crisis. *Latin American Research Review* **XXIV** (3): 7-44.
  1994   Children of immigrants: Segmented assimilation and its determinants. In *The Economic Sociology of Immigration: Essays in Networks, Ethnicity, and Entrepreneurship.* New York: Russell Sage Foundation Press.
PORTES, ALEJANDRO AND RUBÉN G. RUMBAUT
  1990   *Immigrant America: A Portrait.* Berkeley: University of California Press.
PORTES ALEJANDRO AND JOHN WALTON
  1981   *Labor, Class and the International System.* New York: Academic Press.
REICH, ROBERT
  1991   *The Work of Nations: Preparing Ourselves for 21st Century Capitalism.* New York: Alfred A. Knopf.

SASSEN, SASKIA
1988   *The Mobility of Capital and Labor.* Cambridge: Cambridge University Press.
1992   *The Global City: New York, London, Tokyo.* Princeton, NJ: Princeton University Press.
1994   *Immigration and local labor markets. In The Economic Sociology of Immigration: Essays in Networks, Ethnicity, and Entrepreneurship,* Alejandro Portes, Ed. New York: Russell Sage Foundation.
SCHARF, THOMAS
1874   *The Chronicles of Baltimore.* Baltimore: Turnbull Brothers.
SHURKIN, JOEL
1984   *Engines of the Mind: A History of the Computer.* New York: W.W. Norton and Co.
SIEGEL, LENI
1984   Delicate bonds: The semiconductor industry. Mountain View, CA: Pacific Studies Center.
STORPER, MICHAEL
1985   Technology and spatial production relations: Disequilibrium, interindustry relationships, and industrial development. In High Technology, Space and Society, Manuel Castells, Ed. Beverly Hills, CA: Sage Publications.
TUTTLE, WILLIAM M., JR.
1970   *Race Riot: Chicago in the Red Summer of 1919.* New York: Atheneum.
WILSON, WILLIAM J.
1987   *The Truly Disadvantaged: The Inner City, the Underclass, and Public Policy.* Chicago: University of Chicago Press.
WRIGHT, CARROLL D.
1894   *The Slums of Baltimore, Chicago, New York, and Philadelphia.* Seventh Special Report of the Commissioner of Labor. Washington, DC: Department of Labor.

The Urban Enclave and Related Policy Issues

JOAN MONTBACH

Linkages
784 Columbus Avenue
New York, New York 10025

The Fall 1992 Workshop on Urban Enclaves examined two related issues: 1) the continuing and unremitting needs of poor populations in the United States (and particularly in New York City) as revealed through personal biographies, community studies, and policy analyses and 2) the increasing failure of social policy to effectively address these needs. Attention was focused on gaps in the development of urban social policy and on new ways to think about the roles played by the researcher, community resident and the policy makers. Several of the attendees—more specifically, those of us who did not present a paper at this workshop—were asked to reflect on the impact of this workshop on our work. Thus, in this paper I define what were for me key outcomes of this conference, and offer suggestions for new spheres of urban research.

Unlike many of the presenters at this conference who are actively engaged in social science research and teaching, I am presently working as a social service provider. Although I am an anthropologist by training, for the past several years my principal responsibilities have been administrative; currently, for example, I am providing administrative support to two programs in East Harlem: an AIDS outreach program and a residential treatment facility for MICA (mentally ill/chemical abusing) women and their children. Over the past several years I have operated programs for non-profit agencies—programs which address many of the issues raised in this workshop: substance abuse, homelessness, family violence, *etc.*

As a non-profit administrator, I am keenly aware that providers tend to be more concerned with crisis management rather than long-term planning and problem solving. This tendency to "focus down" is due, at least in part, to persistent insecurity and intense competition for funding for social services. It is also due to the continuing crises experienced by the clients we serve. Each case contains the elements of a crisis—is the child in this family at-risk of abuse or neglect? is the parent relapsing? will housing be available for this mother/child dyad at the time of discharge? are workshop attendees getting the message about practicing safe sex? should the curriculum be revised to better reflect the needs of the participants? and of course, where will the money come from to pay for this service? for hiring this staff?

235

Practitioners engaged in the day-to-day management of social service programs are rarely afforded the time or opportunity to reflect on the impact and purpose of their work. Similar problems mar the relationship between the policy makers and the clients whose interests they represent. In defining the rules that govern day to day life in the urban enclave, policy makers are more often guided by consumers (read voters), local level providers, and of course the socio-political environment than they are by research evidence supporting innovative social agendas.

Collaboration between practitioners, policy makers and researchers is often hailed as a means of providing the social service community with valuable insights into the strengths and weaknesses of their program approaches. Rarely, however, is this kind of collaboration ever achieved. (see Reid 1993; Ashford and Lecroy 1991). The dialogue between participants at this conference, sustained in this book, provides just such a valued opportunity.

As a provider who affects and is affected by official policy, one of the key outcomes of this workshop for me was in observing the ways in which the complex web of issues that confront practitioners and decision makers are mirrored in the experiences of consumers of urban services. Discovering ways to manage urban life—to seek solutions and to overcome obstacles—is the task of both the urban resident and the policy maker. Managing urban problems is a challenge for the poor; at the same time formulating policy is a notorious morass—a seemingly incomprehensible remarkable tangle of rules/regulations and conflicting ideologies. Finally, responses to the frustrations and both the urban dweller and the urban bureaucrat are trivialized. More on this below. First, let me identify some of specific contributions made by presenters and responders to this conference from my perspective as a social service provider:

1. A central contribution made by presenters of this workshop was emphasizing the need to put a human face on social problems and describing ways in which this task can be accomplished:

Although the backdrop for many of the issues discussed at this workshop was on the larger political and economic forces that impact local communities, the presenters provided us with an insider's view of the effects of such problems as unemployment, domestic violence, substandard housing, substance abuse on the life of the community. Providers, unlike ethnographers, often see only one aspect of this human face. While social service agencies now espouse a comprehensive (some call it "one-stop shopping") approach to service delivery, most providers have been trained in narrow specialty areas (*e.g.*, substance abuse, domestic violence, child abuse) and continue to define issues and interventions according to their own areas of expertise. Thus, while they may at times offer a voice for the consumer, the providers' focus is often quite narrow. The policy makers, on the other hand, have a wider perspective but too often have very little direct experiences with the individuals whose lives they affect and importantly, most see themselves as mediators—mediating conflicts between interest groups. In the absence of descriptive material, policy makers have a tendency to stereotype and/or

establish priorities which reflect the needs of the most influential constituency.

As discussed in this workshop, personal biographies as a methodological
devise afford informants an opportunity to tell stories about their lives and
afford policy makers access to this information in all its richness. In so
doing, opportunities are provided for exploring strategies used and lessons
learned about meeting one's own needs, and on individual variation in
available resources.

At the same time, a good biography also exposes our informants to careful scrutiny. The person behind the policy is the human face portrayed by
researchers at this workshop. Responsible policy must be based on the realization that problems are not static—the world of the poor often consists of
saddening cycles of victimization and abusive responses, or as Rosa
Torruellas described life in the urban enclave: "a negotiation between the
sustaining and oppressing aspects of family life." At different points in one's
life cycle or from differing perspective, the victim may even be the perpetrator (or the perpetrator the victim) and the policy responses must be formulated to address these evolving needs.

2. A second important contribution of this workshop was the effort on the
part of the presenters to identify specific ways in which changes in social
policy might be effected. Clearly, the urban ethnographer can play an
increasingly helpful role by facilitating dialogue, clarifying, generalizing,
and contextualizing themes identified by various constituencies.

Through devices like "community biographies" information is revealed
about the ways in which resources and the ability of the community to meet
the addressed needs of its populace vary through time (through changes in
demographics, resource base, *etc.*). In their "search for solutions" to urban
problems, policy makers have often failed in the past to acknowledge a community's strengths—for example, the social networks, communities of
interest, and kinship groups, or its need for involvement.

As argued by Freidenberg and discussed by the majority of the participants in this conference, informants—recipients of service—not only can
but *must* participate in the problem solving if workable solutions are to be
designed. The discussion of information exchange is particularly relevant to
our understanding of evolving social policy.

The concept of involving the informant/client in decision making situations has emerged as a political ideal in the past several decades, starting
with the decentralization movements of the 1960s and 1970s; the newest
expression of this ideal is represented by the popularity of the term
"empowerment":

> Certainly as professional caregivers, we can stand back and intellectual-
> ly attempt to explain or talk about these conditions. If we wish to under-
> stand the conditions and how their real pathos and significance, however,
> it is necessary to be open to the meaning of these conditions in the lives
> of those people suffering. Only when we ask, "What is it really like for

you" and to gain some sense of our clients experience can we join with our clients in the search for greater understanding, for new learning, for creative solutions. . . . (Goldstein 1986:355).

Despite, the growing recognition of the need to include the participant in the decision-making process, the presenters spoke meaningfully about the nature of this dialogue, and the need to listen as consumers both frame the questions and supply the answers.

3. A final contribution of this conference was in offering the participants an opportunity to grapple with key questions about causality. What larger political and economic forces have contributed to the rise of poverty neighborhoods like East Harlem? (If one assumes that operationalizing bad policy is/was no one's goal—the workshop's emphasis on considering the historical context for the development of social policy is a sober reminder of the limits to social change.)

In the same way that the personal biography helps us to understand an individual's needs and access to resources, groups of stories are helpful methodologies for revealing reasons WHY segments of the population are or may be disproportionately affected by economic or social forces. For example much of the workshop discussion revolved around structural transformations in which social changes in the arenas of gender, generation and the market place impacted on personal and community biographies.

A biography or history of social policy/biography of policy responses describes the ways in which government is able or unable, willing or unwilling to meet these needs. (Moving beyond description of failed social policies to an examination of how and why they were developed in the first place highlights the key role of consensus and/or power in the establishment of community goals/priorities: clearly, establishing goals/priorities means mediating individual and group goals and ends.)

The usefulness of reviewing social policy in an historical context is that it helps us to realize the transitory nature of social policy and, the not only the possibility, but the inevitability, that solutions are tailored to the contemporary social-political climate—rather than, necessarily, to the resolution of what we may see as a pressing social problem.

ILLUSTRATIONS FROM THE FIELD

At the outset, I referred to parallels between the complexity of managing family life in an urban enclave, and the tangled web of policy decision making. In developing this argument, I have outlined below public policies affecting three constituency groups with whom I have worked over the past several years: 1) victims of child abuse and their abusers; 2) persons affected by HIV/AIDS; and; 3) victims and perpetrators of family violence.

Policy, as I have experienced it (and as it is defined by Webster) either ends up or starts up as a very mundane set of guidelines (*cf.* Webster, policy 1. a principle or course of action chosen to guide decision making 2. prudent management). Virtually every decision made by a public employee is guided by a complex web of "policies" (read regulations). The case studies presented below aim to illustrate this point and highlight ways in which formulating or implementing public policy is responsive to many of the same forces that govern the daily life of many urbanites. More specifically, the following points are made: first, social service providers also have a human face—given the imposed constraints on social services (*e.g.*, fiscal as well as regulatory), social service providers, like the client population they serve, respond differently to their clients—some are helpful and informed, others are not; secondly, in arguing for increased participation in policy development, it is important to recognize situations in which activists do inform policy and to consider the implications of this involvement. Finally, a history of debate around social issues is embedded within many social service policies. In understanding and/or in changing policy it is important to consider the reasoning which underlies existing policy.

1. Child Abusers, like Bourgois's crack dealers are often vilified in the press and popular culture, often justly, but often without a clear notion of who these people are and what offenses they have committed. Research such as that suggested by the participants in this workshop could challenge some of the myths and assumptions about the men and women who are accused of neglecting or abusing their child. What it could also reveal is the role that social service institutions can do, and can't do to change lives.

Edith was the first client receiving services at a new child welfare "intensive-preventive" program I helped build and direct in New York City in the 1980s. Edith had come to the attention of CWA when she gave birth to a "positive tox" baby (indicating that she had been abusing drugs, in this case crack/cocaine, on or near her delivery date). At first guarded, Edith eventually poured out a fairly typical story—the father of her children was a dealer; looking beyond this, Edith saw a man who was—in her eyes, and yes, in my eyes too—capable of kindness, competent and in many ways a caring and involved parent. She was not prepared to leave him even if she could manage her family on her own. Short of leaving him, she was prepared and motivated to do whatever she needed to do to restore stability to her homelife. She was humiliated by the accusation, but honest in her own self appraisal. She wanted to get off drugs.

The program to which Edith was referred, was, as noted, new—it was a model program targeting substance-abusing mothers with babies, and it worked in the sense that Edith and many other mothers in the program achieved the short term goal of getting off drugs. In claiming "success," however, there are some key questions to consider: 1) Although they were in what was labeled a "preventive" program, families like Edith's were already deeply in crisis at the time that supportive services were provided. One can only imagine how these lives might have been affected if needed services were provided in a more timely manner; 2) Despite the fact that Edith did get off drugs, it was a painful experience for her and her family. Who knows how long-term the results will be, who can measure the damage that was already done to this family or in what subtle or not so subtle ways the stigma of having a CWA case will impact on this family.

Given this, it is still important to reflect on why Edith and the other mothers served in this program did change their behavior. Was it because Edith was, as social workers say, in a state of readiness for change, or because the providers reached out to her in a different way. How much does it matter that the staff was made up of young men and women from the community, (many shared social environments that objectively paralleled those of the clients they served); does it matter that this was a new program and that staff were energized at the thought of helping others? finally, does it matter that programs of this type were well financed and supported by the city and that all supported the goal of keeping families together?

Information about what makes a program "work" continues to interest policy makers. Researchers can help ensure that answers to these questions are sought not only in client histories (it is not enough to identify profiles of the high-risk, the engaged client, the resistant client, *etc.*) but also in the program profile (staffing patterns, meaningful services, program culture, *etc.*).

Just as the personal narratives described in the workshops would go a long way towards revealing the variability among consumers of social services, such research could also be used to consider variation among providers and the impact of this variation on change.

2. The identification of a community interests and the importance of dialogue with members of the community are issues which were explored in this workshop. In the world of policy decision making there is considerable variability in terms of the degree to which groups of consumers are included in the dialogue over policy—again, recognizing that the term "policy" refers to both petty regulations as well as national issues.

A situation in which the consumer voice is organized, is insistent and is heard is in the area of services provided to persons affected or infected by AIDS/HIV. This "community of interest" is in many ways a model for effective involvement—the consumers have become the activists/lobbyists and advocates. They have learned the system, and they have developed a range of strategies, tapping their own strengths to communicate their message. At the same time, the very success of the AIDS activist community highlights the constraints and conflicts inherent in policy decision making. One relatively small aspect of the debate over AIDS/HIV services should illustrate the conflict inherent in policy decision making—a conflict which surfaces among even the most like-minded "communities of interest." Persons affected by HIV/AIDS have lobbied fiercely over the years to ensure the confidentiality of an individual's HIV status and his/her right to self-determination in terms of testing. When medical research recently revealed that administering AZT to pregnant women with HIV/AIDs reduced the incidence of transmission to the fetus, a conflict of interest was born—a conflict which is in the hands of the policy maker to resolve. In short, it is now up to the policy maker, who claims to listen to the voices of the AIDS activists to weigh the privacy interests of affected and infected individuals who are resisting the establishment of a policy which mandates testing and treatment of pregnant women against the rights of the infant for the most advanced medical intervention available. Differences among the consumer/advocacy groups will ultimately be fed into an equation in which differences between these constituency groups will be weighed against key political-economic such as the cost of health care.

The fact that like-minded people differ over public policy will come as no surprise to anyone working in the social service field (in every field— substance abuse, domestic violence, housing and homelessness—there are conflicting methodologies for managing social issues); at some level, usually at the funding level by individuals whose task it is to resolve, mediate or overrule the proponents of these various points of view. At the same time, interest groups continue to form, sometimes by the force of their arguments or the courage of their conviction.

3. Finally, the usefulness of adopting a broad/historical perspective to the development of urban policy can be illustrated by examining the changes in urban policy around such pressing urban problems as domestic violence. An exploration of domestic violence interventions overtime reveals that domestic violence was not an invisible social issue prior to the re-emergence of feminism in the 1970s but was "managed" according to the social values of the period. For example, in the early part of the 20th century, responses to domestic violence tended to be relatively pragmatic—tangible services (provision of health services, housing and employment) and legal advocacy were the preferred interventions. Starting in the 1930s an emerging interest in psychotherapeutic responses and a concern for family privacy shifted the responsibility for acting to the individual victim and/or abuser. (Edleson 1991:pp304 2). In my work as Director of a Child Welfare Program in the early 1990s I witnessed and participated in what may be yet, another shift in social policy response; in fact, I was caught between conflicting (evolving?) policies. The families referred to our program were referred because of combined family crises involving both child abuse and domestic violence. Because of a recent policy shift in Child Welfare towards family reunification and preservation, fathers, even fathers who batter, were receiving increasing attention and services focused on their parenting roles. Domestic violence advocates, in contrast, typically reject a family systems/family reunification or rehabilative approach to working with domestic violence abusers and have voiced strong opposition to this kind of family systems approach (Goudner 1993). Conflicts over policy of course complicate

responses and frustrate both the consumer and the provider of the service. Until, if ever, a consensus emerges about most appropriate action there will be voices of disapproval and dissatisfaction. At the same time, this kind of conflict will have served a purpose if, during this period of transition, effective models for intervening with domestic violence case will be reaffirmed or redefined.

CONCLUSION

The histories told in this workshop and the suggested methodologies used to explore and define the continuing strengths and urban residents provide a rich and contextualized analysis of life in an "urban enclave." We learned, for example, that families in the city's poorest neighborhoods share the values of the larger culture: they fear crime, they raise their children to believe in the future and to behave in the present. And, in telling the story of a poor families raising children in poverty in East Harlem, we learn what real problem solving means in a world where there is no such thing as self-reliance. The urban enclave is clearly a place in which public institutions play a long-term and vital role in sustaining (having have replaced the roles played by the community in more traditional societies, see Jones, Turner, and Montbach 1992). Our task at this time in history is to ensure that these public institutions are competent and capable of meeting the needs and expectations of the populations they serve.

Even in considering the many contributions made by participants in this conference, however, we are left with the same burning questions to our immediate concerns that we went in with. The presenters expressed their continued interest in social change in the language of researchers and social scientists (issues like redundancy in the labor market, and inadequate resources in the community). As a service provider, I usually hear different expressions of concern. I hear endless accounts of the humiliations and obstacles that poor urban New Yorkers face every day. We, all of us, nevertheless, wonder how to end this cycle of urban misery. As Del Jones noted in his comments on the workshop, the poor haven't chosen to stay poor . . . the social contract that is supposed to provide for society's dependents, has failed the neediest and offers little encouragement to those struggling to manage a more independent life.

The workshop did not provide us with a blueprint for changing the life condition of the residents of "urban enclaves" but it did suggest an approach for facilitating communication between and among the research, the community and the policy maker was suggested.

At several points during the workshop, Carlos Vélez Ibañez reminded workshop participants to consider "the middle." The "middle" as I understand it, suggests a place in which transactions occur—in this case transactions between the consumers and providers of social services. This theme, which has been sounded increasingly in recent years among anthropologists, suggests a direction in which we, as urban ethnographers, might move; indeed, many of the participants at the workshop are already actively working in this fertile "middle area" (Anna Dehavenon, Terry Williams, Center for Puerto Rican Studies. . .). It was evident from their presentations that their work have has an impact on the life conditions of residents in poor urban neighborhoods. While unarguably affected by macro-structural issues: health care, education,housing and employment, practically speaking, the daily lives of subjects of urban research are apt to be more immediately affected by garden variety social policy issues—such as eligibility criteria imposed on local populations by public or by publicly funded agencies or the geographic location of social services centers and the models or political ideologies governing the delivery of these services. In the short run that characterizes the nuts and bolts of policy decision making, it is important to look in the middle for effective models, and it is important to believe that sometimes effective solutions do exist:

> ". . . it is important to recognize that there are programs that have succeeded in solving difficult problems; we have to be unshackled from the myth that nothing works . . ." "the keepers of the purse strings . . . have to see tangible evidence of effectiveness as a condition for support of any social program" (Schoor in Halpern, p. 646).

As I noted at the outset, my perspective as a provider has sensitized me to the complexity of policy development. Just as the research presented at this workshop shed light on the reality of urban life, research on policy decision making would reveal a complicated web of persons and policies all too often engaged in internal conflict, and all too often operating at cross purposes with the clients they serve. While the contribution made by the participants in this workshop is significant, a formidable next step is to pursue a parallel examination of service delivery and policy decision making at all levels.

REFERENCES

ASHFORD, JOSE B. AND CRAIG WINSTON LECROY
    1991   Problem solving in social work practice: Implications for knowledge utilization. *Research on Social Work Practice* 1 (3):306–318.
EDELSON, JEFFREY L.
    1991   Social workers' intervention in woman abuse: 1907–1945. *Social Service Review* :305–313.
GOLDSTEIN, HOWARD
    1986   Toward the integration of theory and practice: A humanistic approach. *Social Work* 31: 352–357
GOULDNER, VIRGINIA
    1992   Making room for both/and. *Networker:* 55–60.

HALPERN, ROBERT
    1990   Fragile families, fragile solutions: An essay review. *Social Service Review* :637–648.

JONES, DELMOS, JOAN TURNER, AND JOAN MONTBACH
    1992   Declining social services and threat to social reproduction: An urban dilemma. *City and Society* 6: 99–113.

REID, WILLIAM J.
    1993   Toward a research-oriented profession: An essay review of building social work knowledge for effective services and policies—A plan for research development. *Research on Social Work Practice* 3 (1):103–112.

Contemporary Immigration

Issues and Perspectives

NANCY FONER

Department of Anthropology
State University of New York
Purchase, New York 10577

The 1992 workshop on which this collection is based examined the urban ethnography of one particular lower-income urban enclave: New York's East Harlem. Among the many topics discussed were the history of "El Barrio" and Puerto Rican settlement, social institutions in the area, and the strategies, experiences, and problems of the Puerto Rican residents. El Barrio has in fact been one of the most important areas where Puerto Ricans settled when they came to New York.

The 1940s and 1950s marked the heyday of Puerto Rican migration to New York. In 1940, there were about 61,000 Puerto Ricans in New York City; two decades later, in 1960, there were 613,000 people of Puerto Rican birth and parentage in the city.

Now in the 1990s, a new wave of immigration from Asia, Latin America, and the Caribbean is altering the city in dramatic ways. New Yorkers, used to thinking of Puerto Rican as synonymous for Hispanic, are beginning to realize that the city's Hispanic population is very different than it was only a few decades ago. By 1990, Puerto Ricans comprised only half of all Hispanics in the city, down from 61 percent in 1980 and 64 percent in 1970 (Salvo and Ortiz 1994). Dominicans are in fact the largest group of new immigrants to New York. There are also sizable numbers from Columbia and Ecuador, and many from other Central and Latin American countries as well. Even Mexicans are beginning to have a considerable presence; the 1990 census counted some 62,000 Mexican immigrants in the city.

The fact is that since the removal of restrictive quotas from the national immigration law in 1965 immigrants have literally been pouring into the city. By now, nearly 30 percent of the city's population is foreign born, a figure beginning to approach that of the turn of the century (40 percent). Indeed, if we count island-born Puerto Ricans, who are U.S. citizens, as immigrants from a non-English speaking culture, today's figure would be even closer to that of the turn of the century. And although New York, along with Los Angeles and Miami, are the new immigrant cities par excellence, virtually all the nation's major metropolitan areas have seen an increase in foreign-born residents in the past few decades.

The remarks that follow reflect on the workshop presentations as they consider the way the latest arrivals are transforming our cities and are, themselves, transformed in the move. They point to some of the contributions anthropologists have made to the study of immigration in low-income urban enclaves and some of the topics that still need to be further explored.

OPPORTUNITIES AND INTER-ETHNIC RELATIONS

Many of the papers at the workshop touched on the broad social, economic, and political forces outside the community that affected the lives of East Harlem residents. This same perspective applies to new immigrants. Macro-level political and economic forces play an important role in shaping interactions, experiences, and meanings at the micro level.

Consider the job opportunities available to immigrants—opportunities that ultimately determine the context in which they work—and the New York City case in particular. The restructuring of New York City's economy, with the rapid growth of the advanced service sector, has led to openings for new immigrants in low-wage service jobs (Sassen 1988). The growth of financial services has created jobs not only for stockbrokers and investment analysts but also for messengers, janitors, and building cleaners. There is also a demand for workers to service the life styles and consumption requirements of the high-income professional and managerial class—as child-care providers, for example, restaurant workers, and apartment cleaners (for descriptions of immigrants in these jobs see Colen 1990; Margolis 1994). At the same time, what Sassen (1988) calls a downgraded manufacturing sector has generated a wide array of low skilled and poorly paid jobs for new arrivals in small-scale, labor intensive, and often immigrant-owned operations.

Replacement processes are also at work: employment opportunities have emerged in manufacturing and retailing in the wake of the erosion of New York City's white population base. As large numbers of whites retired or left the city, they created job vacancies, some directly filled by new arrivals, others indirectly. Indeed, as many native-born Blacks moved into vacancies in white-collar public sector work created by the outflow of whites, this, in turn, opened up opportunities at the bottom of the employment queue for immigrants (Bailey and Waldinger 1991).

Macro political and economic forces also shape opportunities for housing. A number of papers at the workshop noted how government public housing policies had, and continue to have, repercussions on the lives of East Harlem families, sometimes, as Mencher describes, separating extended families. Elsewhere in the city, in other low-income enclaves, government programs and subsidies influence the availability and cost of housing for new immigrants. Moreover, in drawing people to certain apartment buildings and neighborhoods, government housing policies directly affect daily interactions. Economic downturns (or upswings) can have the same effect. A fascinating study in another part of the country details how changes in Houston's economy affected immigrant housing arrangements and social relations (Hagan and Rodriguez 1992). When Houston's economy went into decline, managers and owners of some apartment complexes sought out Latino tenants, thereby affecting the ethnic mix and ethnic relations in the apartment buildings.

Interethnic relations, in general, is a critical area that anthropologists, with their intensive fieldwork methods, are well positioned to study. Through field research in urban enclaves we can see how people behave and react in concrete situations in settings like schools, work sites, and housing complexes. A key question is how immigrants get along with and relate to other new arrivals as well as established minorities and dominant white groups. What are the sources of conflict? What issues and interests bring them together?

My own research has explored relations between West Indians (especially Jamaicans) and American-born Blacks (Foner 1987). As Alex Stepick (1993) aptly puts it, the two groups stand at arms' length apart rather than warmly embracing. West Indians seek to distance themselves from American Blacks, yet at the same time there are spheres, such as political campaigns and the workplace, where they come together (Foner 1987; Kasinitz 1992).

Actually, my study of Jamaicans in New York found that outside of work they mainly moved in a Jamaican social world. Studies of other immigrant groups make a similar point, emphasizing that recent arrivals and native minorities may not interact much at all. This is the conclusion of a six-city project on changing relations between newcomers and established residents. As Lamphere (1992: 29–30) sums up, important and subtle boundaries compartmentalize newcomers and established residents in the workplace, the school, the neighborhood, and the community. She refers to a "parallel tracking system," with recent immigrants fitting into particular economic niches in urban areas and creating their own social networks and institutions.

We need more "institutional-based" studies, whether in hospitals, factories, or schools, that will allow us to better understand the complex nature of interethnic relations that are being played out in the wake of the new immigration. The studies in the six-city project (Lamphere 1992; Lamphere Stepick, and Grenier 1994) are a good beginning and some of my own research is relevant. In my recent study of workers in a New York nursing home, I found that shared gender, occupation, class, and race brought nursing aides from different immigrant and ethnic groups together in a common work culture, but that ethnicity was a source of division among them (Foner 1994). Beyond interethnic relations, fieldwork among immigrants in places where they live, work, study, and seek services can also clarify the way they cope in their day-to-day lives and come to terms with their new environments.

In this regard, anthropologists can contribute to debates that dominate the economic literature about whether immigrants are competing for jobs with native-born workers, especially Blacks and Puerto Ricans. Through detailed field studies, we can reveal the complex dynamics of hiring practices, employer preferences, and employee attitudes in actual workplace settings, including comparisons of immigrant and native minority views of low-level service work (see Bourgois in this volume on attitudes to service sector jobs among Puerto Rican crack dealers in East Harlem).

NEW MEANINGS AND SOCIAL PATTERNS

When people move from one country to another they begin to see the world and themselves in new ways. Invariably, new social practices and arrangements develop among them as well. Anthropologists have begun to chart these kinds of transformations among different immigrant groups, yet much work still needs to be done.

The impact of American racism is crucial in shaping the way immigrants think about themselves and others. In her paper on East Harlem in the 1950s, Joan Mencher notes that fair and white Puerto Ricans fit more easily into the wider society than their darker-skinned compatriots. Darker Puerto Ricans felt doubly isolated, she says. They had no option but to merge with American Black culture, but, at the same time, found themselves rejected by many American Blacks. In the case of recent West Indian immigrants, they develop a new consciousness of themselves as Black, and a sense of racial victimization, now that they are subject to prejudice and discrimination of a sort they had not encountered back home (Foner 1987; Stafford 1987; Sutton and Makiesky 1987).

In addition to new racial and ethnic identities, immigrants also develop new conceptions—and new patterns—of gender roles. A number of studies show that immigrant women's increased economic independence allows them to renegotiate traditional gender roles and gain greater autonomy (e.g., Foner 1986; Grasmuck and Pessar 1991; Pessar 1993). More research will help to clarify immigrant women's gains as well as the constraints they still experience. Mencher writes about changes in childrearing behavior among Puerto Rican migrants of the 1950s, and this is something we need to know about for recent immigrants, too. The kinds of family arrangements and strategies that immigrants develop here is also another fertile area for research.

In the community study tradition, anthropologists are well-suited to look at institutions and social arrangements in local communities and ethnic enclaves in which newcomers live. Just as social scientists in the 1950s wrote of the making of "El Barrio," we have the opportunity today to construct portraits and histories of other local neighborhoods and areas that have recently been revitalized by the latest immigrants (e.g., Orleck 1987 on Brighton Beach; Winnick 1990 on Sunset Park; Wong 1987 on Chinatown).

In exploring new cultural and social patterns we need to consider members of the second as well as first generation. What are the attitudes, expectations, and aspirations of the children of new immigrants who were born and raised in this country? What are their relations with their families and peers? Traditional theories of immigrant assimilation which predict steady economic and educational progress across immigrant generations may not apply to many descendants of the recent immigrants. Indeed, in her paper, Fernandez-Kelly raises the question as to whether assimilation for the children of nonwhite immigrants will mean becoming Black American, with the enormous stigma and isolation this involves. It is critical to know, moreover, how the children of recent immigrants are faring in school and the kinds of jobs they are taking as they enter the workforce.

TRANSNATIONAL LINKS AND COMPARATIVE VIEWS

While studies of immigrants in American lower-income urban enclaves inevitably focus on their lives in this country, links to the home society remain significant.

It is not surprising that anthropologists have been among the pioneers in emphasizing the importance and elaborating views of transnational connections since they, themselves, often have a foot in both the receiving and sending society. Many—myself included—came to the study of new immigrants after having done research on the same group in the home society (Foner 1983, 1987). A first-hand understanding of pre-migration cultures gives anthropological studies a depth often lacking in research on immigrants in the United States. It allows us to better understand the kinds of changes and continuities found in the immigrant setting—and to have a better feel for what it means to emigrate and settle in a new land.

Urban ethnography in East Harlem made clear that Puerto Ricans living there kept up vital connections to the island. Today, the growing literature on transnationalism shows how recent immigrants, though living in the United States, also forge and sustain familial, political, economic, and cultural ties that connect them to their home societies (Glick Schiller, Basch, and Blanc-Szanton 1992). Immigrants leave children back home to be reared and educated, send millions of dollars annually in remittances, build houses and buy land in their home societies which they supervise from a distance, and participate in political struggles in their home societies (see Basch, Glick Schiller, and Szanton-Blanc 1994).

Finally, as anthropologists study contemporary immigration in urban enclaves we can build on the time-honored comparative perspective as well. As I found in my own comparative work analyzing differences and similarities among Jamaican immigrants in London and New York (*e.g.,* Foner

1983, 1985), a comparative view highlights processes that might otherwise be overlooked or minimized. It forces us, as well, to sort out the conditions under which specific social and cultural patterns develop among certain groups.

The comparative perspective is not confined to crossnational comparisons. In terms of the new immigration to this country, cross-city comparisons of the same immigrant group—Haitians in Miami and New York, to give one example, or Mexicans in Los Angeles and New York, to give another—would be valuable. I suspect that such analyses will reveal many contrasts, partly due to features of the "structure of incorporation" such as ethnic composition, economic opportunities, and sheer demographics in the different cities. It would also be illuminating to systematically compare different immigrant groups within the *same* location as a way to begin to sort out the influence of a wide range of factors that shape immigrants' lives, including cultural traditions, language, and the class composition of each immigrant stream.

What these remarks suggest is that there is a full research agenda ahead. At present, American cities are witnessing a major demographic change in the midst of an enormous wave of immigration. As we study lower-income urban enclaves today, increasingly this means taking into account these latest arrivals on the urban scene as they are transforming—literally remaking—American society.

REFERENCES

BAILEY, THOMAS AND ROGER WALDINGER
1991 The changing ethnic racial division of labor. In *Dual City: Restructuring New York*. John Mollenkopf and Manuel Castells, Eds. New York: Russell Sage.

BASCH, LINDA, NINA GLICK SCHILLER, AND CRISTINA SZANTON BLANC
1994 *Nations Unbound: Transnational Projects, Postcolonial Predicaments, and Deterritorialized Nation States.* Langhorne, PA: Gordon and Breach.

COLEN, SHELLEE
1990 Housekeeping for the green card: West Indian household workers, the state, and stratified reproduction in New York. In *At Work in Homes*. Roger Sanjek and Shellee Colen, Eds. Washington, DC: American Ethnological Society.

FONER, NANCY
1983 Jamaican Migrants: A Comparative Analysis of the New York and London Experience. *Occasional Paper 36*. New York: Center for Latin and American Studies, New York University.
1985 Race and color: Jamaican migrants in London and New York. *International Migration Review* 19: 708-727.
1986 Sex roles and sensibilities: Jamaican women in New York and London. In *International Migration: The Female Experience,* Rita Simon and Caroline Brettell, Eds. Totowa, NJ: Rowman and Allanheld.

1987   The Jamaicans: Race and ethnicity among migrants in New York. In
        New Immigrants in New York, Nancy Foner, Ed. New York: Columbia
        University Press.
1994   *The Caregiving Dilemma: Work in an American Nursing Home.*
        Berkeley: University of California Press.
GLICK SCHILLER, NINA, LINDA BASCH, AND CRISTINA BLANC-SZANTON, EDS.
1992   *Towards a Transnational Perspective on Migration.* New York: New
        York Academy of Sciences. (*Ann. N.Y. Acad. Sci.* Vol. 645)
GRASMUCK, SHERRI AND PATRICIA PESSAR
1991   *Between Two Islands: Dominican International Migration.* Berkeley:
        University of California Press.
HAGAN, JACQUELINE AND NESTOR RODRIGUEZ
1992   Recent economic restructuring and evolving intergroup relations in
        Houston. In *Structuring Diversity.* Louise Lamphere, Ed. Chicago:
        University of Chicago Press.
KASINITZ, PHILIP
1992   *Caribbean New York: Black Immigrants and the Politics of Race.* Ithaca:
        Cornell University Press.
LAMPHERE, LOUISE, ED.
1992   *Structuring Diversity: Ethnographic Perspectives on the New
        Immigration.* Chicago: University of Chicago Press.
LAMPHERE, LOUISE, ALEX STEPICK, AND GUILLERMO GRENIER, EDS.
1994   *Newcomers in the Workplace: Immigrants and the Restructuring of the
        U.S. Economy.* Philadelphia: Temple University Press.
MARGOLIS, MAXINE
1994   *Little Brazil: An Ethnography of Brazilian Immigrants in New York
        City.* Princeton: Princeton University Press.
ORLECK, ANNELISE
1987   The Soviet Jews: Life in Brighton Beach, Brooklyn. In *New
        Immigrants in New York.* Nancy Foner, Ed. New York: Columbia
        University Press.
PESSAR, PATRICIA
1993   Research on immigrant women: Enriching our understanding of work-
        ing-class women on the homefront and in the workplace. Paper pre-
        sented at American Anthropological Association meetings,
        Washington, DC.
SALVO, JOSEPH AND RONALD ORTIZ
1994   *Puerto Rican New Yorkers in 1990.* New York: New York City
        Department of Planning.
SASSEN, SASKIA
1988   *The Mobility of Labor and Capital.* Cambridge: Cambridge University
        Press.
STAFFORD, SUSAN BUCHANAN
1987   The Haitians: The cultural meaning of race and ethnicity. In *New
        Immigrants in New York.* Nancy Foner, Ed. New York: Columbia
        University Press.
STEPICK, ALEX
1993   Pride against prejudice: Conceptualizing race, immigration, and cul-
        ture. Paper presented at American Anthropological Association meet-
        ings, Washington, DC.

SUTTON, CONSTANCE AND SUSAN MAKIESKY
  1987   Migration and West Indian racial and ethnic consciousness. In *Caribbean Life in New York City,* Constance Sutton and Elsa Chaney, Eds. New York: Center for Migration Studies.
WINNICK, LOUIS
  1990   *New People in Old Neighborhoods.* New York: Russell Sage.
WONG, BERNARD
  1987   The Chinese: New immigrants in New York's Chinatown. In *New Immigrants in New York.* Nancy Foner, Ed. New York: Columbia University Press.

The Challenge of Funds of Knowledge in Urban Arenas
Another Way of Understanding the Learning Resources of Poor Mexicano Households in the U.S. Southwest and their Implications for National Contexts

CARLOS G. VÉLEZ-IBÁÑEZ[a]

Department of Anthropology
College of Humanities and Social Sciences
University of California, Riverside
Riverside, California 92521-0132

This paper is written in response to the November 1992 workshop for urban ethnographers held at the Museum of the City of New York, entitled: **Anthropology of Lower Income Enclaves: The Case of East Harlem.** Since the forum treated a number of pertinent theoretical and practical topics, this paper will combine both theoretical and practical approaches to the manner in which the poor should be treated analytically outside of the Eastern Region of high density urbanization and the way in which such treatment lends itself to "applied" educational intervention programs that benefit poor households, their members, educational institutions, and "feeds back" findings and data to enhance the original theoretical constructs used to initiate the process.

I have used the term "Funds of Knowledge" as the central core concept to mean all rural and urban skills, experience, technical knowledge of habitat and survival, and the full inventory of social knowledge that households have developed for survival. These are "distributed" in special ways within Mexican households in the U.S. Southwest and their understanding provides the observer and analyst very different lenses from which to understand the social and economic dynamics of modest income households. As well, not only are these funds of knowledge amenable to analysis but they are also of great utility in creating intervention programs that enhance the

[a] Dr. Vélez-Ibáñez is a professor in the Department of Anthropology and Dean of the College of Humanities and Social Sciences. His address for correspondence is Office of the Dean.

learning relationship between educational institutions and the constituent households they serve. This paper will describe one such effort over a three year period.

Last, this work will consider the various theoretical and applied applications outside of the regional Southwest and the manner in which both theory and practice can be brought to bear in dense urban settings. However, the important work presented in the forum supports and expands the theoretical and methodological foundations upon which this discussion is based.

THEORETICAL AND METHODOLOGICAL FOUNDATIONS[1]

The starting point for analysis for this work is the "political economy" of the border region which embraces a 2,000-mile long political border within a 400-mile-wide belt and 52 million persons living in 10 Mexican and U.S. border states. The region includes the immediate border cities and population centers, but also rural and urban centers affected by the border economy in agriculture, trade, services, manufacturing, and labor use. The United States-Mexico borderlands region has always been economically differentiated because of the economic integration of agricultural markets between borders, the simultaneous penetration of capital and labor intensive technologies such as mining and construction on both sides of the political border, and the accompanying extensive movement of the Mexican population in the region to different labor markets.[2] New capital and technologies have always transformed the regional ecology of the borderlands and at present, as Moore (1988:16) correctly points out, the borderlands

---

[1]Portions of the following characteristics were published in Carlos G. Vélez-Ibáñez and James B. Greenberg, 1992, Formation and transformation of knowledge among U.S. Mexican households, *Anthropology and Education Quarterly,* **23** (4): 313–335.

[2]Beginning with large-scale irrigation-based farming by the Riverine Hohokom peoples between 300 B.C. and A.D. 1450 to the penetration of mining, farming, and ranching by Spaniards and their entire cultural and political structures, the borderlands were very early made to conform to population and technological demands. These were followed by the attempted consolidation by a centralized mestizo population during the Mexican period in the 19th century and later in the same century to the Anglo introduction of large-scale, industrially organized mining, construction, commerce, and animal production. In the present, service, electronic, military, and modified mining and border-related twin plant production are the main methods and means for natural resource extraction and transformation.

As well, most historical periods were also filled with raids, warfare, conquest, and subjection of one population over another. The American period is also marked by large scale land clearing, land speculation, control of mineral, water, and natural resources by national corporations, and state ownership of more than half of the available land area.

forms part of a "border subeconomy" that is part of the internationalization of production and the exchange of populations.

Since 1950, the population of the six Mexican border states has increased threefold; while the four U.S. border states have increased from 20 million to 42 million in 1980. Such growth stems from uncontrolled industrialization on both sides of the border, created by a series of symbiotic economic and technological relations in manufacturing, processing, industrial agriculture, labor markets, and twin plants development (Diez-Canedo 1981, Fernandez-Kelly 1987, Martinez 1983, Garcia y Griego 1983, Tiano 1985, Gonzalez-Archegia 1987, and Porras n.d.). Such relations in the borderlands, continue to shape the formation of Mexican households as well as their cultural and social responses.

U.S. border policy exacerbates such structural conditions and influences how Mexican households on both sides cope with changing economic and political fortunes. Whether yesterday's Mexican national becomes today's U.S. citizen is very much dependent upon the region's economic health. Even ethnicity among U.S. Mexicans in the Southwest and its attending political implications is of very recent origin and largely a product of post-Depression border policies (Vélez-Ibáñez, forthcoming).

Thus even "poverty" must be contextualized within the borderlands region as a highly fluid and dynamic characteristic with U.S. Mexican populations periodically entering and leaving what appear to be "underclass" sectors depending on the economic relations between nations, the ups and downs of world markets, and the manner in which they influence labor markets of the region, and cross-border relations between Mexican households in northern Mexico and the southwestern U.S. The actual distribution of U.S. Mexican households in labor sectors is that 1 in 5 households are part of the primary labor sector in income, stability, and security of employment. In such households there is a significant percentage of middle-class households for whom scarcity is not a primary struggle but rather indebtedness due to ease of credit. Further, 3 of 5 households have working class income

Throughout the borderlands areas of northwest Mexico and southwestern United States, the Mexican population has been part of major transformations. It has been a population subjected to constant demographic shifts, ecological pressures, and economic uncertainty. The 1 9th and 20th centuries are replete with periodic large movements of Mexicanos moving north and east and west, enlisted or attracted by farming, mining, and railroad recruiting agents and contractors, or pushed out by the Mexican revolution, U.S. depressions, natural calamities, and great economic changes.

Periodically, as the borderlands economy cools off, Mexican labor has been voluntarily or forcefully pushed back across the border when no longer needed. During these cooling periods and during periods of high industrial and building development in various states, Mexicanos migrate from New Mexico, Arizona, and Texas to California and most recently from California, New Mexico, and even Wyoming into Arizona.

that is largely derived from employment by several household members, members having two jobs, and using scarce resources in innovative and creative ways. Also more households contain more adults than non-Hispanic white households, and thus there are more earners per household. This advantage, however, is offset by a larger number of children per household, greater unemployment than among the non-Hispanic white population, and, probably for the first 10 years of a household cycle, intermittent employment. Finally, approximately 1 in 5 households are in poverty, and poverty is concentrated among female-headed families of the 45-year-old cohorts to be described, persons over 60, and children under 18.[3]

Such labor and income dynamics create a fluidity of employment constraints as well as opportunities in which Mexican households are simultaneously under varying degrees of economic stress but as well create the conditions by which information, data, skills, innovations, inventions, and creative solutions are sought after to solve problems of daily existence. While increasing separation between knowledge of the household and occupations is one manifestation of the way local populations respond over the loss of control over the means of production, it is also probable that the sheer necessity of adjusting to shifting technologies and structures of labor in the borderlands region, also forces households to use previously held knowledge as well as to import knowledge not previously known. Thus some households in the span of a single generation may shift from a totally rurally based means of subsistence to a totally urban environment in which the previous knowledge base is not only used but crucial in adapting to the new urban situation. This is especially true during times of grievous economic or political crises such as after failed labor strikes as was the case for U.S. Mexican miners in Arizona who became cowboys to make ends meet because they were already skilled in ranching technologies. The knowledge base that allows such shifting, I have termed "Funds of Knowledge."[4]

Yet such processes as well are further complicated by demographic increases, and all indicators clearly show that the U.S. Mexican population will more than triple that by the year 2050 given that the population increased by more than 50 percent between 1980 and 1990. Since

---

[3] The probability of poverty in households headed by a single person is twice as great as in those headed by a married couple. Of U.S. Mexican households in poverty in 1980, only 17.1% were headed by couples and close to 40% were headed by single persons (Stoddard and Hedderson 1987: 66 and 68; Bean and Tienda: 355 and 371). Similarly the National Center for Health Statistics' Hispanic and Nutrition Examination Survey (HHANES) study showed that 63.3% of female headed households were below the poverty level but only 26.1 of dual headed households were in poverty (Trevino *et al.* 1989:9).

[4] See Vélez-Ibáñez and Greenberg, (1992), Formation and Transformation of funds of knowledge, among U.S. Mexican households, *Anthropology and Education Quarterly*, **23** (4) 313–335.

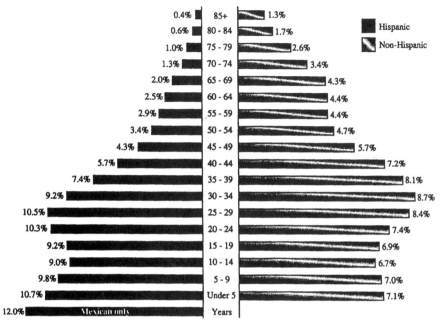

FIGURE 1. Age of the Population: 1990 (SOURCE: U.S. Bureau of the Census, Current Population Reports, p. 7, *Hispanic Americans Today*. U.S. Government Printing Office, Washington, DC, 1993:2).

Mexicans are the youngest at 24 among all groups (Puerto Ricans are at 27 and Central Americans and South Americans at 28.5) with quite a percentage of those between zero and 14, it does not take a great deal of statistical knowledge to know that large cohorts are waiting in the wings to enter schools.[5] "Population Pyramid" of FIGURE 1 illustrates this even more dramatically; when a "Mexican" 0 to 5 age bar is added the bar percentage jumps to 12% of that cohort, which is almost 75% larger in proportion to population than the Anglo population of the same age in large part due to birth rates almost twice that of the Anglo population.[6]

This stress on the increasing numbers of the population over time, its youthfulness, and the large numbers of children either waiting to enter school or already in the "pipeline" is central to understanding the distribu-

[5] U.S. Bureau of the Census, Current Population Reports, P23–183, *Hispanic Americans Today*. U.S. Government Printing Office, Washington, DC, 1993: 2. All figures and enumerations in the discussion are taken from the same source, pp. 2,3,4, and 7 except when noted.

[6] *Persons of Hispanic Origin in the United States:* August 1993, U.S. Bureau of the Census, Current Population Reports, 1990 CP-3-3, U.S. Government Printing Office, Washington, DC, 1993: Table 1:5 and Table 5:157.

tion and effect of the various "illnesses" from which the population suffers and in some cases suffers more than other populations of the region. From every reputable source available who comments on the population, there is no doubt that the single most important predictor of its mental, physical, economic, social, or cultural well being is the acquisition of a quality educational experience.[7] While there are too many other factors to exclude out of hand such as structural factors like plant closings, "restructuring of the economy," English language acquisition, the opportunity structure, the ages of the cohort in question, recent migration status, and commoditization and ethnocentrism, these by themselves largely are not as successful in predicting the well being of most of the Mexican population either born in or migrated to the United States.

However, what is more important is that while there have been significant improvements in educational attainment in the last 20 years, these are continually setback by the horrendous dropout rates of 45 to 50 percent in many areas where the population resides, including the midwest. Thus for the U.S. Mexican population a large number of adults persist with less than a 5th grade education: 15 percent for Mexicans and half as many with a Bachelors degree or more, with the accompanying inequities of median income among households: $22,477 for Mexicans and $32,311 for Anglos. Too many Mexicans are under the poverty line (27.4) while only 9 percent of all Anglo families suffer in poverty.[8]

THE SETTING[9]

Within the City of Tucson there exists an incorporated analog of its poorest households concentrated within the City of South Tucson. Composed of 6,535 residents, most of whom of very modest means, the City of South Tucson is surrounded by a population of over 400,000 in the City of Tucson. South Tucson is 76.5% U.S. Mexican, with a mean income

---

[7]Alan Rowe, 1991, Note on education and self-worth among Anglo American, Black American, and Mexican-American men in San Antonio, *Perceptual and Motor Skills*, 73 (No. 2) October: 433–434. The study from a sample of 164 White, 168 Black, and 149 Mexican-American male regular drinkers supports the hypothesis that education beyond the high school level is related to higher perception of self-worth.

[8]*Persons of Hispanic Origin in the United States:* August 1993, U.S. Bureau of the Census, Current Population Reports, 1990 CP-3-3, U.S. Government Printing Office, Washington, DC, 1993: Table 1:5 and Table 5:157.

[9]Portions of this section was previously published in Carlos G. Vélez-Ibáñez, U.S Mexicans in the borderlands: Being poor without the underclass, in *In the Barrios, Latinos and the Underclass Debate*, J. Moore and R. Pinderhughes, Eds. New York: Russell Sage Foundation, see pp. 206–213.

of $10,026 and with 38% of the population below the poverty level.[10] In contrast, for the City of Tucson's Mexican population (22% of total population), the mean income was $18,241. Of over 2,100 housing units in South Tucson, 43.5% were owner-occupied with 3.18 persons per unit and 56.5% were rental with 2.82 persons per unit. South Tucson's tax rate is based on 16 cents per 100 dollar evaluation while the City of Tucson's is 1.00 dollar per 100 dollar evaluation (*Tucson Daily Citizen*: 1-6-88) so that land values are relatively low and "start up" homes are possible. It is one square mile in area, running from 40th Street on the south to 26th street on the north; 12th avenue on the west to the railroad tracks—roughly Second Street—on the east.[11]

Incorporated in 1936 there have been periodic disincorporation attempts in part because of its reputation as a poverty-concentrated city and in part because of operations associated with illegal activities. Its unemployment rate in 1989 was three times that of the City of Tucson, and this ratio has remained constant since 1983.[12]

In 1979, one South Tucson resident dubbed prostitution, as "South Tucson's major industry (*Citizen* 4-15-89)." For years the community had the reputation of being a haven for vagrants, prostitution, alcoholism, street crime, and police authorities who used speed traps as the means of assuring revenue for city budgets. The central street—South Sixth Avenue was noted for the taverns and bars that were reputed by local wags to provide abdominal operations without anesthesia or quick appendectomies for customers without charge. In the pre-drug era of the seventies, heroin could be purchased with relative ease and alcohol and drug addiction was not unknown. Having lived in the area for some years, the author can attest to the necessity of turning on water sprinklers to remove unwanted sleepers from Saturday night's fun.

But for South Tucson Mexican households this one mile square pocket of modest income was their home, and unlike the populations described in the "underclass" model who are considered apathetic, apolitical, and passive, this population revitalized its community over a space of ten years. In

---

[10] This is using as a base the 1986 federal definition of "poor" as a family of four with an annual cash income of less than $11,203 (*Magnitude and Persistence of Poverty among Latinos*:2). For South Tucson, 34% of the population is under 18 and only 11% is over 60.

[11] Jance C. Berry, South Tucson, *Tucson Daily Citizen*, 4-1-87.

[12] The percentage of unemployment in 1989 in South Tucson was 13.1% while it was 4.5% in the City of Tucson; in 1990 through August, it was 12% in South Tucson and 4.0% in Tucson city. Unemployment for South Tucson is directly tied to the economy in the City of Tucson so that variance in each is reflected in increases or decreases in the other. For 1983, the unemployment rate in the City of Tucson was 8.6% while in South Tucson it was 23.2%; and in 1984 it was 4.5% in the city of Tucson and 13.2% in South Tucson (*Special Unemployment Report for January through December 1989 (Final) For Arizona Local Area Statistics*: Pima County, Department of Economic Security, State of Arizona: 1990)

spite of the fact that economically and occupationally South Tucson's households were among the poorest in Arizona, they nevertheless made important political decisions that changed the face of community in substantive ways. Thus as the following clearly shows, the applicability of the "underclass" populations even within contexts of ecological poverty seem not to be fruitfully applied to U.S. Mexican populations.

Ten years after being anointed with the dubious honor of having prostitution as its major industry, major sting operations were conducted in which the crime of prostitution although sporadically present was almost wiped out by the vigorous efforts of city authorities and the community. In 1986 there were three homicides, 11 rapes, and 52 robberies. Crimes were reduced by the shelter for the homeless but complaints against vagrancy and liquor laws violation increased.(*Citizen* 9-11-87.) Further crime crackdown in 1988 reduced all crimes by 26%. By 1987, murder had dropped 66%, rape 70%, robbery 30.1%, aggravated assault, 54.2%, larceny was down 13.6%, autotheft down 15.6%, and arson down 28.6%.(*Citizen*, 2-12-88). Further in 1988, crime decreased another 16% from 26% the year before with reduction of larceny from 440 to 395, auto theft from 38 to 31, aggravated assault from 60 to 49 with the rest remaining the same except for "date rape."

In 1986, more than a 100 new businesses opened up, and no space was available in the city's light industrial park. Business loans, block grants of $230,000 for 20 new or renovated business had been awarded since 1984, voluntary associations like the Lion's Club and others provided both funds and energy to support community reform and change. The clean up of the lots and homes of absentee owners, 60% of whom did not reside in South Tucson vastly improved the physical environment of the city and at present, school children canvass the tiny municipality for unsightly trash. South Tucson spent 1 million dollars on street lights and burglary dropped 30% for 1986 (*Tucson Daily Citizen* 12-9-87). Proportionally, South Tucson's burglary rate is lower than Tucson's. A new library, city park, and municipal complex were built and together with the parish church and the two elementary schools of the municipality, city wide celebrations are held through the calendar year.

A St. Patrick's Day celebration and street march is held annually, which is a mixture of Mexican Catholicism, Mexican Independence day, and the wearing of the green—all a Mexican adoption to fit in to the United States with play offs of Spanish surnames—Ochoa, Otero, and Obregons. A Norteño Music Festival and Street Fair for the Benefit of Pio Decimo neighborhood center drew 15,000 person (*Citizen* 8-11-89). Equally, an annual Christmas Party in front of Ramon Gonzalez's house, which he began in 1970, in celebrating its 19th year drew 1,500 persons on Christmas with the poor children of the area receiving two gifts each.

These various accomplishments, however, rest not just on a sense of acquired community spirit but in fact much of the energy stems from the ability of U.S. Mexican households to mobilize scarce resources in relatively efficient ways. In fact, even with all of the community improvements, South Tucson is still a community of poor to moderate-income persons. The revitalization process resulted from the efforts of clustered householders born in South Tucson.[13] As our findings show from a recently studied sample[14] of 30 households, the poorest household may barely survive, but as long as it has some access to familial resources the type of debilitating poverty that destroys the social fabric of familial relations may be avoided in even the most modest of U.S. Mexican households.

CENTRAL FEATURES AND DYNAMICS OF HOUSEHOLD CLUSTER IN POVERTY CONTEXTS AND THE LIFE CYCLE[15]

The central feature in the formation of household clusters in poverty contexts seems to be the ability to locate consanguineal and/or affinal members in relatively close proximity but generally not within the same home. For the most part in our sample, each associated household in a cluster either owned or was purchasing its own home. Especially in the South Tucson area, land values are relatively low, construction knowledge is rather plentiful or available within clusters, information of the lowest prices for materials is shared, and the actual labor for construction is exchanged for use. As well, 20% or more of real individual household income in our sample is derived from unreported sources such as childcare within clusters and from outside sources such as income earned from housecleaning, informal labor, weekend sales, swapmeets, and barter.

[13]Third generation South Tucsonans like Mayor Dan Eckstrom, Gilbert Mariscal, Jr., and others were at the core of the revitalization efforts and themselves belong to large clustered households that figure importantly in the many restaurants that operate in South Tucson, *Tucson Daily Citizen*: December 9, 1987).

[14] Fifty-three household heads were purposively selected for their place in the development life cycle. The study specifically selected households that were representative of a stage of household development in which dependent third and fourth grade elementary school children were present in the household and thus adult functions were primarily focused to income mobilization. It was also likely that such a sample would encounter single and double parent households, persons likely to be non-U.S. born and first generation, and given the grade level of the children, likely to also have had the opportunity to have generated household relations of the type already described.

The mean educational level of the 53 household heads was 7.6 with a mean age of 40 of whom 81% were born in Mexico and mostly from the State of Sonora (70%). They had established a U.S. residency mean of 11 years and earned a mean income of $14,544, which differs little from a comparable community age cohort.

[15] Portions of this section was previously published in Carlos G. Vélez-Ibáñez, U.S Mexicans in the borderlands: Being poor without the underclass, in *In the Barrios, Latinos and the Underclass Debate*, J. Moore and R. Pinderhughes, Eds. New York. Russell Sage Foundation, see pp 206–211.

A second feature that is important to note is that no household cluster is ever exclusively made up of persons in dire economic need. When poor persons are looked at from this point of view, they should be understood as *individually poor* but not part of a cluster that is necessarily impoverished. As long as external circumstances are held relatively constant with even minimum employment available, access to male labor in the case of single parent female households somewhat predictable, and moderate opportunities for social exchange with others in slightly better economic circumstances in existence, then even impoverished *individuals* may avoid the worst features of being poor. On the other hand, if a combination of circumstances occurs such as a sudden immigration raid, unemployment, or illness striking portions of the cluster, then the entire network may be endangered and the already "at risk" individual forced to seek institutional remedies.

A third and crucial feature in understanding the functions of such clusters in poverty conditions is their functions within the dynamic of the life cycle in which age and generational considerations are also importantly linked to when and how individuals are impoverished. Whether poor adults are at the beginning, middle, or end of their household life cycle will in part determine the quality of poverty and its survivability. Thus poor young adults who are married with small children but are minimally employed will more than likely have access to their own parent's housing. In this case, parents provide a subsidy to poor offspring for that period of time in which income is poor, mobility limited, and shift in occupation very small.

However, adults in the middle of the household life cycle in which income is still at poverty or near poverty level will be very hardpressed to either subsidize offspring or elderly adults. It is at this point that the "clusters" appear to break down functionally and relationally and do not develop to lineal depth to include an elderly core. In fact, it is highly likely that this type of "mid-adult" household will maintain tenuous exchange relations with collateral kin of brothers and sisters and same generation cousins.

Yet, one other dynamic is present that will finally define the quality of mid-adult poverty; that is, if collateral relations are in the same economic circumstances. As has been already stated, it is seldom that entire networks are impoverished even in South Tucson. However, in those circumstances in which collateral relations are as badly off then there is a tendency towards centripetality of relations with little social exchange expected or desired. On the other hand, the dynamic quality of the economy of the borderlands is such that it is highly unlikely that the "underclass" economic circumstances of urban poverty ghettos described in the literature are duplicated even in very moderate contexts like South Tucson.

In the case of the elderly, the quality of poverty is also conditioned by institutional subsidies available but also the existence of lineal relations. While income may be very moderate among South Tucson elderly and subsidies basically only maintain minimal health and nutritional levels, for the most part such elderly will own their own homes, have paid off most debts, and have some income provided by adult children. This assistance is usually provided for the caretaking of children. On the other hand, there are circumstances in which poor elderly do not have either lineal or collateral relations to provide an edge to their poverty. In such cases, the elderly couple may become heavily reliant on public subsidies and especially so if it is the one surviving part of the household. Yet for the most part, in all the samples used to carefully analyze the household clusters of in South Tucson and Tucson both poverty and modest income elderly were usually incorporated within a descending generation household of either daughter or son.

Lastly, a combination of social dynamics and contextual constraints determine the quality of poverty among South Tucson and most U.S. Mexican households. Households may be poor in economic terms, but household poverty is relative to the economic cycles of the region as well as to the assistance and reciprocity of other households. Single heads of households fluctuate in stability ranging from periods of despair in which appliances, are sold in order to pay rent, to periods of stability during which income in combination with assistance from relatives 60 miles away may give them enough money to refuse public assistance.

THE EXPERIMENTS[16]

Since genius is not necessary to conclude that there is a direct relationship for U.S. Mexicans especially[17] between income and education, the focus of work undertaken for four years in collaborative projects between the University of Arizona's Bureau of Applied Research in Anthropology and the College of Education focused on taking advantage of the strategic funds of knowledge of U.S. Mexican households of Tucson, Arizona in order to revitalize the relationships of various sorts between home and school and in fact perhaps even redefining them to the extent that they benefitted students, parents, teachers, and administrators.

What we have experimented with is not a panacea nor is it a solution to the myriad educational problems that the U.S. Mexican population faces,

---

[16] Much of the description of the Experimental description of the various projects are taken from the project proposal: Promoting Collaborative Learning and Educational Delivery and Quality among "At Risk" U.S. Mexican, Native American, and African American Elementary School Children in Three Sites: Adrian, Michigan, Tucson, Arizona, and The Hopi Reservation. C. Vélez-Ibáñez, Luis Moll, James B. Greenberg, Brackette Williams, and Norma Gonzalez. Bureau of Applied Research in Anthropology and Division of Language, Reading and Culture, College of Education. Submitted to the Kellogg Foundation, November 30, 1992.

[17] Carlos G. Vélez-Ibáñez (n.d.:314) *Border Visions of One World An Anthropology of U.S. Mexicans of the Southwest.* University of Arizona Press: Tucson, Arizona: 400pp. In press.

but this is an attempt to change the context somewhat for learning of whatever type to take place in a more culturally conducive manner. There are a number of assumptions underpinning this effort and they consist of the following: learning is a social process; that is, ideas, references, iota, and concepts are transmitted and generated within an emotive and cultural context and thus rely not only on what has been termed as pedagogy for accuracy and utility but on the unseen and often undiscovered relationships that are indigenous to that process. Second, within formal educational institution such contexts are part of the prevailing social relations arranged by the institution and buttressed by the current ideology of education such as "meeting the needs of the individual," "teaching the whole child," and sundry other modes most of which stress individual achievement, merit evaluation, and measurable individual success.

FUNDS OF KNOWLEDGE AND DENSITY OF EXCHANGE RELATIONS

Few such institutionally created modes, ideologies, or their attending social relations have been attentive to the way in which U.S. Mexican children the social relational context for learning and the flow of constant information to which they are exposed and with which they experiment. As well, this learning process has much less to do with measurable rewards but rather move to do with relational evaluation, indicators of commonality and reciprocity, and measures expressed by exchange relations that are not necessarily gauged to a measure or in units of precision.

For U.S. Mexican children, it is highly likely that this is the case based on recent work.[18] Such systems of evaluation are embedded within the cluster of familial relations that I have termed "household clusters," which are linked extended collateral households made of up of a series of affinal and consanguineal relations that are geographically proximal within a mile or so of each other. These household clusters are usually densely interactive systems of exchange in which goods, favors, and information pass between them and children especially spend large part of their non-school days passing between and amongst them.

But what is also noteworthy is that these household clusters contain "Funds of Knowledge" that have been accumulated within the dynamic regional economy of the U.S. Southwest so that vast arrays of information, skills, and strategic knowledge are also embedded in their repertoire. Children are often found to be experimenting, accumulating, accessing, and discarding aspects of these funds as very much part of the daily dense

[18]Carlos G. Vélez-Ibáñez and James B. Greenberg, 1994, Schooling processes among U.S. Mexicans, Puerto Ricans and Cubans: A Comparative, distributive and case study approach, pp. 275–278 *Handbook of Hispanic Cultures in the United States: Anthropology*, T. Weaver, Ed. Houston, Texas: Arte Publico Press.

social exchange relations of the entire cluster. Thus U.S. Mexican children enter schooling processes having had the benefit of constant and intense social exchange relations, having their expectations, and having been exposed to a wide array of strategic information such as that in TABLE 1.

Therefore two salient cultural resources are readily available to educational institutions that may assist learning, the relationships between school and home, and ultimately the manner in which teachers interact and define their roles and statuses with students, parents, and ultimately with themselves. These consist first of the "Funds of Knowledge " present within most household clusters, and second, the dense and reciprocal social relations through which such knowledge is transmitted, transformed, and utilized. In order to gain access to these resources and utilize them in the most efficient manner possible a series of "Funds of Knowledge" projects were initiated between 1988 and 1992 in cities of South Tucson and Tucson, Arizona among U.S. Mexican and Yaqui "at risk" elementary school children.

The term "at risk" students is used to describe students from economically poor backgrounds, who have limited proficiency in English, who have high absentee rates, or who move frequently from school to school. These students are identified in the professional literature as those who are most "at risk" for dropping out of school.[19] During the "Pilot" (1990–91) and "Demonstration" (1991–92) phases of the W.K. Kellogg project" Promoting Collaborative Learning and Educational Delivery and Quality among "At Risk" U.S. Mexican and Native American Elementary School Children in Tucson, Arizona," the Bureau of Applied Research in Anthropology at the University of Arizona, in collaboration with the College of Education, also at the University of Arizona, have established a framework for validating the resources of "at risk" students, and have provided a viable strategy for teachers to come to "know" their students. The underlying premise for these projects has rested on the contention that, for the most part, existing classroom curriculum and pedagogical practices seriously underestimate the important learning resources that "at risk" students carry with them into the classroom. Teachers in the Pilot and Demonstration projects were continually surprised by the unanticipated quality and quantity of learning resources readily available even within

---

[19] In Tucson, Arizona, the predominant "at risk" schools in the Tucson Unified School District, the largest district in the city, are located where high concentrations of U.S. Mexican, Native American, and African American populations reside. For example, in one neighborhood on the southside of Tucson in which over 80% of the population is U.S. Mexican, 90.5% of the local elementary school is of the same origin, has an above district absence rate, has a higher mobility rate than the district, has 99.35 of the children in free lunch programs, has 40% of limited English proficiency, and finally has most of the indicators of academic achievement including mathematics, language, reading, word analysis, vocabulary, and listening are in the 30th percentile or below between the second and sixth grades.

Table 1. Funds of Knowledge of U.S. Mexican Households (*Fondos de Conocimiento*)

Agriculture	Economic and Strategic Information
Ranching and Farming	*Business*
Horsemanship (cowboys)	Real estate (rentals and selling)
Animal husbandry	Market values
Crop planting	Appraising
Vegetable gardening	Contracts
Veterinary	Loans
Knowledge of mice, crickets, cockroaches (insects)	Mortgages
Knowledge of domesticated and wild animals	Property management
	Institutional familiarity
	Credit checks
	Marketing
	Labor laws
	Organization of production (construction)
	Building codes
	Accounting
	Federal regulations
	Computational skills
	Literacy skills
	Appliance repair (refrigerators and washing machines)
	Bicycle shop and go-kart builder
	Welding knowledge
	Sales (candies, bicycles)

Material and Scientific Knowledge	
Construction	*Repair*
Carpentry	Airplane
Read blueprints	Automobile
Masonry (bricklaying)	House maintenance
Plumbing	Plumbing (toilets)
Building fences (chain link)	Bicycle
Electrical	Heating and air conditioning
Coolers and heating installation	Washing machine and refrigerator
T.V. cable installation	Appliances
Painting, exterior and interior	Tractor (on farm—farm
Plastering	implements)
Design and architecture	Welding
Estimates of materials and calculating costs	Fences

Table 1. *(Continued)*

Construction	Repair
Measurement skills and leveling estimates for sewer	
City codes	
Planning work site	
Assembly of labor	
Management skills	

Arts	Medicine
Arts	*Folk Medicine*
Music	Folk veterinary medicine (cure or mastitis with crickets)
Composition	Folk cures for asthma (knowledge of chemistry of same)
Instrumental (guitars, violins) Vocal (sight reading, 200 ranchero songs, writing music, lyrics)(memory, fractions, tempo, rhythm,harmony, melody, recognition)	Herbal knowledge Diagnostics— Knowledge of anatomy and biology of animals
Orchestration	Kinds and classes of animals
Band organization	Kinds and classes of plants Kinds and classes of herb mixes

Social Exchange and Culture	
Social Skills (Exchange)	*Childcare*
Commensal Activities Cooking	
family	Children caring for children
cluster	Children playing at childcare
ritual	Adult childcare as part of exchange
intimate	Experience of a variety of adult caretakers by child
public	Learning limits of expected behavior
visitas	
Organizational Information personnel listing allocation of labor	
Visits	
Child exchange and care	
Household support or management (paying bills, smart consumer, budgets, etc.)	
Institutional knowledge (school, INS, welfare, church, banks, utilities, hospitals, *etc.*)	

Table 1. *(Continued)*

Social Skills (Exchange)	*Childcare*
Moral support (advice)	
Interpersonal skills	
Conflict mediation	
Caring for the sick, the elderly	
Maintaining social networks	
Networks as communication system	
Brokage system (children facing the institutions as interpreters)	
Child/adult relations: *respeto*	
Recognizing the flexible social boundaries outside immediate household: trust, reciprocity, *etc.*	
Qualitative role playing	

Education and Religion

Education	*Ritual and Religion*
Parents assistance with homework	Catechism (First Communion)
Household pedagogy of household tasks	Bible reading
Training programs of household adults	Liturgical knowledge
Formal and informal	Moral knowledge and ethics
Job training	Cosmic Information
Musical training	
Religious training	
Learning by example and observation (mechanics)	
Ranch and farm as school	
Reading of manuals, national geographic, *Time, Newsweek*, history books, blueprints, Life, encyclopedias, Good Housekeeping, bills, catalogues, self-improvement books, shopping lists, business literature, contracts, school assignments, etc.)	
Writing of letters, poetry (Spanish)	
Covert theory	
Self discipline and practice ability	
Good listening skills	

seemingly economically poor households and families. The projects demonstrated that the involvement of students' and their households' "funds of knowledge" in the formation, design and implementation of rigorous learning modules showed that children bring with them valuable learning resources that can be tapped for classroom instruction. This involvement can improve not only class participation but the learning environment and relationships between teachers, students, and parents.

The project template that guides all of the activities is that change in student performance among minority populations is directly associated with change in the relationship between home and school. The best agents for this change are teachers who themselves become convinced that minority children and their homes are repositories for what we have termed, "Funds of Knowledge." This transformative process engages the cultural core of teachers, qualitatively multiplies relationships between home and school, and unfolds as a long term dynamic between teachers, administrators, parents, and students.

Our contention that "at risk" students come from families that are rich in what our previous work has termed "funds of knowledge" was cogently and decisively demonstrated in these two phases. "Funds of Knowledge"[20] are the inventories of information and knowledge that are contained within every household and include an impressive array of skills, survival strategies and home practices that may be utilized by the classroom teachers to appropriately contextualize mathematics, reading comprehension, and composition lessons. The Tucson-based Pilot and Demonstration Projects showed that "funds of knowledge" often reflect the historical derivation of adaptive strategies rooted in southwestern ecology and subsistence activities and that this knowledge base is retained by portions of both Yaqui and U.S. Mexican populations.[21] The projects showed that using home contexts for learning for "at risk" U.S.Mexican and Native American children provides teachers with specific "funds of knowledge" which can be utilized as resources or references for learning. Too often students are presented as not ready for instruction in the early grades. Evidence is cited of a low level of parental education, low income, presumed low educational aspirations, a supposed lack of emphasis on learning and achievement at home, and an

---

[20] See Carlos G. Vélez-Ibáñez, 1988, Networks of Exchange among Mexicans in the U.S. and Mexico. Local level mediating responses to national and international transformation, *Urban Anthropology and Studies of cultural Systems and World Economic Development*, **17** (1) Spring: 27–51; Also, 1989 Transmission and patterning of funds of knowledge: Shaping and emergence of *confianza* in U.S. Mexican children. Paper delivered, Society for Applied Anthropology Annual Meeting, Santa Fe, New Mexico, April 5–9. See also (1994) Plural strategies of survival and cultural formation in U.S. Mexican Households in a region of dynamic, transformation, in *Diagnosing America*, S. Foreman, Ed.

[21] In order to cope in "risky" contexts, and to adapt to changing circumstances our sampled household members became generalists and possessed a wide range of

assumed absence of learning opportunities for children at home.[22] The projects demonstrated that in contrast to the deficit model of student's households, students come equipped with an impressive inventory of experientially based learning foci, and, as the Pilot Project's final report stated, teachers developed "fundamental attitudinal changes in regard to parental concern for their children's education."

Educators may assume that "at risk" students are not only not ready to learn during the primary grades but also are not ready to read, and have only a rudimentary knowledge of numerical manipulation. Such assumptions prompt teachers to implement curriculum around easily manipulable second language tasks such as teaching letter sounds—"oral language"; repetitive computational skill acquisition without a practical context in real space, activity, and time, and recitation without comprehension, cause-effect reasoning, interpretation, or inference. Thus, learning is largely "decontextualized" and non-rigorous, a situation which is antithetical to the processual manner in which children emerge as interactors within their own social and physical environments.

As schools nationally have undertaken efforts to bridge the home/school distance, our project will further provide a viable strategy for teachers to come to "know" their students. Teachers are not given second-hand information via inservices and training. Rather, they learn directly *from* the households *about* the households and in the process undergo profound cultural change. In part, teachers become learners and students of parents and their children as "participant observers" which is the key anthropological method to which the teachers have been exposed intense-

---

complex information. They understood as our other work showed, the characteristics of the local ecosystems: soils, plants, pests, hydrology, and weather. Given the frailty and complexity of arid land environments in the Southwestern region, water management, flood control, and climate variations were important parts of the knowledge base for survival. Equally, knowledge of animal husbandry, range management, and veterinary medicine were part of the "natural systems" of household information as is knowledge and skills in construction and repair in order to avoid reliance on specialists. This required bodies of knowledge about building plans, masonry, carpentry, and electrical wiring, as well as formulas for mixing cement, mortar, and adobe. In addition, folk medicine including the knowledge of home remedies, medicinal herbs, first aid, and a knowledge of anatomy seems quite common.

Taken together these largely rural skills, experience, technical knowledge of habitat and survival which demanded originality and manipulation, made up, and, in part, still make up part of the repertoire of information which we have termed "funds of knowledge" for much of the Arizona-Sonora U.S. Mexican and Native American population.

[22] This assertion was recently repeated by the Arizona State Superintendent of Public Instruction and quoted by the *Arizona Daily Star*, July 21, 1989.

parents and their children as "participant observers" which is the key anthropological method to which the teachers have been exposed intensely. The role reversal incurs profound cultural change in the "schooling" culture of the institution and the expectations for and about learning between teachers, parents and students. Simultaneous to such cultural change is the creation of quality multiple ties beyond the teacher/parent/student "professional" relationship. Thus teachers become friends to parents, fictive kin to children, and both parents and children establish newly formed relations of *confianza* (mutual trust) with the school. Such changes become "internal" to the schooling cycle so that they have long-term, longitudinal effects to be assessed in the future.

The demonstration project and other work[23] clearly showed that "at risk" students have been exposed to and have manipulated their environments along the learning dimensions we have described as "funds of knowledge" and the method for their understanding and utility rests on the methods tried and validated. Moreover, regardless of language, comprehensive learning resources are readily available within the home environment which can be used to enhance learning in the classroom. "At risk" children have had the benefit of observing and participating in such diverse areas as home construction, automobile and bicycle repair, growing gardens and other horticultural practices, holding yard sales, veterinary medicine, cross-border trade, reading receipts and contracts for non-English literate parents, organizing familial celebrations, travels to relatives in Mexico and the reservation, and hunting and dressing animals, among various other activities. They are taught to manipulate and experiment in many of these domains. Children in these households are not only ready to learn but have already mastered instructive arenas far beyond the recognition given by school authorities.

OPERATIONAL ACTIVITIES

The operational activities served to develop innovative home-to-school resources in order to improve the school performance of a sample of students in each of the "at risk"schools. The basic mechanism for such innovation is for classroom teachers, who were given basic training in anthropological perspectives and methodology, to research and organize

---

[23] The domains of the "Funds of Knowledge" found in a sample of 30 household, U.S. Mexican households is contained in the Year I Final Report to the W.K. Kellogg Foundation.

home resources for classroom use.[24] This involves a fundamental change in former paradigms of teacher-home interaction in that the teacher role has been switched from one in which the agenda of the school predominates to that of becoming a learner. In fact, the nomenclature of "home visit" is a misnomer, in that the teachers are involved in a process of much greater

---

[24] We approached the school sites above as a team—consisting of two teachers from the CLP project, the same fearsome foursome of Gonzalez, Greenberg, Moll, and myself, and assorted graduate students.

We received the wholesale cooperation of the administrators of the three school sites and proceeded after a great deal of discussion, negotiation, and providing information to teachers, recruited 14 teachers from the three school sites in grades K–5.

The training elements themselves consisted basically of the following:

1. The description to teachers by teachers was absolutely essential of both the strengths and the pitfalls of the entire process. The CLP teachers explained their many discoveries which were essential, the awful time consuming process of fieldnote writing—some had tried it themselves, the difficulty of integrating material to learning modules and so on.

2. The ethnographic training itself was accomplished over a period of ten weeks and held at both the university and the school sites depending on the schedules for teachers. In this first training process, teachers were remunerated for time spent and for expenses, but Saturdays, after school, and any time they could squeeze was devoted to their training sessions.

Therefore we had to be very efficient in the ethnographic sessions and participant observation training that we conducted so that we used video, audio, and on the job practices to gain an insight into the method.

3. The questionnaires were designed around getting to and at household funds of knowledge and included questions directed toward their own literacy practices, knowledge and skills, labor history (which was crucial), daily activities, and questions also focused for and to children such as where they played, with whom, what they made, created, cooked, washed, and so on. It was crucial here to learn **the differences between what one thinks one thinks, what you think others think, and what you think you do, and what you think others do.**

4. Fieldnotes and Observation were the two most concentrated and difficult training ideas and methods to impart. We discussed the shifts and changes that occur in front of one in the field, the way in which fieldnotes allow us to "see" what we normally miss, how fieldnotes and their quality change over time as we practice our observations, and as well as just the sheer technical practice of going from non-grammatical, verb oriented initial fieldnotes—to expanded fieldnotes done in private—to fieldnote summaries—and finally to "grounded theory" questions these provide.

5. Practice Sessions were difficult; all of which were videotaped, first one with the other, simple 5 year old recollection device was used, and practice families were selected for the teachers to initially try their newly learned skills.

6. The collaborative home ethnographic visits then ensued by the end of the tenth week with children selected from their own classes. Usually three to four children from each class was selected for "treatment" and represented so that high, middle, and low achievers were elected, letters sent out to the parents asking them if they could participate allowing the teachers and anthropologists in their homes first to explain the project, and then to participate in it.

Together we then proceeded to ethnographically visit each household and went through the usual phases in fieldwork: painful introductory, participation, *confianza*, and integration phases, the last of which after a few months; teachers could literally not hope to leave the home under two to three hours.

depth and breadth than a simple "home visit." The teachers are, in actuality, participant-observers within the concrete lived experiences of their students. They establish a dialogue with the households which we have documented to be an emancipatory experience for both parents and teachers. The teachers came to know the community empathetically and emotionally. The affective ties which were elaborated during the household visits forged a link between home and school which has formed a solid basis for continued connections.

One significant finding from our Pilot and Demonstration projects was that the exceptional teachers were eager to become participants, observers, and fieldworkers in the discovery of the "funds of knowledge" and to transform such funds into meaningful learning modules.[25] The basic mechanism for teachers to effectuate successful interaction and collaborate on curriculum units has been within the setting of the "teacher labs."

As a key component to the mediating process between home and school, collaborative teacher-directed laboratories were initiated during various projects. The prototype for these "labs" had been developed and used successfully in previous work.[26] Labs are settings within which teachers mobilize **their** collective "funds of knowledge" about teaching and share resources for the development of instructional innovations. These resources include not only the teachers as mentors for each other, but the sharing of research literature, observations of classroom practices, assistance from university colleagues, and, of course, the households' funds of knowledge. In brief, these labs are settings to help teachers think about their work, develop and tap into their own pedagogical funds of knowledge, take full advantage of resources in their environment, and assess the development and trajectory of the work. In addition, evidence from these labs during the Pilot and Demonstration projects show that they have the potential to stimulate teacher transformation and enhance project ownership. One desired outcome for the projects was that participation of some teachers will spread to whole schools and that the teachers will become the leaders and trainers for the rest of their schools. This, indeed, was an outcome at one of the schools involved in the Pilot project, where all teachers are now involved in

---

[25] For example, the outstanding Funds-based, learning module developed by a participating teacher was one which was developed as the aftermath of parents visiting the classroom and demonstrating the construction techniques of building a home. This created the student interest in reading blueprints, figuring out the geometry of angles, the appropriate planning of infrastructure such as water, electricity, and sewage lines, and eventually led to interest in developing an entire learning module on the planning of an entire city. Such a learning module included the learning of basic design, architecture, broader infrastructure planning, and demographic and population movement.

[26] See Moll, Vélez-Ibáñez and Greenberg:1990, Community Knowledge and Classroom Practice: Combining Resources for Literacy Instruction. Final Report, Community Literacy Project.

making home visits, and where parents, seeing new avenues for strengthening ties with the school have shared their "funds of knowledge" through such projects as the school's landscaping.

Our projects have made two important innovations in the planning, implementation, and assessment of project activities. First, the training activities conducted by the project have transpired through both small groups and large group interactions. The small group orientation was the initial mode of inservice, but became problematic in one school due to the wholesale participation of the majority of teachers. This required large group methods such as weekend retreats, large group seminars, and school-focused meetings. Second, teacher-administered planning and implementation groups have taken over many of the activities originally developed by project personnel, and teachers involved in the Pilot project have participated in training teachers for the Demonstration project. In essence, these groups eventually took responsibility for the institutionalization of the program within each school and changed the institutional relations between project personnel, school administration, and teachers. After the first six months of the demonstration project in Tucson, Arizona, Teacher Planning and Training groups came into existence, and became sufficiently empowered to plan, determine, and implement the household visits, the use of ethnographic data for classroom use, and the construction of learning modules.

LEARNING AND DISCOVERY OUTCOMES

The various experiments proved to have generated intensive and extensive processes for teachers, anthropologists, educators, administrators, and parents and children, eventually creating a dynamic in which the learning modules themselves became so central to the activities in some of the schools that the ramifications are still being felt at this moment in a variety of ways. Built into the learning modules were four conceptual templates that had to be met: computation, composition, critical thinking, and the scientific method. Each learning module that resulted from learning household funds of knowledge proved the efficacy of the idea of constructing each module within the templates. Household-derived modules consisted of early elementary school children experimenting with dietary production, constructing cities, experimenting with plants and generating household taxonomies, creating books, and many other such examples. Thus the making of candy as one class module followed this sequence that began with the household observation:

> 1.0 Household Observation: During observation child observed selling candy, and candy making and selling is discovered to be an important "informal economy" enterprise in which family members produce, package, and sell candy in Arizona and Sonora.

2.0 Classroom Demonstration by Mother. Actual production and demonstration including discussion of nutritional and dietary benefits of U.S. and Mexican candy as well as its taxonomy.

3.0 Class agrees to make candy.

3.1 Literature in English and Spanish Reviewed including origins, international dimensions, processing and nutrition, slavery, and monocrop societies.

3.2 Hypothesis created of probable outcomes: probability theory introduced, charts created, computational exercises, and "project" write up of activities.

3.3 Production teams are organized: Quality Control Set up, Prediction of Sales using cost inventory, analysis, charting, and computer as means of predicting outcome.

3.4 Manufacturing set up: review of "factory system," maquiladoras, division of labor, and cottage industry

3.5 Sales force set up: presentation of products, self, and territories, and canvassing: Arizona versus Sonora health regulations.

3.6 Sales conducted: Accounting and computation of results.

4.0 Evaluation and Assessment: Small group reports created, Skills assessed: computation, literacy, critical skills, scientific method as feedback.

5.0 Results: all computational and composition skills tested; scientific method and reporting process completed.

CONCLUSIONS

The method was incorporated by the entire faculty in one school and made part of their planning process and time to be used. The other schools as well were strongly influenced and in all three schools the trained teachers became trainers themselves for other teachers interested in the method. Given conservative attitudes in most schools, such innovation was remarkably well accepted.

What other more salient implications however resulted and continue to result from these experiments. First, the teachers themselves changed in their relationship to themselves, children, and parents and school. They not only gained control of their labor but of the relationship to their labor. They had exchanged roles as teachers to that of students with their students and their students had become teachers as had their parents. Their household roles changed to honored guests or Aunts or Uncles with attending duties as co-godparents, invitees to rituals, and other commensal activities such as barbecues, birthday parties, picnics, and yard sales.

Second, the parents changed in their relationship to teachers and their own children. They made explicit their participation in the learning process but as well came to understand that their "funds of knowledge" were of value and could be utilized for their children's benefit. They no longer considered their knowledge superfluous to school knowledge. In so doing they recognized that they could be full partners with teachers and the school rather than objects to invite to the yearly PTA meeting.

Third, the children changed in their relationship to teachers and parents. They could look upon their parents as knowledge bearers equivalent to their teachers but also came to perceive their teachers as equivalent to caring parents. Younger siblings in the same school demanded that their teachers visit them as had their older brothers and sisters. Classroom participation increased in general, discipline problems abated, and performance has been gauged as improved, especially among some students who were usually withdrawn.

Fourth, the political relations between home and school changed. Parent participation in school activities improved, especially in demonstration projects tied to learning modules. As well, parents sought out teachers before problems of the household affected children's performance. Thus thicker relations of mutual trust came to be formed so that the schools themselves seem to be thriving enterprises with a constant movement of teachers into neighborhoods and parents into the schools .

However, at a much deeper cultural and cognitive level the impact on teachers especially have taken two transformative potentials: first, there is a definite shift in their definition of culture and the second, the alternative view of Mexican and Yaqui households as "deficit" or at risk, or disadvantaged, or culturally poor have been radically changed.

Teachers no longer looked at culture as an assembly of tacos, dances, and frijoles but viewed households as repositories of strategic information and relationships. They learned that households operated within the clusters already described and experienced them first hand. They learned more importantly than everything was the manner in which their own students participated in multiple domains, in multiple dimensions, and the extreme time depth of the funds of knowledge they were able to dip into if an when they were given an opportunity. They received insights into the true cultural history of their students not reduced to stanine scores. They did not stop their inquiry because a parent did not have a job and allowed them to continue probing until the teachers truly arrived at an understanding of the many daily cultural negotiations that parents and children in modest contexts have to undergo. Culture from this point of view emerged as a dynamic and processual concept which teachers gained in experience and which as importantly could be used to enhance the learning experience of their students.

Equally well, in contrast to a deficit "at risk" model, the "Funds of Knowledge" idea introduced them to the breadth and wealth of learning resources that can be used for classroom enhancement. Rather than teachers going into the household to "teach" parents, teachers became learners and in so doing avoided the subtle but unmistakable message that "we are coming into your home to teach you how to survive." They have gained in the process *confianza*—mutual trust—which upsets the unequal status relation between themselves and parents. Teachers become a valued source and resource for parents and children but this becomes only possible when the myth of knowledge that teachers impart becomes recognizable as only another way of surviving and no more important nor of value than all of the funds of knowledge that their students and parents have already inherited, developed, created, and discarded.

REPLICATION OF THE MODEL IN URBAN ENVIRONMENTS

If this model for learning would be incorporated within the urban enclaves described by others in this broader work, obvious negotiations would have to occur. However, the funds of knowledge in operation in "El Barrio" for example are broad and applicable. Among the Puerto Rican population there are myriad examples of rurally based knowledge carried into the urban environment, of constant cyclic visitation to Puerto Rico, of labor extensive experiences, and multiple levels of knowledge as well. As a simple example, the amazing taxonomies of flora present in many Puerto Rican households can easily be used for scientifically oriented learning modules and as can the immense variety of economic practices learned in the constant movements between New York and Puerto Rico be used to create the same kind of modules described in this work. There are little other than environmental constraints that prevent similar experiments from being carried out.

But more importantly there are also theoretical boundaries that need to be touched in relation to this experiment. Some have suggested that urban conditions of poverty are seldom total—that is that no form of domination is ever complete over a population.[27] From this point of view, oppositional cultures emerge in those spaces so that optional cultural forms arise and with them optional traditions—a deconstructed "reconstruction" of events, behaviors, and unknown historical relations.

But this point of view places too much power in the dominating and not enough in those being affected. This point of view licenses without intent an idea that somehow domination "slips" and allows cracks so that those dominated have the opportunity to invent alternate options and histories that act in opposition. This eliminates agency from those dominated and induces a kind of victimization that may provide a kind of morally superior position to those dominated but allows them no agency. Agency is allowed only by the fissures in the "dominating" process and not by the conscious organizational and mobilizing ability of cultural creators.

Thus the experiments conducted here illustrate clearly that agency is normative rather than passivity. That with a little innovation, agency by not only seemingly powerless households and seemingly powerless teachers and administrators, and communities can arise and do arise from within and not just stimulated from without. Last, however, while a great deal of focus is

[27] Raymond Williams, 1977;108–127 *et passim*) *Marxism and Literature*. Oxford: Oxford University Press.

centered on such categories of persons as "at risk," the working poor, culture of poverty, the underclass, and urban enclaves, such categories have a tendency of reducing human populations to categories often integrated into the professional literature and define the potential agency of persons of modest income. Such experiments as those conducted here contradict such reductionism.

REFERENCES

BEAN, F.D. AND M. TIENDA
  1987   *The Hispanic Population of the United States.* New York: Russell Foundation.
BERRY, J.C.
  1987   South Tucson, *Tucson Daily Citizen*, 4-1-87.
DIEZ-CANEDO, J.
  1981   *Undocumented Migration to the United States: A New Perspective.* Translated from the Spanish by Dolores E. Mills. Albuquerque: Center for Latin American Studies, University of New Mexico.
FERNANDEZ-KELLY, P.
  1987   Technology and employment along the U.S.-Mexican border. In *The United States and Mexico: Face to Face with New Technology.* Cathryn L. Thorup, Ed. New Brunswick, N.J.: Transaction Books.
GARCIA Y GRIEGO, M.
  1983   *Mexico and the United States: Migration, History, and the Idea of Sovereignty,* No.7, December 1983, El Paso, TX: Center for Interamerican and Border Studies, The University of Texas, El Paso.
GONZALEZ-ARCHEGIA, B.
  1987   California-Mexico Linkages, First Annual California-Mexico Business Conference. Los Angeles, California: October 28–29, 1987, Unpublished MS.
HISPANIC AMERICANS TODAY
  1993   U.S. Bureau of the Census, Current Population Reports, P23–183, U.S. Government Printing Office, Washington, DC, 1993: 2.
MAGNITUDE AND PERSISTENCE OF POVERTY AMONG LATINOS
  1988   Claremont, CA: The Tomas Rivera Center.
MARTINEZ, O.
  1983   *The Foreign Orientation of the Mexican Border Economy, Border Perspectives,* No.2, May 1983, El Paso, TX: Center for Interamerican and Border Studies, The University of Texas, El Paso.
MOLL, LUIS, C.G. VÉLEZ-IBÁÑEZ, AND J.B. GREENBERG
  1990   Community knowledge and classroom practice: Combining resources for literacy instruction. Final Report, Community Literacy Project.
MOORE, J.
  1988   *An Assessment of Hispanic Poverty: Is There an Hispanic Underclass?* San Antonio, TX: The Tomas Rivera Center.

PERSONS OF HISPANIC ORIGIN IN THE UNITED STATES: AUGUST 1993
1993   U.S. Bureau of the Census, Current Population Reports, 1990 CP-3-3, U.S. Government Printing Office, Washington, DC: Table 1.5 and Table 5:157

PORRAS, A. SALAS
(n.d.)   Crisis, Maquiladoras y Estructura Sociopolitica en Chihuahua, Sonora y Baja California. Unpublished MS.

ROWE, A.
1991   Note on education and self-worth among Anglo American, Black American, and Mexican-American men in San Antonio. *Perceptual and Motor Skills* **73** (No.2) October: 433–434.

STODDARD E.R. AND J.HEDDERSON
1987   *Trends and Patterns of Poverty Along the U.S.-Mexico Border.* Las Cruces: Borderlands Research Monograph Series, New Mexico State University.

SPECIAL UNEMPLOYMENT REPORT FOR JANUARY THROUGH DECEMBER 1989 (FINAL) FOR ARIZONA LOCAL AREA STATISTICS (1990)
1990   Pima County, Department of Economic Security, State of Arizona.

TIANO, S.B.
1985   *Export Processing, Women's Work, and the Employment Problem in Developing Countries: The Case of the Maquiladora Program in Northern Mexico.* No. 22, November 1985. El Paso, Texas: Center for Interamerican and Border Studies, The University of Texas, El Paso.

TREVINO, F., D.B. TREVINO, C.A. STROUP, AND L. RAY
1989   *The Feminization of Poverty among Hispanic Households.* San Antonio: The Tomas Rivera Center, February, p. 9.

TUCSON DAILY CITIZEN,
1987   September 11.

TUCSON DAILY CITIZEN,
1987   December 9.

TUCSON DAILY CITIZEN,
1988   January 6.

TUCSON DAILY CITIZEN,
1988   February 12.

TUCSON DAILY CITIZEN,
1989   April 15.

TUCSON DAILY CITIZEN,
1989   August 11.

U.S. DEPARTMENT OF COMMERCE
1980   *Tucson, Arizona: Neighborhood Statistics Program, 1980 Decennial Census.* Washington: Bureau of the Census.

VÉLEZ-IBÁÑEZ, C.G.
1988   Networks of exchange among Mexicans in the U.S. and Mexico: Local level mediating responses to national and international transformation, *Urban Anthropology and Studies of cultural Systems and World Economic Development*, Vol. 17 (1), Spring: pp. 27–51
1989   Transmission and Patterning of Funds of Knowledge: Shaping and Emergence of Confianza in U.S. Mexican Children. Paper delivered, Society for Applied Anthropology Annual Meeting, Santa Fe, New Mexico, April 5–9.

1993   U.S Mexicans in the borderlands: Being poor without the underclass, in *In the Barrios, Latinos and the Underclass Debate*, J. Moore and R. Pinderhughes, Eds. New York: Russell Sage Foundation, 195–220.

1994   Plural strategies of survival and cultural formation in U.S. Mexican households in a region of dynamic transformation. In *Diagnosing America*, S. Foreman, Ed. Ann Arbor: University of Michigan Press.

n.d.   Border Visions of One World: An Anthropology of U.S. Mexicans of the Southwest. Tucson, Arizona:University of Arizona Press, 400pp. In press.

VÉLEZ-IBÁÑEZ, C.G. AND J.B. GREENBERG

1992   Formation and Transformation of Knowledge among U.S. Mexican Households. *Anthropology and Education Quarterly* 23 (4): 313–335.

1994   Schooling processes among U.S. Mexicans, Puerto Ricans and Cubans: A comparative, distributive and case study approach. In *Handbook of Hispanic Cultures in the United States: Anthropology*. T. Weaver, Ed. Houston, TX: Arte Publico Press.

VÉLEZ-IBÁÑEZ, C.G., L. MOLL, J.B. GREENBERG, B. WILLIAMS, AND N. GONZALEZ

Promoting Collaborative Learning and Educational Delivery and Quality among "At Risk" U.S. Mexican, Native American, and African American Elementary School Children in Three Sites: Adrian, Michigan; Tucson, Arizona, and The Hopi Reservation. Bureau of Applied Research in Anthropology and Division of Language, Reading and Culture, College of Education. Submitted to the Kellogg Foundation, November 30, 1992.

WILLIAMS, RAYMOND

1977   *Marxism and Literature.* Oxford: Oxford University Press pp. 108–127.

Subject Index

Index of Contributors

†Deceased.